Karen Lamb teaches literature and communication at the Australian Catholic University and has held teaching and research positions at the University of Queensland, Monash University, and the University of Melbourne, where she taught in literary studies, media and communication, and cultural studies. Her research interests include Australian literature, life writing, and the cultural context of authorship. She has edited a book of Australian short stories, and published book chapters and articles on Australian authors, including a book on Peter Carey. She lives in Sydney.

THEA ASTLEY

INVENTING HER OWN WEATHER

KAREN LAMB

UQP

First published 2015 by University of Queensland Press
PO Box 6042, St Lucia, Queensland 4067 Australia

uqp.com.au
uqp@uqp.uq.edu.au

Edited by Jacqueline Kent
Cover design by Sandy Cull, gogoGingko
Cover photograph by Christopher Ellis
Author photograph by The Melbourne Headshot Company
Photographs courtesy of Ed Gregson and the author unless otherwise noted
Typeset in 11/15.5 pt Janson Text by Post Pre-press Group, Brisbane
Printed in Australia by McPherson's Printing Group, Melbourne

Cataloguing-in-Publication Data
National Library of Australia
Lamb, Karen, 1956– author.
Thea Astley : inventing her own weather / Karen Lamb.
Astley, Thea, 1925–2004.
Women authors, Australian—Biography.
Novelists, Australian—Biography.
ISBN 978 0 7022 5356 0 (pbk)
ISBN 978 0 7022 5500 7 (pdf)
ISBN 978 0 7022 5501 4 (epub)
ISBN 978 0 7022 5502 1 (kindle)
920.72

University of Queensland Press uses papers that are natural, renewable and recyclable products made from wood grown in sustainable forests. The logging and manufacturing processes conform to the environmental regulations of the country of origin.

For my daughter, Laura

Contents

PART 4 PERSONAL WEATHER

Prologue

There was never a time when multi-award-winning Australian novelist Thea Astley was not a writer. She began as a child, published on the children's page of the newspaper where her journalist father worked; as a teenager she wrote for her school's magazine; at university she joined Barjai, a group of young writers and artists that, in time, became one of the better known cultural organisations of the era, largely for having nurtured talents such as hers and poet Barrett Reid's. She was able to pursue her ambitions as a writer within this small informal group; by the time Astley was in her thirties the effort she made to 'carve out a good sentence', as she called it, was the consequence of more than two decades of writing.

Her first novel, *Girl with a Monkey*, published in 1958, dazzled with insight and wit. Further novels appeared almost every two years throughout the 1960s. By 1963 Thea Astley had her first Miles Franklin Award for fiction for *The Well Dressed Explorer*, a humorous but scarifying portrait of a philandering journalist. This firmly established her reputation as a sharp-eyed satirist of Australian social mores. By the end of the next decade she had picked up a further two Miles Franklin Awards (for *The Slow Natives* and *The Acolyte*) and a healthy clutch of other major literary prizes. Yet Astley spent her life suffering from an acute sense of being a writer who was out of favour, a sentiment that sits curiously alongside her visible success. When she received the Patrick White Award in 1989 – intended for writers who might not have received the recognition they deserved – Astley regarded it as confirmation of her failure.

While eccentric, this attitude can be understood. Astley's early literary role models, even from within her own family, were male (her artist-musician grandfather, her journalist father) and she also began writing at a time when, as Astley would later explain, women were supposed to emulate a 'masculine style' to succeed; that is, they were expected to conform to the ideals of strong narrative lines and the superior virtue of brevity. In Astley's writing there are tensions between the vulnerability of female existence and the manner of its telling.

It is astonishing to think that even by the mid-1980s Astley was already as much of a household name as any Australian writer can be, that is, in Australia. 'Australians loathe success that doesn't take place in a scrum,' she once said.[1] But what becomes of a writer's work when that writer is no longer alive? The relentless commerce of publishing, the thirst for the new, dictates much of that answer. Thea Astley was being published – and reviewed – in the United States, as well as in Australia. In all she wrote sixteen works of fiction in just under half a century. *Drylands*, published in 1999 when she was in her seventies, won her a fourth Miles Franklin Award (a feat shared only by Tim Winton).

Astley's books offer a rare and sustained engagement with the social and political realities of Australian life over more than forty years, particularly for women. She was no Christina Stead balancing typewriter on knee in shabby hotels across Europe, but at home in Australia Astley established an output in the same class, rarely taking time off before moving on to her next manuscript. She has influenced a generation of Australian women writers such as Helen Garner and Kate Grenville and is known for her support of the many younger writers who came within her orbit as a teacher.

Astley was a child of the Depression and she lived through World War II as a teenager; she was no stranger to 'personal weather', as she called it, the highs and lows that sweep through a life. Early experiences shaped her fiction: the Catholicism of the 1930s and 1940s; the presence of American GIs in wartime Brisbane. She also observed unhappy marriages; absent fathers; bachelor celibates; misfits and 'runaways' risking safety for the tropics. Her strong women of the later books (*It's Raining in Mango*, *Reaching Tin River*, *Vanishing Points*, *Coda*, *Drylands*) manage without men but with stoicism and a certain panache. Sometimes Astley's own anxieties and self-doubt creep into her prose, driving the narrative with particular force. Like the work of Christina Stead, Astley's novels and short stories have a strong autobiographical element which she readily acknowledged: 'They are 90% ME,' she wrote, adding that, 'When you're writing a novel, you're not writing about anything really except yourself' and, 'I work from life, as I know it, as I have known it.'[2] Astley's characters can be like members of an extended family, reappearing from novel to novel. A typical Astley protagonist has drifted unawares into middle age (Astley herself once claimed to have been 'arrested at forty-two'). Their will is seemingly suspended, their memory animated by usually hostile past events, while they await the decline of the ripened body.

In her work as in her life, Thea Astley was a fatalist. In public she could display a strange mixture of bombast and anxiety, be sentimental – reduced to tears by a recalled scene – yet blunt in her opinions, often mumbling a shambolic apology. She was a tangential thinker; her mind darted helter-skelter across an exotic range of concerns, but she was also possessed of a practical logic and an acute mind, and these were the housekeepers of her imagination.

This picture of a successful Australian woman novelist nevertheless has a shadow across it. There are many full-length literary biographies of Australian women writers, from Miles Franklin and Christina Stead to lesser-known writers like Eve Langley or Jean Devanny. Until now, inexplicably, a biography of Thea Astley was not in this list, ghosting her with the same neglect she felt in life.

Do writers welcome having their biographies written? History tells us that many have not. F. Scott Fitzgerald called biography 'the falsest of arts' and Henry James swore he would avoid such 'literary scavengers' as biographers.[3] Thea Astley was not strongly in favour of biography or against it, but she did regard herself as a very private person. When I contacted her in the mid-1990s about writing her biography she was happy to be interviewed, but, she said in a smoker's rasp, 'Don't write your address on the back of any envelopes, will you? People might see – might know – that we are in touch.' *But aren't we?* I couldn't help thinking. It took a moment to digest conspiracy and invitation in the same breath. I did come to understand this strange and contradictory behaviour but it is worth recalling this moment because it frames the central paradox of a work such as this: the story of a public person whose life was intentionally private.

Astley's novels and stories have always fascinated me. They show a masterful blend of whimsy, the absurd and the deeply serious; her prose is energised by her irascible wit and there is a visceral, almost sexual energy in the nature of its swoops and silences that appeals to me. There is a pleasing perversity in the way she could bring seeming opposites into unison. Because writing this book took so many years, and I, too, have experienced many of life's various upheavals, my enjoyment of her work has deepened.

When I began, I simply wanted to know more about the public writer Thea Astley. Of course Astley only went public as part of being a successful writer who receives awards and is a guest at book festivals, literary conferences and international symposiums. Astley would have characterised these as necessary obligations, despite the obvious pleasure she took in being part of them – or even being the star attraction.

Once she had left the working life that meant residing in Sydney, Astley chose remote places to live but she was not a hermit: she loved people, loved gossip. She was married for more than fifty years to Jack Gregson and gloried in recounting what she considered the absurd dreariness of domestic routines. The late-life gravelly voice, the wit, the warmth and engagement that distinguished Astley in person are not easily forgotten. She had the knack of making people feel that they were happily encountered confidants, special people with whom she needed to share herself.

Those who thought that they had come to know Thea Astley from such encounters were often surprised to find that others had the same experience. This is especially true of those students, writers or other young folk whom Astley tended to regard as protégé-children. Yet there was often a one-way intimacy in these friendships that belied their apparent candour; sometimes the chosen ones could see that perhaps they did not know Astley so well after all. They did and they didn't, to use a characteristic Astley phrasing. They knew her jokes, her gestures, fronts, defences. They knew how kind she could be – but they did not share in her private emotional world. Few did: from the start it belonged to her writing, as is true of many writers.

Astley grew up feeling at odds with the demands of her social world. She developed a defensive habit of mind early in life: her parents didn't especially get on, she had to handle the dictates of the strict Catholicism of her childhood in the 1930s and 1940s, then loneliness as a young woman teaching in remote rural towns in the far north of her home state of Queensland and in the Mary Valley, closer to Brisbane. More than her circumstances seemed to justify, Astley came to see herself as set apart from others. She became guarded, nursed well-worn hurts and humiliations, vulnerabilities, anger and guilt. All these things were expressed in her fiction.

Thea Astley is one of those writers who invite portraiture – such is the indelible impression of her personality inhabiting her prose.

This is the seduction of reading, this attraction between writers and readers that biography can give expression to. This book's portrait of the novelist includes the imperfect, glancing impressions of those who met and befriended Astley, those 'hints from everyone', as Christina Stead once called them.[4] Beyond skeletal facts, 'hints' are often all there is. Like many writers before her, Astley destroyed much of her written correspondence. For most of her life she preferred talking on the telephone. It is only because her death was more sudden than expected that some letters and other items were salvaged. In the end it was Astley who delivered the final instalment of her story, in her last novel, *Drylands.* It is a loosely assembled collage, but a knowing self-portrait.

Perhaps many of us carry around a sense of the world as insensitive to us, holding on to a story of ourselves that seems plausible, bearable, all the while pleading a special case: ours. It is true that I have tried to look in on Astley's private world and can offer only an interpretation of her life, but I have done so in the hope of understanding her lifelong private conversation with herself and how that shaped the distinctive body of work that is Thea Astley's literary legacy.

PART 1

THE HINTERLAND

I

The hinterland of childhood

There were many corners – she learned a lot about the eternal warfare of couples. It rather put her off.

Drylands by Thea Astley, 1999[1]

Nearly thirty years into her writing life, at the 1986 Adelaide Writers' Festival, Thea Astley was, as always, preoccupied with weather: not the furnace-like heat so characteristic of Adelaide in March, but what might be called 'personal weather', part of the climate people created around themselves, their mark on the world. She had written about this, in various ways, for many years. Her preoccupation with physical weather, its strictures, limitations and effects on her characters, had always been deeply metaphorical. She liked to describe her characters charting what she called 'the approximate geography of the dream' while dealing with the inclement elements of life.[2]

At the time she was living near Cairns in the tropical north of her home state of Queensland. She had already entertained an audience about her strange love-hate relationship with that particular region's climate: we 'wait for the big wet', she said, and it comes 'striding over paddocks and hits roofs like gravel trucks emptying'; 'landscape and sky are like a boil waiting to burst, skin crawls, salt stings your eyes and you itch'.[3]

At the age of sixty Astley was an arresting figure, her agility as she moved to the microphone giving a clue to her energetic personality. During that festival she could be spotted around the tents, among other writers, the familiar cigarette in hand, at ease.

This was an exciting and important time for her: she was balancing her public exposure as an established novelist with the potential she still saw in her future as a writer. She was a guest at major arts festivals, the winner of three Miles Franklin Awards and she was also achieving longed-for recognition overseas. The publication of her most recent novel, *Beachmasters*, in the United States would be followed in less than a year by *It's Raining in Mango*.

This particular festival was therefore a special moment in an already long writing life, and Astley had been writing long enough to appreciate how few and far apart such moments were. Her voice, a deeply accented rasp with more than a hint of the broad vowels of her home state, was a world away from the plummy politeness of her early television and radio performances in the 1960s. She knew how to use that voice: her ability as a performer lit up public readings. If Astley hadn't been a writer, she could have made it as a stand-up comic – she had that kind of timing. So when she leaned forward and nervously lowered her voice to the crowd, 'I should explain, I suppose, that I'm not a very accomplished traveller', this unusual candour sent a ripple of excited interest across the audience. Astley used the personal pronoun in a casual, familiar way; it was an intimate sharing of what it might be like to be Thea Astley, Australian novelist.

She talked about the writing of her short story 'Diesel Epiphany' about a journey in a 'rail motor' – a motorised railway carriage very common in Astley's youth – perhaps because it was so characteristic of her own preoccupations. Rail trips across Australia's vast state borders had always held all the elements of narrative for Astley: human beings in a small spaces forging strange alliances, all with a rueful acceptance of their own banality. In a railway carriage anyone could be a 'people freak' – Astley's favourite term for herself – could listen in on the frank conversations which were natural theatre to her ear. She was no doubt irritated (perhaps with a high sense of drama) by all the inconveniences typical of 'cattle class' travel, especially other people's selfishness. 'Diesel Epiphany' is a story that is superficially about train travel, but is really about having the last word. After the travellers alight and head to town, the climax of the story describes a different kind of banality. Bored people are standing in a bank queue when the sound of a light baritone, the music of a Bach cantata, breaks through.[4] The singer is a typical Astley 'screwball' and in her work she would give voice to them all: hippies, unfrocked priests, outcasts. Couples, with their 'hissed domestics', were a special case. Above all else, Astley loved to observe that most familiar of human relationships up close.[5]

It was a fascination that grew quite naturally out of Astley's own childhood. By the time she came to know her parents beyond the familiar 'Mum' and 'Dad', Eileen Adeline Lindsay and Cecil Bellaire Astley had taught her a lot about marriage, or at least a certain kind of marriage. At a very young age, then, she had the central preoccupying theme of her novels. It was not the success or otherwise of such unions that fascinated her. Rather it was marriage itself that delivered to Astley, complete, the small-world whole-world perspective so essential to her as a novelist.

For Astley, the endless negotiation of the self with the other, intrinsic to marriage, came to stand for all the negotiations inherent in the passage through life: with family, with the Church and belief, with the social world and the politics of it, and inevitably with the personalities who would enter and leave her world. Astley, who had a lifelong affinity with numbers and logic, saw marriage as the perfect algorithm for a lifetime of experience, containing sex, choice, boredom, inertia, entrapment, despair, acceptance and love.

Looking back at Astley's childhood, it is easy to see why she, like her parents, stayed married and lived a regulated domestic existence much like theirs. She wrote sharp social commentary into her novels, but their emotional strength lies in the way Astley captured the nuanced, intimate, fallible moments of couples living a humdrum existence, together yet apart.

She was negatively drawn to this for the most understandable of reasons: in her early emotional world there was certainly care, but also an absence of closeness. Intimacy and emotional frankness – things she craved – were not part of ordinary life in the household in which Astley grew up. The Astleys were stoics, though Thea as a child was vulnerable and exposed to differences within the home and allegiances outside of it – particularly religious ones – that she could hardly have been expected to understand. They marked her life unmistakeably.

Thea Beatrice May Astley was born in Brisbane on 25 August 1925, a sister for her older brother, Phil, then aged four. The name 'Thea', meaning 'gift of the god' or 'goddess' (Thea was the Greek goddess of light), was a logical choice for Astley's pious mother, Eileen. If Astley could have read the future, to see the renowned editor who would give her a start in writing would share her middle name 'Beatrice', meaning 'traveller' or 'voyager', she might have preferred that name.

Brisbane in the 1920s bore almost no resemblance to the skyscrapered commercial city of today. It was considered the hick cousin of Sydney and Melbourne. Throughout Astley's childhood and young adult life, being a Queenslander conferred a particular kind of status, sometimes negative. Migrants, from the 1940s through to the 'ten pound Poms' of the 1960s, were drawn to this place's exotic mix of shambolic suburbia and hillside wooden shacks high up on stilts all set amid lush tropical foliage. Some foreigners saw the place as unspoiled, others as backward, depending on their background and personal circumstances. For the locals, however, loyalty and acceptance of 'home' led to parochial defensiveness. It was an attitude that became inseparable from what it meant to be a Queenslander. For Thea, Queensland was a home she loved to love, and loved to hate. Brisbane and memories of her childhood there created an intense emotional world for her writing.

She is not alone. Other well-known Australian writers have written about growing up in Brisbane, including Thomas Shapcott, Matthew Condon, Rodney Hall and Rhyll McMaster. And David Malouf has written of Brisbane's gullies and vistas, how the senses become drenched in tropical downpours, and the steepness of the streets make buildings cast long shadows, a town built on hills, a river that changes direction so often it seems like many rivers. The Queensland child in this dilapidated and makeshift world, he wrote, was somehow more exposed to the vulnerabilities of the world beyond it.[6] From these same origins Astley created an emotional geography inseparable from her sense-memories of home. The emotional aura of the Astley household made the two very different worlds seem imaginatively inseparable.

The Astleys had settled in Waterworks Road in the relatively new suburb of Ashgrove. The suburb was only five or six kilometres from the city and accessible by tram, the major mode of transport, and it developed around a long and winding main road. In the late nineteenth century this had been the road used to drive livestock to market. While the area was originally noted for its genteel rural estates, it was the new Waterworks Road that redefined life for the first residents who lived along it. By the time Astley left the suburb it was readying itself for the post-World War II baby boom and an influx of thousands of families looking for relatively cheap houses near the city.

The atmosphere at home when Astley was a primary school child was quietly tense, characterised by silences between her parents, punctuated with many arguments. Sister Mary, who taught young Thea at Rosalie Convent primary school, could see that Cecil and Eileen Astley were not much of a match.[7] Astley's mother made frequent visits just to talk to Sister Mary, who remembered conversations with one or the other parent but never both.[8] In the days before school counsellors family tension was not for discussion.

For Astley's parents, marriage was disappointing, after what had been a promising romance. When Eileen first met Cecil she saw at least a superficial resemblance to her own father, for Cecil Astley was also a journalist. However, beyond that, the resemblance was not particularly obvious. Canadian-born Cornelius John Lindsay, Eileen's runaway father and Thea's maternal grandfather, left his family for the 'wild' city life and, as his granddaughter Thea would say pointedly, his wife never forgave him.[9]

Eileen Lindsay was born in 1897 and from about the turn of the century until the 1920s endured a very straitened upbringing with her two sisters in a single-parent household. The Lindsays were related to a well-to-do family from Ballarat, Victoria – Eileen's great-grandfather was Judge O'Dee – but this did little to alter the poverty of her small family group. The derogatory term 'deserted wife' epitomises what would have been the practical and emotional reality.

Thea and her older brother, Phil, came to understand their mother as a troubled personality, and they slowly understood how her background was very different from their father's. Eileen was embarrassed by her lack of education and made amends by reading the classics by candlelight late into the night. Phil and Thea watched shame flicker across a great many of her actions and hard-set attitudes. She seemed too aware of social pride. Instead of the merely customary politeness of returning generosity, every little favour or act of kindness had to be returned in greater measure: a gift of jams meant a jam-cake for the giver.[10] This developed into an exaggerated solicitousness, awkwardly annexed to anxiety, ideas about God and duty, and guilt – behaviour that would affect the lives of both Phil and Thea.

Eileen's father had, however, been modestly successful in his writing and was a reasonably well-known figure in Sydney journalistic circles throughout the 1930s and 1940s.[11] Cornelius, known as Con, published articles in *The Bulletin* and was a member of the Dawn and Dusk Club, a bohemian society of writers, formed in the late 1890s, which met for drinks and conversation; Henry Lawson was a prominent member. When Eileen's father moved to Melbourne he quickly gravitated to similar circles, joining the Bread and Cheese Club, an all-male club based on 'mateship, arts and letters' and associated with prominent book collector J. K. Moir and his set. During the 1940s the club was an important champion of Australian writing, publishing books that dealt particularly with regional and bush Australia. Con later edited its left-wing magazine *Bohemia*, for which he wrote a column under the pseudonym 'Mr Grouch'. He was well liked, with a larrikin sense of humour and irreverence towards artistic pretension. He could puncture egos in a flash. One day, enjoying a quiet drink in a Melbourne wine saloon, discussion turned to the famed bush balladists of the 1890s:

> Drinker: 'Con, did you know Henry Lawson?'
> Con: 'Who didn't?'[12]

Thea Astley didn't really need to meet her grandfather Con (in fact she did so once, when she was about thirteen, a couple of years before he died); he was a 'type' she grew up knowing.

By the time Con died in 1940, Eileen, who had married Cecil Astley in 1918, would have appreciated the irony that her own husband of choice was a man whose interests were almost identical to those of the father she barely knew. Eileen was three years older than her young journalist husband. He was conservative in his habits, seemed settled. In Cecil she could enjoy a little of the allure of a man in the same profession as her absentee father, but one who might offer the security she had lacked as a child.

The family of Cecil Astley was English. Cecil's father, Charles, born in Deptford, Kent, in 1869, had migrated from England at the age of eighteen. He lived briefly in New South Wales, where he married Mary Rankin at Wagga Wagga in 1894. The couple then set sail for Tasmania, where Cecil was born in 1896. Charles was extremely versatile. A highly regarded violinist with the Hobart Philharmonic Orchestra, he moved his family to Queensland's Darling Downs in 1902 and became a well-known painter, woodcarver and potter, as well as a teacher of these crafts. Cecil, an only child, would have watched his father establish himself and make his mark in a growing arts and crafts movement in Toowoomba, Queensland, and the nearby Warwick Technical College. Charles's artwork was praised and valued: the Queensland Art Gallery purchased his 1926 watercolour *Rose of Evening* and an intricately carved wood hallstand.[13] His work has survived and is still traded in the contemporary art world – two watercolours were sold for nearly 7,000 British pounds in 2011.[14] Charles's painting *Condamine at Warwick* gave Astley a placename for her to use in her novels, one that resonated with her grandfather's artwork and her memory of him. Condamine would become the setting of several novels.

Thea inherited her grandfather's gifts as a fine pianist and as a teacher. Charles was something of an experimenter with style in his painting, and Thea as a writer never gave up working on style. Most of all Charles Astley passed on a passion about Australian culture. His was quite unlike other immigrant British households with their morose backward-looking glances at the 'home country'. Charles Astley stamped that independent spirit – the joy of valuing where you are, not where you come from – on his entire family, and Thea grew up with pride in being Australian. Charles Astley made a prodigious series of paintings of seascapes, early settlers' homes, swagmen and the Australian bush. Because he was also a teacher these views made him a pioneer in his field, encouraging Australian artists to use their own locale as a subject. He fought for recognition and funding, since the cost of art equipment and materials was a real threat to his art at the time. Charles obtained local clay – unheard of then – and pressed it himself.

Throughout his childhood Cecil grew up with a father whose artistic reputation was building. Two-year-old Thea stood proud among her family at the presentation of the potpourri jar Charles had designed for the Duchess of York on her 1927 visit to Australia. The inscription on the pot 'Laugh and the world laughs with you' acquired pathos, since Charles died, aged only sixty-one, just two years later.

Cecil was then in his early thirties. After his father's death Charles's achievements were kept alive in conversations at home. There was no boasting or pretension in this; as parents Cecil and Eileen wanted young Phil and Thea to appreciate their grandfather's habits of self-discipline as much as his art. In years to come, Astley would say little of Charles and his art unless prompted, though she grew up knowing about his achievements. The novelist Patrick White once tossed off a remark to her that Queenslanders were 'back in the woods' when it came to 'the visual'.[15] Astley said nothing.

As a young man Cecil had wanted to write, and at just nineteen years of age, in 1915, he published a ditty (not unlike Charles's cheerful potpourri jar inscription):

Comin' into Work

You a-comin' in.
Me a-goin' out.
Passin' ev'ry day
In life's roundabout.

Passin' by to work
Not a word to say:
Only smilin'-like,
As we meet each day.

Winter comin' on.
Rain a-fallin' fast:
Courage in me hands.
Passed the word at last.

Held me gingham up—
'Come in from the wet':
Then you smiled an' spoke.
An'— I'm glad we met.[16]

He managed to get it published in *The Bulletin.* At that time, the magazine had separate sections of its literary pages devoted to writing from Queensland, titled 'Queensland Gossip' and, rather disparagingly, 'Bananaland'. Cecil kept writing and soon some more poetry and a short story were accepted.

Facing the inevitable choice between his own literary ambitions and the necessity to earn a living, as well as personal responsibility for a wife and young family, Cecil took the only job he could that enabled him to work with words: he became a journalist, joining the staff of the newspapers *The Queenslander* and then *The Courier-Mail.* His experience led his daughter to understand that journalism could be the enemy of literary ambition.

Cecil became a sub-editor, a job that was highly responsible and utterly preoccupying. The newspaper routines of going to press were, by today's standards, gruelling and the day's shift long. Cecil had taken the job to support his family, but he hardly saw them. He left home in Ashgrove at around five in the afternoon and didn't finish his shift until the early hours of the morning. The working culture among the subs meant socialising after their long night, then spending their daytime hours playing sport. Cecil was not a member of the sporting group, but subs generally were regarded by other newspaper workers – including reporters – as a different breed. Belonging to a separate and all-important part of the news process, they cast a watchful eye over the work of their fellow journalists. Cecil set himself further apart when he was promoted to senior sub-editor, preferring to wear a suit and tie instead of the more casual clothing of his co-workers. He looked every bit like the popular image of a newspaper sub-editor, bent over pots of glue and working intensely with stories and galley proofs. Newsroom histrionics were not for Cecil: he was private, quiet; he preferred to work under close direction from his superiors. Even though subs were known to be sharp-minded with better than average general knowledge, Cecil's colleagues wondered about this man with an unusually strong intellect, apparently so intent on dealing with the matter at hand.

He took the job very seriously and personally. A sub-editor was responsible for a section of pages with deadlines at exact times, in minutes, in succession. There was no possibility of extension of time for alteration. Correctness in spelling, grammar and punctuation was paramount and the sub was the all-important end-line in the editing process. The job could be stressful but it seemed to suit Cecil's temperament. Because correct use of language was close to his heart, he approached his duties with fervour. He must have known that the subs' desk was a waiting-line to nowhere, with no hope of promotion.

As senior sub-editor he seemed content to carve out a reputation on home ground. The censure of 'Cec' Astley was feared by junior colleagues, perhaps because he was known as a 'man of extraordinary wide knowledge' with a 'finer sense of language than you would sometimes find in a sub-editor'.[17] His small physical size seems at odds with a photograph of him at about this time: sitting, the impression is of a reasonably tall, upright, stern and constrained man. Cecil was like his father, Charles, in having the instincts of a teacher. When it came to cadet errors, he was cruel to be kind: embarrassing mistakes were quickly dealt with and not passed on to the editor. His daughter's firm attitudes about language standards owed as much to her father's legacy as to her own traditional education, which she often cited.

By the early 1960s, when writer Hugh Lunn was a cadet at *The Courier-Mail* and first met Cecil Astley, the chief sub-editor was close to retirement. The years had made him seem ornery and angry.[18] This could have been interpreted as personal unhappiness, but Cecil was politically engaged and felt life's injustices very keenly. Like many workplaces, the world of newspapers often delivered a microcosmic view of the abuses of power. When Thea was a teenager Cecil warned her against a career in journalism because of the nepotism he saw within it. Nevertheless, Thea Astley claimed to have been once tempted by journalism when she was about twenty-one, but was saved from a job at the Brisbane *Telegraph* because she was considered too old.[19] What she saw was that journalism had brought her father teasingly close to words, but not to writing.

Cecil's principal interest remained literature: 'daily work' was something else, a sense of a divide that Thea also inherited. That cheerful 'stickability' of his early *Bulletin* ditty 'Comin' into Work' had served Cecil well in its way. He had strong values about effort and service to pass on to his children and they were the values he and Eileen shared. Both parents encouraged Phil and Thea to read widely, to play music and listen to music with real attention, to pursue and develop their abilities. When eight-year-old Thea was encouraged to publish her first piece of writing in 'Bubbles Corner' of *The Courier-Mail*, parental approval would have been undemonstrative: it was important to be humble about one's gifts.

Music was highly valued in the Astley home. Thea soon learned to play the piano, working her way through studies and pieces by Heller, Clementi and Beethoven. Later she would claim to have 'written the hands' of her favourite music teacher, Arthur Sharman, into the character of Bernard Leverson in *The Slow Natives*.

But Cecil also knew how to enjoy family life. Beach holidays held the Astleys close in a way that the daily routines of their life in the city could not. In these rented 'sea-rotted houses' at the beach, usually at Kirra near Coolangatta on the Gold Coast, Cecil would finally relax and even sing shanties.[20] Thea and Phil saw a different Cecil, a different Eileen. These were the happiest occasions for Phil and Thea. Back in town, Cecil occasionally took them on news-related outings (such as viewing the damage caused by the 1930 Brisbane floods when Thea was only five) but it was nothing like the free-spirited loose time of these holidays. It was a rare treat to spend time with Cecil, something Astley did not do again until her university days.

When Cecil was in the house his presence was large; on the light side, he was irresistibly drawn to the 'one-liner, or the smart-arse crack', and he relieved the tense and rather staid atmosphere at 358 Waterworks Road.[21] The tension in the marriage gave an edge to these witticisms, and Cecil, while funny, could also be a standover merchant, a bit of the 'bully of the Lawson type', as Astley would later describe him.[22] Eileen was the ever-present parent who needed a confidant. At first this was Phil, who from early teenage years was becoming increasingly religious and close to his mother, then it was Thea's turn to stand by her mother's side. Cecil was a stronger and more dominant personality than Eileen and he and his daughter shared a strong interest in writing and literature. Thea was naturally more ebullient than her older brother, and drawn to her father, especially as he encouraged her to read 'almost anything at all'. Later in life Astley would fondly recall him reading *The Magic Pudding* aloud to her. She identified from an early age with this male approval, under the watchful eye of her mother, Eileen, whose demands in the end were of a moral kind.[23] Cecil and Eileen were diligent, good parents but 'conservative'. It is not clear exactly what lay behind the friction in the Astley household: possibly Cecil's long working hours, which left Eileen alone for extended periods. They might even have quarrelled about the size of their family, for Cecil was an only child and Eileen had two sisters. There was a four-and-a-half-year gap between Phil and Thea, which was unusual for the times, and the Astleys were a small family by Catholic standards. In any event both children tried to make sense of their family situation, and responded as their temperaments dictated.

Photographs of Phil in his teens show a slightly built boy, standing at the end of the line where the shorter boys were placed; his bony, angular face was better suited than most to the thick-rimmed round spectacles he wore. He attended St Joseph's College, Gregory Terrace, a highly regarded fee-paying Catholic college for boys. Phil was softly spoken and by the mid-1930s, when he began the four years that would take him to senior, he had already acquired a shy, some would say effeminate, manner. Perhaps at this early stage Thea developed a protective attitude towards her brother. More than seventy years later, when the writer Michael McGirr began writing about his experiences of depressive illness during his own years as a priest, when he knew Phil well, Thea insisted that he not use Phil's name in the book.[24]

Phil thrived at Gregory Terrace. He avoided sport and soon became known as one who 'worships at the altars of Bach and Haydn'. He became a school prefect and debater but his personal intensity belonged to religious matters always. By the end of his school years, in 1938, he was the President of the St Vincent de Paul society and active in the Holy Name Society. The school's motto '*Servire Deo Sapere*' ('To serve God is to be wise') suited Phil, who would forever link intellect with belief; when in the school newsletters he promoted the Catholic Truth Society pamphlets it was because he believed they were instructive for 'an educated laity' which he saw as 'essential in this twentieth century'.[25]

Despite seeming success, Phil struggled with self-esteem. The God he believed in dictated that either he be devout or be unworthy. Thea watched this painful process, unable to offer much support. A gap of temperament made their four-year age difference seem larger, a kind of affectionate and benign estrangement that left both children having to negotiate separately their respective roles within the family. Despite all, they were and remained close for life.

In families, emotional and sexual identity is secreted in a hidden world of childhood. Often there is a kind of cross-modelling of child to the parent of the opposite sex. David Malouf expressed this, writing of his older sister in a poem dedicated to her: 'You were like father/ I like mother/ a happy compromise/ … I wrote you out of my childhood.'[26] The Astley family was like this: the effeminate and increasingly devout Phil and the acute-minded, robust Thea were in their way intensely close but very, very different. It was a difference that at least one of their parents, the devout Eileen, had a vested interest in. Thea couldn't help becoming a younger sibling who was curious and observing.

If Phil struggled with his own sexuality, it was in private: such things were not openly discussed at the time and certainly not in a conservative Catholic household. In the years to come it was that kind of forced silence that left its mark on Astley, though she gave voice to such dilemmas in her novels when she wrote sympathetically, as she often did, about gay priests. In their internal dialogue, she could comment indirectly on the plight of those who, like Phil, took this path in life. In many of the novels, such characters tend to escape to remote places – a comment in itself – and it is Father Lingard in *A Boat Load of Home Folk* who reflects: 'I never had to think, to worry, to examine. I accepted the lot.'[27]

Curiously, Astley never expected anyone to connect these perceptions with Phil. More than fifty years later, when Astley's daughter-in-law had only just met Phil, she commented to her husband, 'Ed, you didn't tell me Phil was gay!' Astley snapped the topic shut with quiet phrases about Phil's delicate mental and emotional states, while Thea's husband, Jack, would often speak of Phil affectionately as a 'funny thing'.[28] Nobody spoke of sexual orientation.

The attitude of the Catholic Church towards homosexuality precluded open discussion: it was considered a sin against the unitive and procreative sexual activity approved by the Church and regarded as an act of depravity, therefore a moral evil to be fought with the vigour of faith. As a teenager growing up in the early 1930s, Phil would have seen little in Australian public life to encourage any different view. In another decade or so, after World War II in Europe at least, some homophile – as they were called – advocacy groups would emerge but in Australia throughout the 1940s and the Cold War atmosphere of the 1950s there was little acceptance of – indeed there was open hostility towards – homosexuality.

Like all children, Phil and Thea were immersed in the climate of their own small family world. Eileen was ambitious for them, her attentions shaped somewhat by her own insecurities and lack of formal education. Yet Eileen's hopes for Phil and Thea were not so much aspirational as religious, attended by an intense concern for their moral future. This would prove a fearsome combination for her children.

Phil crept quietly into his middle teens while his younger sister watched what she would one day call his 'vagaries of personal weather' and sought out those many corners where she might escape the 'warfare of married couples'.[29] Thea did what was expected of her in terms of religious observance but unlike Phil she did not especially seek to understand her God, nor at the age of nine or ten to question the rituals of Catholicism by which the family lived. At home devout families might recite the Rosary every night, others perhaps weekly, and nobody was supposed to eat meat on Fridays. The strictest rules, as Astley would one day remark, were saved for sexual matters: chastity before marriage and sex for procreation as well as a complex set of rules governing marriage, annulment and divorce. Marriages between Catholics and non-Catholics were for a long time called 'mixed marriages' – between a believer and a so-called heretic.

James Scullin, the Australian Labor prime minister elected in 1929, was of Catholic background and so as a religious group Catholics were perhaps less set apart from the rest of the population than at other times in Australian history. The Depression of the 1930s also brought a credible voice via the *Catholic Worker* newspaper to those who saw their mission as defending the needy and the poor.

In one of the 'many corners' Thea found reading. If it can be said that Patrick White fell into a puddle and found God, then it could be said that Thea Astley fell into fiction to see whether God even existed.[30] Some people try to discover the existence of God in the physical world; she read fiction as a way of determining such a presence in the human moral and imaginative world. In books, Astley hoped to find God in a form she could accept.

Reading was her escape, a salve, and proof positive that a world existed beyond her own. Books were also a form of consolation. When she was eight, she went to Melbourne with her mother for six months during a temporary parental separation. Whether because of Cecil's overtures or because Eileen remembered her own lonely life in a single-parent female household, she returned to the marriage. However, in those unfamiliar surroundings, young Astley grabbed whatever books were around. What she chose to read might be partly responsible for what came next. At eight years of age Astley read *Les Misérables* by Victor Hugo.

Some individuals seem uniquely primed to have certain impressions made upon them from the start in a way that others do not. Thea Astley seems to have been such a child. The reading of Hugo was not simply a literary feat: the corners of Astley's psyche were squared by that novel. Its story of convict Jean Valjean is a nineteenth-century crisscross pattern of injustice compounded by misunderstanding, lit up by acts of desperation and depravity, but there is also love, kindness and a kind of 'life justice' in the fortunes of the main characters.

Close to the end of her life, Astley still talked about the novel in detail:

> I still remember that terrible scene where [policeman] Javert chased Jean Valjean through the sewers of Paris, it made a fantastic impression on me – never wanted to work in sewers [laughs]. The bishop [Myriel] scene … Jean Valjean brought back with missing candles by police … funny how I can remember this, given I was eight … [He says] 'Oh no, I gave them to this gentleman. He was here.' One of the best lessons in charitable behaviour I've ever had in my life.[31]

The experience of reading such a tale allowed Astley at a very young age to intuit aspects of human experience of which she was already aware. Her reading might have been of that intuitive kind young people sometimes do, where the emotional and psychological reality of the work brushes against the edges of a developing sensibility, long before the child can hope for complete understanding of what is being read. Such reading is not so much precocious as prescient, pointing the way to other truths that the child will come to recognise.

Hugo's novel showed its young reader in another hemisphere that the universe had an order that could be subverted; that a human being could be misunderstood, misjudged and die in the process; that alienation was sometimes inescapable; and that if you hoped to win over the odds, the chances were you would die a slow spiritual death. The basics of all this somehow lay nascent in the eight-year-old girl, the first intimation of a conversation Thea Astley never stopped having with herself about universal human experiences, morality and belief, making her life as a writer seem inevitable from this very early point.

It does seem melodramatic to suggest that the harshness of Hugo's world had its resonances with a young girl in Brisbane, Australia, in the 1930s. But Astley was growing into and experiencing troubling aspects of her own self, and a lot of difficult things were visible too, even to children. Cecil's presence – even if he did not speak of the news of the day – had an impact because the daily news throughout the 1930s and much of the 1940s was harrowing. He was sorely tested by much of what he saw and read in his working life and the emotional weight of bearing those events in a civilised silence must have taken its toll on him and been obvious to members of his family.

Cecil and Eileen's conservative approach to the upbringing of their children did not conceal differences of insistence and emphasis, especially in matters of religion. Eileen's brand of Catholicism was rather severe and unforgiving. It was 'a peculiarly obsessive, categorical and intolerant brand of Irish–Australian Catholicism', full of confusing ideas – at least from a child's perspective – about sin, forgiveness, judgement and punishment.[32] At a very young age, Thea and Phil were learning to focus on intention and action, and to reflect on the effects of their own choices.

Brisbane, like the rest of Catholic Australia, was in the grip of the charisma of that fierce defender of his faith, Melbourne-based Cardinal Mannix. A controversial figure for decades, by the 1940s he was a recognised leader of the Irish community in Australia and highly regarded by the members of his faith. He made public statements about his attitudes towards work, unions (which he supported though he disagreed with strikes), loyalty and the Catholic–Protestant divide, much of which would have been either the subject of discussion at the Astley home, or integral to Eileen's approved way of worship.

Thea enjoyed her local school, the Sisters of Charity convent of St Michael's, which was close to Ashgrove in the nearby suburb of Rosalie. The sisters who taught there stayed at the senior Catholic convent school All Hallows' in the city and caught the tram to Rosalie. For Thea, St Michael's provided a ready-made connection to a quality Catholic post-primary education. She stayed there until the equivalent of today's Year 8, in what was then an extended primary system.

In this year Thea, like other academically able students, was coached for a scholarship to gain entry into the private Catholic senior school system; other students would go on to state high schools. But to achieve the best results, all was not left to the final year of primary school: one teacher would often take one class for all subjects, and for many years in succession. This way, the teacher developed knowledge of individual students and their families, could take a special interest in the personality or ability of a particular child. Thea had much to be grateful for here: for four important years she received exactly this special attention, and from a very young and enthusiastic nun.

From the start Sister Mary noticed that the physically diminutive Thea was a special student, not just a bright child but one with unusual ideas and abilities.[33] She could see that Thea was outstanding academically across the curriculum but she also noticed that she seemed able to pursue and to articulate individual ways of thinking. It so happened – against the odds – that Sister Mary valued independence of thought. It would not be the first time that Astley would benefit from the forthrightness and intellectual independence of the nuns who taught her.

Unfortunately, Astley's young peers were not so forgiving, either of their perspicacious classmate or the approving young teacher. They looked askance at what to them seemed quirky ways. Resentment hovered at the edge of tentative friendships: already Thea looked unlikely to be one of the group. She was making the first of her choices about the price of belonging – a lifelong obsession with outcasts and misfits lay ahead. Catholicism had shown her community and comfort in ritual but when it came to 'group' versus 'true self', it seemed to her that a different bargain was being struck.

She set herself apart.[34] It's hard to imagine those students seeing the reader of *Les Misérables* as 'just an ordinary reading kid', as Astley always described herself when asked to look back at her childhood.[35] The other children felt that either she was superior, or she held herself to be superior. In Australia that meant much the same thing, translated to being 'full of yourself', or 'up yourself'.

Even a bold-thinking child is vulnerable and Astley was not at this age even really bold; she did tend to be the first to speak up, but this was part ebullience and part anxiety. To her young peers it might have seemed like attention-seeking. As an adult, the same tendencies led her to awkwardly twisting her hands in unfamiliar social situations, the ever-ready witticism fired like a distracting cannon shot. It was a way of using attention as camouflage.

Sister Mary saw before her eyes this peculiar child's stubbornness turn into bold-faced courage. She watched as her young pupil read loudly and with confidence to her peers, stoically enduring their whispered derision. Sister Mary believed that here was a child whose personality was going to need 'space' and recognition.[36]

Teacher and student remained close; Thea even became known as a 'teacher's pet'. Their relationship was important emotionally, all the more so for being outside the home, with Thea away from her own mother. The nuns had begun to suspect that Eileen was demanding of the mother–daughter relationship, that she was perhaps expecting too much from such a young child. Sister Mary was therefore all the more inclined to give young Thea the freedom she needed to express herself. This comfort and support even attracted Astley to the idea of becoming a nun.[37] There seemed nothing to fear in self-sacrifice, but then she was the beneficiary. The problem, Astley would grow to realise, was on the giving side. This balance of giving and receiving was the equation that the novelist she became tried to solve.

The nature of love – selfless love – became her obsession for life. Picasso once identified this kind of anxious intensity in Cezanne's work, which fascinated him less for its formal artistic aspects than for the anxiety that drove Cezanne to paint so many similar things. Astley's response to her childhood experiences had the same quality, and it never left her. The emotional core of her work was always this 'hinterland of childhood' – a phrase that meant a lot to Astley – a subtle geography of hurts. When it was pointed out to her that her early story 'Cubby', published in the 1961 edition of the short story anthology *Coast to Coast*, had been the impetus for her novel *The Well Dressed Explorer*, about an unlikeable philandering journalist, she challenged the assumption. The one note of sympathy in the novel is the link to the lost world of innocence described in 'Cubby', and there for anyone who really understood the book.[38]

Astley regarded childhood as not just a 'hinterland' but also as a 'sovereign state'. Like a favourite poet Charles Baudelaire, she, too, felt that true genius was recaptured childhood but she gave it another name: 'primary magic'. In *The Well Dressed Explorer*, the character George Brewster tries to repeat one of those breathless being-in-the-present moments, which, by their very nature, can never be repeated: 'Never would he have a moment quite like that again – but he did not know it. All his life George was silly enough to believe primary magic could be held and repeated at will; and like so many people benignly silly, he was often lucky.'[39]

Elements in this archaeology of self can be found in Astley's subsequent versions of vulnerability, delusion and disillusion, her collection of characters in childlike states: Peter Pan philanderers, idealists, benign zealots, naïve intellectuals, misfits and oddballs.[40] They reminded her of the outsider status that children on the verge of puberty often experience, turning them into observers and witnesses.

It is the children in her novels who often give voice to the 'tacit war between men and women' she came to know growing up with Cecil and Eileen.[41]

As Astley entered the next phase of her life she became transfixed by self-doubt, her own vulnerability and anxiety. She did not in any realistic sense grow up an outsider, nor was she an 'oddball', but she felt like a 'bit of a misfit'.[42]

She would always look to wider social and political matters to explain these strong personal reactions, observing: 'I believe ours is the age of the misfit. Because I grew up in a period when conservatism was rampant and one had to fit a pattern, I allow my feelings to take over when I write about misfits. I always develop an enormous sympathy with them.'[43]

As Astley matured, her early experiences continued to make her angry; she continually explored the extremes of human behaviour. That tendency was her way of expressing the gap between how she was forced to behave and what she actually felt, making the resentment in her writing not always or even necessarily about the plight of 'oddballs' but, rather, about the displacement of individual will.[44] As a girl of ten in the mid-1930s, Astley had every reason to be thinking about choice: she was already confronted with her religious brother Phil's choices, his future in the Church, but she was also thinking about her own life and how different she could make it.

2

Suspected of reading

He was a beanpole of a man with a long amused face and rimless glasses. An unlikely planter, they said. He was suspected of reading.

Beachmasters by Thea Astley, 1985[1]

Given the close relationship between Sister Mary and her bright and unusual young pupil at St Michael's Primary, it is not surprising that the very best efforts were expected of young Thea in the all-important Year 8 primary scholarship exam. Everyone, including Astley herself, knew that the results would determine her chances of access to quality senior schooling, which Cecil and Eileen could not provide given what Astley came to call the family's 'shabby-genteel' existence. There was no question of going to a school outside the Catholic system.

When the news came about their daughter's scholarship as a day boarder at All Hallows', relief would have mingled with pride. Thea could live in the family home even though her school day would be long. Not only was All Hallows' considered a cut above the major state high school (Brisbane State High), it also had a superior reputation among Catholic schools. The Sisters of Mercy who founded the school were the most significant religious order of nuns before the expansion of Catholic education in the 1920s. Conditions at the school in the late 1930s were, however, hardly luxurious and the school's appearance had changed little since the original 1861 bare quadrangle of tall buildings, daunting for a young teenager used to a local parish school. Physically, the school insisted on its place in the city of Brisbane, since the buildings were a prominent landmark on the hillside bank of the Brisbane River, as well as being adjacent to the proposed site of the Story Bridge overlooking Kangaroo Point. The teachers were religiously dedicated and believed in educational rigour, but the school motto '*Dieu et Devoir*' ('God and Duty') revealed the overriding ethos of school life.

Astley entered this very formal environment, leaving behind the friendly chatter of her primary school classroom. The difference in scale would have been overwhelming. It all seemed so severe. The full boarders conducted much of the school day in silence, beginning with silent prayer, followed by study, Mass and breakfast, after which they were allowed to speak. Astley had been a teacher's favourite and she missed the one-on-one attention; here she was being asked to fit into a large multi-staffed convent, a girl among many, albeit 'a scholarship girl'. To win a scholarship to such a school was an admirable academic achievement, but Astley was only too aware that she was among many children of well-off families. She was adrift, uncertain, constrained. Awed by the enormity of the change, perhaps clinging to the world she had just left, she continued to keep in touch with Sister Mary: she needed an ally, and perhaps also someone to complain to about the new school.

Life at home had been conservative but this new school was all formality. Even the uniform announced restriction: a 1940 photograph of Astley in her second year shows her wearing a long-sleeved dark-coloured school dress with a high, wide collar. The uniform (retained until 1954) was both physically limiting and utterly impractical in the heat and humidity of Brisbane, an absurd transplantation of British couture. Astley felt that a great deal of importance was placed on outward show, and that the students were always being watched for 'irregularities' in conduct.

What made things worse for Astley was that formalities and restrictions were always presented in terms of care and protection, and privilege. This combination was morally disturbing to Astley, whose father rejected any expression of class privilege, and it affected her understanding of politics for the rest of her life. She had earned her privileged place: perhaps that was different? Nobody, it seemed, expected the girls of All Hallows' to take on any responsibility beyond their academic studies. When waiting on tables or kitchen work were necessary, girls of Astley's age from the Fortitude Valley public school were called in.

The sight of her contemporaries labouring on her behalf was an excruciating experience for Astley, all the more so as she realised that chance of a different kind from hers was playing itself out in the lives of these less fortunate girls. She had earned her place at the school, she knew that, but unusually for her age, she was mindful of the role that luck played in life. She had Cecil and Eileen and their support at home, she had Sister Mary and she had the much-needed scholarship. There was really no need to feel guilty, but the growing knowledge that the school's prized quality of charity could be so selective left its mark.

But absolute charity was not always the order of the day. In the late 1930s 'a ruler and a strap' were used if school rules or practices were infringed in any way. As a former student recalls: 'Convent girls were exhorted to be humble of heart, unselfish, patient and submissive … the religious practice was governed to a great degree by absolute obedience to the laws of the church. A deep sense of guilt was felt at any deviation from the straight and narrow … no meat on Friday; no hats in church … Latin Mass …'[2]

Within the school, other demarcations divided the social territory. Throughout the 1940s there was a distinct social separation between day students and full boarders. Often this was most obvious in school sports and other group activities, so that as a day student Astley never quite identified with belonging to the school in the same way that boarders did. It always seemed to be the full boarders who rehearsed and performed plays in the school's concert hall, morality plays with melodramatic and pious names such as 'Every Soul' or 'Magnificent Deception'. But she did not necessarily mind this observer role: it offered a rare privacy of thought among the throng.

The school newsletter *Jottings* was full of daily comings and goings, busy with jolly news of school excursions; the girls were not expected to venture into the wider world on their own. (In her first year Astley went to see the Marber Minstrels with the school – an excursion that her parents would hardly have considered, even if they could have afforded it.) All this jollity had the air of being forced, an attempt perhaps to distract from the grave talk of war. The convent, Astley came to understand, intended to remain cloistered. Occasionally Astley and her friends would stage a 'breakout', daring themselves to a milkshake after school in the city at the Pig 'n' Whistle in Queen Street. To be seen drinking these concoctions with suggestive names like 'Keep it Dark' in the company of equally privileged non-Catholic schoolboys was forbidden and could mean expulsion from All Hallows'.[3]

If there was a balancing factor, a reason to toe the line, for Astley it was the spirit and dedication of the teaching nuns. She was grateful for their genuine interest in the abilities of their students.

Consistency and continuity mattered to her, particularly because the relationship between Cecil and Eileen could be bitter, and, as at primary school, one nun in particular became all-important. Astley did not encounter Sister Mary Claver until 1941 when she was in sub-senior year and travelling on a bare C in English: perhaps an indication of how difficult her transition to All Hallows' had actually been. Sister Claver was a large, comforting, motherly woman, 'an amazing enthusiast, a lover of books and language'.[4] She was not a strict nun but the students hung on her every word. She did not reject strong-willed students, especially if they were intellectually gifted, as was the unusual young woman in her English class. Whenever any argument was up for challenge, Sister Claver – and increasingly the other students – began to look to Thea Astley.[5]

After one year with this teacher Astley won the school's McDermott Prize for Matriculation English. As if to herself, as much as for Sister Claver, she wrote a dedication in the novel she won as a prize: 'Kindness is more important than cleverness.'[6]

The young teacher nurtured what she saw as a special talent and a student–teacher bond formed that would last a lifetime. The support was unwavering, one-on-one, and was of the reassuring kind Astley had always needed, especially now that she was beginning to realise it was not enough to be clever.

Astley was starting to find solace in the companionship of words. Unlike primary school, here was competition for the sisters' approval and at least one classmate was a serious literary rival challenging Astley for top spot. Writing, wanting to write, was accepted as natural in a school that had a serious investment in literary and intellectual passions. Thea Astley was by no means considered an oddity and was made to feel that the world might welcome this interest of hers.

Students saw the sense of vocation in their teachers and were encouraged to consider the profession as a possible occupation. In the early 1940s seniors from previous years who were now teaching assistants returned to help in the school. To them Astley seemed a bright girl just a few years younger than they were. She was not outwardly confident but it was clear she was 'self-possessed' of her 'internal world'.[7]

By the time Astley was fifteen some of this confidence had given way to introspection; her internal world interested her most, its remoteness from daily life. She began to express these feelings in the poetry she published in the school magazine. It was only her second year at All Hallows' when she articulated this disquiet:

Unrest

I find no solace in the haunting days,
That creep so slowly by;
Nor in the cool black scarf of Night's pathways,
Nor in the sky
So calm, serene ...
It has no knowledge of my twisted soul
Seeking peace in vain.
Tortured by fears of my own making –
Fancies of a fevered brain.
I seek to fill my mind with other thoughts,
A tree, a limpid pool, an evening sky,
Striving to find comfort in their grace.
And all this misery unexpressed by sigh,
Will wreck my soul, will spoil, will mar, will break,
My heart is like a bird trapped in a cage,
With no escape.[8]

In years to come Astley would dismiss this as 'teenage acne', an adolescent expression of how she saw her emotional world, but the poem also shows formal mastery.[9]

The set of behavioural codes and practices that dominated her life seemed to debase the validity of what Astley was actually thinking and feeling. As each year passed she was more aware of how limiting this protected world could be: it was a stage-managed existence. Students had little to do but study and observe; they were not expected to converse with the priests who came to visit. Astley saw how obedience was all, that a whole parish society could be 'totally controlled by sociological attitudes' delivered by men – ill-educated 'bog Irish priests', as she later called them.[10]

Despite the fine education All Hallows' offered, the conflict between her two modes of being was emphasised by the conservative and religious attitudes of her mother. It was now impossible for Astley to separate the two, something that would cause her enormous anxiety and hurt. The conflict was close to home rather than genuinely internal: Astley was relatively confident in herself of her own views. But the situation pressed in close; in 1940 Phil was preparing to join the Society of Jesus (Jesuits) at Loyola College in Watsonia, a suburb of Melbourne. Unlike his sister, he was seeking a life of stricture and conformity.

The innate differences between brother and sister were opening up. Of course Thea was to some extent in awe of Phil's decision, sharing the family's pride at having a priest in the family, and Phil seemed to survive on the strength of his commitment. At fifteen, Astley had no sense of what joining a religious order might mean, except for the comfort and protection such institutions offered their young devotees. Later in life, as her brother's frailties surfaced, she became more and more nervous and fearful for Phil, though she only expressed the full extent of her feelings nearly sixty years later, and privately, after his funeral.[11]

One thing, above all else, became a bridge between these two who lived in such vastly different ways: music. It was a shared passion and a way of understanding each other. Phil loved sacred music and was a talented organist. Astley was studying piano privately. The fact that her favourite nun, Sister Claver, had a singing voice that was legendary in its way also helped forge the only possible link for Astley between the religious life, her school and her own passions. The school placed enormous emphasis on music, with several choirs, including a nuns' choir, and school orchestras. Mass was in Latin and sung.

It was on these terms that family and Church could coexist in some kind of harmony. For Astley music was a language equal to and beyond words and would always be so. Her novels are full of musical references, and she chose musical terms for titles: *A Descant for Gossips* and *Coda*.

However, she did not choose a musical career because she knew it was very likely to lead to teaching rather than playing or composing; besides, she was not really comfortable in formal musical performance. Music was emotional and exposing of self; what she wanted was camouflage. Poetry was perfect for self-expression because it required the same exactness of skill as music without the need for performance.[12]

Astley's ideas about writing are understandable given the literary models she grew up with. The private world of the self belonged to the idealised Romantic aesthetic of a Wordsworthian solace in solitude and nature. She enjoyed consciously imitating these expressive poetic forms. As she entered her late teens, she wrote out her thoughts on such things:

To You – The Poet

You stood apart from others – weaver of dreams,
For your soul found joy in the light of a star;
You felt with pain the splendour of a hill, Or your spirit went flying
    afar,
Caught in a mad delight on the screaming wind,
That lashed white on the grey of the sea. You knew, too, the sorrows
    of men, All the care that can be.
I have seen you gaze on a stream, your eyes filled with delight
At the slow-moving ripples that weave
Their way through the reeds. There can be no sight
But it fills you with joy or with pain;
You breathe dreams and live them. Again,
As you watched the last ragged autumn-leaf falling,
Or the first fragrant bloom of spring,
You mourned with the tear-furrowed wrinkles of age,
You rejoiced with the laughter of youth –
Such emotions can these things bring.
And I saw, as you looked on a sun-dappled vale,

Your joy – and your sight dimmed with tears;
And I gazed in your eyes to see …
The dreams of a thousand years.[13]

Not only were the ideas important: competence and skill in creating emotion on the page, not just expressing it, were very important to her. They were part of the legacy about effort and discipline in art that her artist grandfather Charles had left and that Cecil and Eileen endorsed. That said, much of the poetry Astley wrote in her late teens is typically adolescent hand-on-heart, poems titled 'Dreaming' or 'Fantasy', with images familiar from English poetry of the Romantic period, which she clearly studied closely. Astley was discovering some of the less obvious pleasures of language; if the words were arranged delicately enough they could hint at an emotional hinterland.

As a discipline, writing was a very welcome substitute for the dictates of home or insistent religious practice. Here was hope that an individual might, privately at least, find expression in a life outside the Church's control. With Phil established in a religious vocation, this conviction was more important than ever for Astley. In writing, confusion could be measured; the fissures of loyalty between faith and self-belief could be expressed, if not mended.

Catholicism was nevertheless an overwhelming presence in Astley's day-to-day life. The faith had a strong national credibility in the years leading up to and during World War II, especially in Brisbane. Catholic Archbishop James Duhig (whose photograph was the only one to make it into the All Hallows' journal one year) was a major public figure in the Catholic Church of wartime Australia. Duhig 'spoke for the northern capital, but he spoke for Australia'.[14] His public concerns were more social than theological, and his views about social responsibility and welfare influenced the growth of the Catholic Action groups of the period. His editorials were published in *The Catholic Leader* and were read widely by parishioners such as

Cecil and Eileen. Duhig was a mixture of the quixotic and imperious, holding often lively but ambivalent attitudes towards many aspects of life. Though he approved of the American soldiers' presence in Brisbane, for instance, he thought they were a bad influence on the moral behaviour of young Brisbane men and women. He was opposed to drunkenness, advocated quality wine instead of spirits, and was not himself a teetotaller.

In the Astley household Duhig was a hero for being a great supporter of culture, especially the visual arts, and a patron of many cultural organisations. Astley was at a critical age – sixteen – for finding a personal resonance in this endorsement that seemed to sanction free self-expression. Catholic cultural societies would become a very important link to the world beyond school, coming as they did with parental and Church approval. Astley was growing up to see that taking a position was important, though different from activism. Later in life she spoke out publicly on many issues – literacy, censorship, the funding of writing. For someone who later claimed to have got 'through university on three sherries', it was as overt as she was prepared to be.[15]

Astley's senior years at All Hallows' brought many changes. The war forced school life into unwelcome union with the outside world, even as the nuns tried keep the routines stable. As physical culture squads exercised in groups and girls studied hard for their external examinations, the material realities of war were making themselves felt. It was announced that the school annual would now have to go without pictures for years because of the expense of photo processing.[16] The school newsletter began reporting the progress of comfort funds for soldiers, marking the anniversaries of war breaking out and describing progress in 'the still troubled Pacific conditions'.[17]

From early in 1942, teenage schoolgirls could hardly ignore the presence of American servicemen in Brisbane during the Pacific War. Even All Hallows' ran a friendly excursion to Brisbane's Hamilton wharves to see the flagships and destroyers, and like her schoolmates

Astley waved cheerfully while she autograph-hunted the American sailors.

She was seventeen and beginning to develop all-important social confidence. Even within school she had begun making jokes, taking on Cecil's habit of larrikin humour, experimenting with other ways of being true to herself. Some of the more extreme rituals of Catholic daily life were easy for Astley to poke fun at, and so was the sermonising. Astley paid close attention to the language used and later wrote of its 'dogmatic assurance' delivered in a sing-song of 'poetry and fancy'.[18] This scorn for overt religiosity remained with her. Even the recitation of the Rosary in Astley's first novel was seen by the main character as 'such mechanicalness and so little piety; it was like being present at a series of verbal gymnastics'.[19]

Astley and her close friend Jean Baker had developed something of a reputation for pranks, but went too far on at least one occasion. All girls were forced to take Epsom salts daily, thought to prevent constipation. The remedy was very popular and the substance relatively cheap at about ten pounds per ton. The two girls were easily able to overdose, and it was practically the only way to be away sick from classes. Always it was ritual literalness that irritated Astley and somehow the daily dose of salts epitomised that. It amused her to 'raise the stakes' by taunting some of the more literal-minded nuns, leading to amusing little scenes:

> Sister: 'Where is your Penny Catechism [a cheap and simplified summary of Church teachings]?'
>
> Astley: [Theatrical display of looking quizzical, pulling out – in slow motion – a Latin book, a French book, a mathematics text] 'I've got a threepenny catechism. Will that do?'[20]

Somehow she was managing to be cheeky without getting into serious trouble and had the confidence of knowing that she could afford these minor transgressions. Playing with semantics came under the heading of impudence, not rudeness, nor rebellion. The nuns regarded her as polite but with naughty-schoolgirl tendencies. Like Cecil's wisecracking, it was a larrikinism without intent.

Astley's novels tell us a great deal about these early years of her schooling. A lot of time in school was spent on describing the trajectory of the soul but what she had taken for granted as a child now seemed odd: little was said of the reality of life or the actual feelings of the individual. Astley's mocking style was used to deflect from incursions into her private world, and this double consciousness became part of her. She was perfecting 'the art of self-containment' that she wrote into the character of Elsie Ford, her first alter ego in *Girl with a Monkey*.[21]

It was as if twin modes of existence now governed Astley's behaviour: bursts of theatrical gregariousness and the flight to shelter. Only later in life did she talk about such defences in relation to Catholicism, of how she became aware of her own repetitive 'examination of conscience, intention and purpose'.[22] The nature of things, the effects of things, the incompleteness of things, all were intensely observed in minute detail; for a personality such as Astley's this meant being aware, then being aware of being aware. She would spend a life battling nerves and 'little phobias'.[23]

At the time, at school, relief came in a surprising form: the sung Latin Tridentine Mass. It was another cherished bond between brother and sister. Throughout their lives, however much the form of Mass was modernised by the Church, both Phil and Thea revered this earlier incantatory form.[24] During Mass Astley enjoyed a sense of community while secretly enjoying her private thoughts. She would be silent but she could observe. She would later write of the rituals of the Mass as slavish and manipulative in its symbolism, but she also knew how they calmed the mind.

The Mass was, as others have observed, 'a language few understood but one that communicated the power invested in it by tradition'.[25] There was an undeniable sense of majesty about it too. All Hallows' boasted an assembly hall with a vaulting ceiling, which made for even more spectacular gatherings. Late in life Astley missed the smell of incense and a kind of poetry in the early versions of the Bible.[26]

But what marred the celebration of Mass for Astley was the behaviour of the various presiding priests. Astley was forced to watch the forthright, astute and hardworking nuns who taught her as they dissolved into obsequiousness in the presence of these visiting priests. Their subservience, she felt, was an example of the iniquitous clerical hierarchy. The views of the male clergy towards women of the Church – or women generally – seemed to undermine so much that was on offer educationally. These sentiments are summed up in many of Astley's stories, but with particular savagery in 'The Curate Breaker': 'Father Rassini was a suave man of God ... who believed strongly in the superiority of the clergy, the philosophic inferiority of all laymen, and the non-existence of women except in some cloudily defined area known as auxiliary where he believed them to be tea-makers for God.'[27]

At the time, as an obedient pupil, Astley would have been aware that she, too, was 'performing' obedience, whatever her thoughts. Her mind became her personal armoury in a fight that for the moment required no actual rebellion. She slipped cheekily past many official conduct rules, preferring ironic digs at the status quo. It was less risky and more fun. This serious academic student was a wit and known for it. Dinnertime was theatre time. In years to come the writer Helen Garner would marvel at Astley's disarming social comfort when sitting at tables in pubs or the like, at how she seemed to know when and when not to perform.[28] This understanding probably started here. Astley was now a senior, enjoying the approval of a young student audience. Day boarders took meals at the school and the posting of 'table sittings' was a daily excitement. One by one, the lists went up on the noticeboard.

'Who'd you get?' Girls swivelled around to friends. 'Who did you get?' Astley always heard, rather than read, her own name as she arrived to escalating squeals of delight: *'Thea Astley!'*

It was a name that meant her table was in for some storytelling.[29] These were delightful moments in what was a dour time.

Big changes in the school arrangements were in place for the following year, 1942, a special year in the wartime history of All Hallows' and a critical one for Astley herself. Brisbane was now the headquarters of the American General Douglas MacArthur, his base for the Pacific War. Even though the actual fighting was still remote, the possibility of air raids on Brisbane forced All Hallows' to split campuses and evacuate students (including Astley) to Warwick, 160 kilometres southwest of Brisbane on the Darling Downs.

Astley was now in her final all-important matriculation or university entrance year. The relative freedom from the control of parents at home, even for just one year, was a great boon and Astley felt more than ready for the change. She loved her parents and had never quarrelled with them but this was a sanctioned parting. She wasted no time making it as different from regular school as it could be. Already sporting a certain status as a crack storyteller, she increased her status as a rebel: she was spied by more timid students at break times playing poker in the dugout trenches with her friend Jean Baker.

It was all very exotic compared with the quiet life of a prewar All Hallows'. Girls practised air-raid drills in make-do trenches 'while the plaster saints managed to look the other way'.[30] Moira Knudson, two classes below Astley, watched this well-known senior from afar, aware of the gossip that she was always jotting things down on the back of tram tickets. Moira had a madcap sense of humour, was rebellious and naturally drawn to Astley, who discovered that despite their age difference Moira was a kindred spirit. Perversely, Astley found her time at All Hallows' was becoming strangely liberating; friendships were unusual and more intense. Astley could hardly have imagined that more than forty years later, while researching her 1982 novel *An Item from the Late News*, she would smoke her way through north Queensland with Moira.[31]

Astley's life in at Warwick was a pleasing balance. There was the academic work, the usual anxiety about achievement and nerves about the future, but Sister Claver, who had accompanied the girls, was a reassuring mentor. Astley's academic ability was not confined to her expertise in English. She needed Maths to matriculate and actively enjoyed Maths and Logic as much as rhetoric and structural thought. Indeed, references of various kinds to mathematical theorems and algebra are scattered throughout Astley's novels.

Her results were English (A), Latin (B), Modern History (B), Maths 1 (B), Logic (A).[32] This meant that she could enrol in Arts, Commerce or Surveying. Astley chose Arts and a career in teaching, not because it was 'all that women could do' as she was inclined to say throughout her life, but because it was the natural choice for someone whose instincts were already suited to engaging others. Her decision was influenced by many things, not least by her gratitude for the expert teaching she herself had enjoyed.

Astley's lively rationality made it hard for her not to criticise the more dictatorial aspects of the Catholic faith. She was unable to accept anything at face value, logically separating ideas and moral values from one another, a habit of mind encouraged by the nuns themselves. But she remained apprehensive about the Church's moral governance of the lives of so many (and her own). Her approach to Catholicism became permanently split between nostalgia for the rituals of the sung Mass and virulent antagonism to religious moral policing. Sexual maturity would bring with it an even greater sense of the gap between what was preached and what was real.

Astley wanted to understand the *mise-en-scène* of her experience of Catholicism; her brother Phil's vocation and her mother's religiosity made her own less than wholeheartedly approving responses difficult to deal with. Here was Phil, training to become one of those superior male figures of the Church she had come to detest. She began to wonder about the role that ego played in adherence to religious principles. Even if she couldn't articulate this, it seemed that ego was a frequent visitor to the house of the Lord. Later in life Astley expressed this in the words of the character Sister Celestine from *The Slow Natives*: 'Could it be, she wondered, that there was too much joy in her relationship with her Creator, that sanctity was more arid than she had supposed and all this abandonment of self was a sensual – dreadful word! – pleasure, a subjective one that should not be tolerated?'[33]

The way Astley personally dealt with and shaped her experience of Catholicism was both very personal and idiosyncratic. All Hallows' had become for her microcosmic in the same way that reading Victor Hugo had been in her youth. She saw beneath the codes and practices of religion with a singular sensibility and acuity of mind that made the small-world whole-world connections for her profound. It fed her imagination. The impact of *Les Misérables* stayed with Astley in her senior years to calibrate carefully her own set of faith values. She never re-read the novel because she never needed to.

'I hope I've become more tolerant – kindly – being kind, to me, is a form of spiritual exercise,' Astley once commented, relegating organised religion to performing a 'cosmetic dab on the upper right cheek-bone'.[34] She fashioned for herself a set of principles that were religious in an entirely personal moral way. This makes Astley's use of religious terms (acolyte, vespers, wafer, martyr) or the mechanics of religious ritual in her work seem like accoutrements. She said as much herself: when asked about Catholicism's influence she would always deflect that it was good for the 'metaphor glands'.[35] Of course, this avoids the extremely personal aspect of her response to what she regarded as mindless zealotry and which she would come to consider as her first experience of an '-ism'.

A deep personal disillusionment underpins many of her characters' utterances about religion. The elderly Miss Paradise in *A Boat Load of Home Folk* laments being expected to 'kowtow and behave and fawn and debase [her] individualism' (in the hope of having 'God's ear'), and in *It's Raining in Mango* Connie is encouraged to believe that 'God had [an] enormous interest in her. A direct line to the Lord'.[36]

In religious terms Astley's characters, like Astley herself, often felt set up for a fall. As a writer her ferocity attached itself to matters beyond religious ideals and forms (and Catholicism) but she remained profoundly interested in a human being's desire to believe. No matter what had happened to her, she never stopped believing in God. She would joke about being 'close to the Godhead' or that a certain person 'couldn't get God on ISD [international calling]' but belief in a controlling power was for her connected to so many things that could not be resisted: her past, music, hope. 'How can chemicals explain the spirit of Mozart or Beethoven?' she asked on ABC radio's *Search for Meaning* program. And Astley never stopped engaging in the act of prayer.[37]

In her thirties Astley became interested in Pierre Teilhard de Chardin and his idea of an Omega Point, some ultimate level of consciousness, a version of belief beyond the material that could be taken as a facsimile for Christian belief.[38]

When Astley declared in 1976 at the age of fifty that she did not miss the Church, she meant that she did not miss organised religion. 'One doesn't miss a power function that supports disparity in wealth and conditions,' she wrote. But she added about St Paul that 'much as one dislikes the old chauvinist – his idea of charity is a good concept'.[39] So while she would write of this 'tragic face of the Christ figure, essentially human and sympathetic', the real trauma lay in the dismal outcomes of faith for humanity.[40] As Astley grew and matured, it seemed to her that the secular search for love and the religious love of God were worlds apart (a 'spiritual rigidity that absolutely precluded warmth and love', as she would write in *The Well Dressed Explorer*).[41]

Astley never lost this deep suspicion of the ways in which symbols become agents of mass control. Almost any large group associated with the Mass was to her a mob, mindless, standing as a metaphor for society at its worst. Being 'mollified by ritual' was a poor exchange for individual will.[42] If this was in favour of a greater good, Astley remained suspicious of the motives. What remained with her were the tenets of humility, personal modesty and discretion. This, too, made her uncomfortable with herself: she was struggling with her own ego and how the exercise of one's gifts, the desire for self-expression, sat with such teachings. Catholicism would yet become a battleground of self-worth.

Ruminating on such things can be immobilising; viewed in such a way the Church looks like a natural home for neuroses, 'importuning God over and over … as if rote meant result …' (as she would describe Mass in *The Well Dressed Explorer*).[43] In years to come Astley would relive these sentiments in interviews, commenting how, for example, 'Guilt, failure and unhappiness are a terrific impetus to writing.'[44] As always, the intensity of her remembered feelings of this time were more explicitly expressed in her fiction, as in the words of Connie in *It's Raining in Mango*: 'All her life had glittered with moments when the words uttered were not those meant …'[45]

Astley was also disconcerted about the social attitudes towards sexuality. At school it was 'the only one of the ten Commandments that people went on and on about' – the most dishonest face of the Church.[46] Years later, she recalled her teenage confusion: 'All of a sudden you're fourteen and you think, "Heavens, I had a dirty thought. This sort of guilt doesn't seem healthy to me."'[47]

Was she the only one who had these feelings? Or did this double-life of mind and body beset others? What about the priests and nuns? What about their sexual needs? Time and again she posed such questions in her fiction. Belle in *Reaching Tin River* says, 'Christians have a terrible duality to deal with when confronted with the body – the spirit and the flesh at tugowar …'[48] Then Jessica Olive rails against the Church in *It's Raining in Mango*: 'All my liturgical loyalties, those reverences for the simple dogmas the poor unfortunate sisters drummed into me at the behest of a male hierarchy, have been my undoing as a human … That terrified obedience you and your brothers in Christ exact is directed largely at women. Women. You've neutered us. Made us nonhuman.'[49]

At seventeen, Astley was a young woman confronted by a set of beliefs that seemed to offer no place for sexual desire, none for longing – and she longed for and desired a great deal. On the verge of leaving All Hallows', Thea Astley was interested in being as full a human being as she could be. She was highly numerate as well as literate, self-disciplined and academically successful. She was formally educated when that was not common for women. How well had these years at All Hallows' equipped her for life? Astley had grown into a lean and lithe young woman – slim, long-limbed, with an easy athleticism. She had hair that could be brushed into abundance; her mouth was full, wide, and shapely. Eyes full of wit and mischief held their gaze under dream-heavy lids. Astley was excited by change and knew it had arrived. Catholicism, she no doubt suspected, would continue to make her life complicated. She left All Hallows' respectful, grateful, and secretly seething.

3

Barjai: A meeting place

We believed in one another. In the way of effect being the cause of the effect, we learned from one another, gained that sense of authority that makes brave the urge to go beyond horizons, 'returning bronzed as from a myth.' We had come out of a war into the light, not needing the nudge-nudge wink-wink of sly grog or dope. We were high on the prospects of the new world being made.

Barbara Blackman, *Glass after Glass: Autobiographical Reflections*, 1997[1]

Thea Astley returned to Brisbane from Warwick at the end of 1942, mourning the loss of the familiar that All Hallows' had been as well as the excitement of her very different last year. North of Rockhampton had been declared a war zone, the New South Wales state border was closed to civilians, and Brisbane itself was under the restrictions of a 'brown-out', a limit to external lighting. With American servicemen moving about the town, Queensland's ramshackle capital had metamorphosed into a bustling, cosmopolitan city. Commerce was at the heart of it and local businesses did not waste the opportunity to meet the demands of this ready-made clientele, though they had to deal with very limited licensing options. In the short term, there was the effect of a sudden social uplift – entertainment for the troops meant more clubs and more social activity generally – but the period was also one of social disturbance. Astley would recall the 'shock of khaki' upon her return to Brisbane, the olive and blue of the American forces' uniforms being the most dramatic sign of the changes that had taken place since she was last there. Their presence would continue to affect that city for the next two years.[2]

Studying Arts at the University of Queensland, Astley hoped, would enable her to meet the like-minded people about whom she had been dreaming, people who did not necessarily share her background. To her dismay, the university world into which she stepped in 1943 was in many respects as enclosed, if not more set apart, than the convent she had just left.

The university had changed very little physically or socially for decades. The campus was housed in Old Government House, dignified by the lush palms and trees of the city's botanical gardens bordering the university grounds. The main entrance was on George Street, one of the city's main commercial streets crammed with offices and hotels. Astley would recall with bemusement how lectures were in the reception room of the Old Government House building.[3] A large modern university was being planned for outlying land near St Lucia (the present site of the University of Queensland) and news of the laying of the first stone in 1937 had captivated Brisbane. It remained an unrealised dream until well after the war had ended, so that in 1943 it was American troops, not Australian students, who were the first to occupy the prefabricated and half-built structures that would one day become Brisbane's new university.

Astley's combined Arts/Teaching degree involved night-time study, as well as full-time day study at university, which was considered a significant privilege. There were more than three hundred students in the Faculty of Arts, split between day, evening and external students; the day enrolment was more like eighty-five. Only a small proportion of these would have majored in English. Because she was attending teachers' college, Astley was an evening student, though she returned to day status in 1946.

Tuition fees had to be paid: a three-year Arts degree cost around fifty-three pounds. Astley was glad of the Senior Teachers' College scholarship at Kelvin Grove that made study financially possible for her, an able student without means. Unfortunately this meant that her lectures and study had to be arranged around her teaching commitments, first at Ipswich, Mt Crosby, and the outer bayside Shorncliffe where Astley stayed at the Villa Marina boarding house, the same name she would use for a boarding house in her 1990 novel *Reaching Tin River*. At teachers' college, the division between day and evening students was marked – a reminder of the day girl/boarder distinction at All Hallows'. The rule was: seniors and juniors must not mix. Even university social events were planned separately for the two student groups.

It was impossible to ignore the practical impact of the war. The police and civil defence authorities, for example, had requested that the university avoid 'night assemblies' due to the brown-out light restrictions.[4] David Malouf, nine or ten years old at the time, later wrote, 'Though we hardly knew it at the time, our city was having its moment of greatness, its encounter with History: General MacArthur had arrived and the whole Pacific campaign was being directed from his office in the A.M.P. building.'[5]

Pride in Brisbane's prominence was one thing, but there were less glamorous complications. Astley walked into her teacher training college only to find it doubled as headquarters for the 53rd squadron of the Australian Air Training Corps with young men learning Morse code.

She soon found that the teaching college was a 'very sober place' under the charge of the principal, an ex-World War I colonel who ran the college as far as possible along military lines.[6] The front steps were out of bounds to all students. Women had to wear stockings (difficult to come by), which catapulted Astley and her mother into an urgent shopping trip.

The presence of American soldiers had quite an impact on

social mores too; Astley watched as it brought into focus the double standard about the sexual conduct of men and women. Young boys would go to the cliffs around Redcliffe on a search for condoms, called 'frenchie hunts', but well-brought-up young women like Astley were not supposed to be sexually active, let alone with visiting American soldiers. Astley claimed years later that she 'didn't know a single Yank' and was likely 'the only teenage girl in Brisbane who didn't!'[7] 'Anglo–American' relations preoccupied Brisbanites.

At university Astley saw how gossip controlled social behaviour; it further circumscribed what women could and couldn't do. A female student lying sideways on the university lawn and revealing the curve of waist to hip was thought to be 'fast'.[8] In her books set in this period, Astley would make a link between the American GIs, sex, degradation and perpetual sexual inequality. Here is Miss Trumper in the 1968 novel *A Boat Load of Home Folk*:

> Still lush in her mid-thirties, but desperately discreet about the exact position of time's finger ('I was never good at telling the time!'), she had sported an American Colonel of distinction with iron-grey temples for three mad weeks of invasion summer. Verna Paradise had gone crazy, dyed her hair orange, plastered her eyebrows, built out her bust ... Now Trumper could hardly believe it of herself. She had never been the racy kind. But the Yanks were different. Soft as honey. The Brisbane streets filled up with slouch hats once more after the forage caps had gone, so that girls who had lost their hearts or their good sense at bus-stops and good-byeing railway platforms were jolted back to terrible sanities.[9]

In Astley's later works the GI presence remains intact: Connie's son Reever in *It's Raining in Mango* is the product of a wartime affair; Belle in *Reaching Tin River* seeks out her American father in the US; Kathleen in the late novel *Coda* reminisces about her wartime romance with an American.

Astley was one of many for whom the American presence in Brisbane left a strong impression that remained with her for life. The same link – scents of the feminine mingling with death and dishonour – is made in David Malouf's quintessential Brisbane poem 'The Year of the Foxes': '… and Brisbane ladies/ rather the worse for war/ drove up in taxis wearing a G.I. on their arm … the rare spoils of '44; old foxes/ rusty red like dried-up wounds and a G.I. escort.'[10] Astley had been primed by All Hallows' to accept unequal moral standards for women but it was disillusioning to see that the world beyond the convent had its own version.

Powerful wartime loyalties made local reaction to the American presence in Brisbane double-edged: with so many soldiers to be fed, housed and entertained it was a boon for local businesses. Though there were serious accommodation shortages and food was rationed, the US forces were protected to some extent by being well paid. And as in all wars, the black market was thriving. The realisation that an up-tempo Brisbane was due to this transient foreign occupation would have done nothing to ease local ill-feeling. Hostilities had been sufficient to cause an all-out brawl at the Grand Central pub between American and Australian servicemen, known as the Battle of Brisbane, late in 1942, killing one Australian solider and injuring many. The impetus for the brawl is thought to have been the simmering tensions over how alluring the cashed-up American soldiers had become to young Australian women at the time. In her novel *A Boat Load of Home Folk* Astley appears to cast moral disapproval on her female Yank-dating characters Miss Trumper and Miss Paradise. In 1943 the poet Judith Wright encountered the effects of this Americanised Brisbane:

> The well-filled olive-and-blue uniforms of US Army and Air Force and the doughboy caps and skittish sailor-collars of the Navy seemed the only signs of wealth. Beside their sleekly-fitted opulence, the sloppy and worn khaki of the comparatively few

> Australian soldiers not fighting the wars in New Guinea looked a bit like Brisbane itself.[11]

If the streets of Brisbane were packed with men in uniform, it was a different story at the university. Astley was learning that, in the 1940s with a war on, a university education had social implications for a woman. Even a decade earlier, a student had learned, 'To be a blue stocking in the Australia of this time meant that a girl had an inordinate interest in learning, a strange disregard for male attention, and risked most foolishly the fate of not being attractive to men.'[12]

In the 1930s universities had abounded with men, now war had tipped the gender imbalance in favour of women. In all probability, Astley's experience of young men was limited to the sneak-out milkshakes with schoolboys of her own age. Like most women of her generation, Astley had grown up with ambiguous messages about men. 'Man was the enemy as well as the provider. Don't talk to strange men …'[13] But these men she had been taught to fear were not around. Of the seventy or so students to graduate in Arts alongside Astley, an unprecedented two-thirds were women. The Arts faculty had simply 'emptied of men' and now had 'exotically low' class numbers.[14] It irritated Astley years later to know how quickly this situation reverted when returned servicemen on war education allowances took up study, entrenching male domination of staff at Australian campuses right through the 1950s and 1960s.

Astley was horrified that being in the majority did so little to change the prevailing sexist attitudes towards women. Wartime restrictions probably didn't help social matters: the 1942 bombing of Darwin had made the Brisbane authorities anxious enough to impose brown-outs nightly. The university magazine persisted in regarding university life as a cavalier romance, with men in the lead roles, something that Astley and her contemporaries knew was comically remote from reality:

> No longer can the Varsity's lusty sons come forth at night, ready to do battle with the elements, in order to meet the fair damsels on a

> social footing … Alas the heart of Romeo can no longer play 'Auld Lang Syne' 'neath his breast as he walks a fair damsel around the grounds when the shades of night are firmly drawn.[15]

Astley realised that her fellow students felt, as she did, that they had little personal freedom; most were still financially dependent on their parents. When it came to matters of dress, the university Faculty Board set the standards. Social activism hardly existed and changes were confined to absurdly petty and marginal issues. In her early months as a university student Astley had read about such a 'win': men would now be allowed to 'attend lectures wearing shorts' as long as 'tie and stockings' were also worn.[16] On-campus segregation was also firmly maintained, with separate clubs for men and women.

Sport was still the most socially sanctioned activity, where the 'lusty sons' of the university could display their much-vaunted masculinity. However, Astley realised that men and women could mix socially at certain clubs that reflected her own interests, those dealing with music, drama and debating, though even here social expectations were still the arbiters of female morality. Astley and her peers spent much of their time ducking and weaving through often ambiguous demarcations of what was considered feminine behaviour.

One of Astley's contemporaries, the writer Amy Witting, whom Astley later befriended, recalled how women of her generation were 'thrust into competition with men' but left somehow feeling 'robbed of womanhood' by the very teachers who had been ambitious for them to achieve.[17] Witting was at the University of Sydney and a member of literary circles that included poets James McAuley and Harold Stewart. An interest in literature did nothing to moderate an atmosphere drenched in sexism, said Witting: 'Women were a subject race. You were accepted only on the most humiliating terms: you had to be somebody's girlfriend, or you were a dead failure … A logical mind as sexual bait was about level with facial hair.'[18] That last sentence drew an appreciative howl from Astley when she and Witting shared these memories twenty years later. It wasn't that Astley disliked men; even in the 1940s she was closer to feminism than she realised, despite her discomfort with the term in middle age.

Astley was now surely aware that the convent had been busy refining her brain for the intellectual long haul but had offered no training on how this might relate to matters with the opposite sex: men did not want women for their brains. Even her course of study had been gendered as lesser. The study of literature, her Arts major, would never be publicly esteemed in the same way as the study of Medicine or Law. But Astley allowed nothing to rob her of the pleasure she was finding in her literature studies. The courses were rich and thorough tours through English literature: Chaucer, Marlowe, Spenser, Milton, Dryden, Keats, Wordsworth, and Carlyle. Poetry, essays and drama were dominant. Astley won two prizes in English during her degree studies: The Ford Prize for the best poem in English in 1944, and the Henry Monteith Prize for English two years later.

Little Australian literature was on offer: the single reference was Percival Serle's *An Australasian Anthology*, first published in 1927. But change was coming. One day Astley walked by the campus notice board to see talks about Australian literature advertised. The 1940s Commonwealth Literary Fund Lectures series about Australian writers and academics to universities had begun. Astley would have seen Frederick Robinson present his lecture in Australian literature at the University of Queensland in 1944. Nationalist sentiment was taken for granted in the Astley household and she knew how it pleased Cecil to see the work of the bush balladists and convict novelists as early subjects. In these years Astley and her father had time to indulge a shared love of Australian literature. It was serendipitous since she was also thinking more about writing, beyond her poetry.

At the same time Astley was discovering European poetry and modernism. Like others at the time, she would not have wanted Australian literature to become defined by images and symbols that isolated it from other modern sensibilities, the experiments in visual arts and literature that were taking place overseas. The national literary bounty, long overlooked, had competition. Students took up their national literature in one hand while others were grabbing T. S. Eliot, W. H. Auden and French symbolist poetry in the other. Loyalties and tensions over nationality and style are best seen in Astley's own writing at the time. Stylistically at least, she was still imitating English Romantic poets, studying, hearing more and admiring much of the classical bush repertoire of Australian writers like stories of Henry Lawson and Barbara Baynton, while thrilling to the excitement of the language of an interior world that came with modernism.

As Astley entered her second year of Arts in 1944 it was becoming clear to her that literary and cultural matters still engaged relatively few people in Australia, including among the student population. As little as three per cent of students took an active interest in the university's literary magazine *Galmahra*. Compared with Astley's experience at All Hallows', this was an apathetic reaction that even the editor lamented.[19]

The irony of the title *Galmahra*, from an Aboriginal word meaning 'spokesman of a tribe', was probably not lost on Astley at the time. In her first year *Galmahra* was not published because there were so few submissions of an acceptable standard.[20] In her desire to be published Astley turned to the support of her Catholic background. She wrote to the poet Paul Grano, then President of the Catholic Poetry Society:

> Dear Mr Grano,
> I'm sending along these poems (as I dare to call them) in the hope that one or two may meet with your approval. When I read my own puerile work I feel horrified to think that I dare criticise anyone else's. However, I really would appreciate your opinion – as scathing as you like – because I do want to learn wherein to improve.
> Yours sincerely,
> Thea Astley[21]

This was a brave move, one she would repeat over her lifetime with other writers, sometimes with disastrous and crushing results. But this was her first real attempt to move beyond the opinion of her peers or the protection of teachers' affirmations. The fact that she did this when she was still craving a teacher or mentor shows what she was prepared to risk if it meant moving forward in her writing. It was important that Grano was not a peer, not even close. He was an established poet about to publish *Poems, New and Old* (1945) to a good critical response.

Astley needed to belong socially to a group that shared her literary and cultural values, and she needed to feel safe too.

Grano was directly and indirectly involved in several Catholic writing groups, some set up under the guiding hand of Archbishop Duhig. Two of the most prominent were the Catholic Poetry Society and the Catholic Writers' Movement (CWM). The latter was known to Astley; All Hallows' had run essay competitions on their behalf. Grano was influential beyond Catholic circles, and knew many other writers, such as C. B. Christesen, Brian Vrepont and James Picot, with whom he would set up the journal *Meanjin* (first called *Meanjin Papers*).

In her second year, Astley also decided to join the CWM. She set off for the Movement's monthly meeting at the Catholic Aquinas Library in Queen Street, Brisbane, hopeful that a new chapter in her life was finally beginning. She found that the meetings were fairly formal affairs, regular and minuted, but she attended for the whole of the next two years. She became a well-known member of the group and was asked over the Christmas–New Year period of 1944–45 to travel interstate to Melbourne on CWM accounting business. Only in 1946, when she was out of the city of Brisbane on a teaching appointment, did her involvement lapse.

The atmosphere in the CWM was still relatively constrained, with large doses of talk about 'the faith'. However, Astley discovered other meetings of like minds. Once again, the presence of American soldiers was the new ingredient in Brisbane's cultural life. Now new unknown American writers and readers from overseas, joined, albeit briefly, the local literary scene.

Judith Wright had just begun helping Clem Christesen with the new journal of literary and social comment *Meanjin Papers*, in which readers now found contributions from American soldiers appearing alongside the Australian content. Christesen had been working as a journalist with *The Courier-Mail* and in government after completing his studies at the University of Queensland, as the magazine was without full financial support. This would change quickly in its favour, and he and *Meanjin* would shortly move to Melbourne.

By comparison, the university's literary culture remained conservative. The student magazine *Semper Floreat* dismissed the first issue of *Meanjin Papers* as 'largely coloured by the war, a little bitter on the tongue' but now at least it recognised a strong counter-current.[22] Astley no doubt noted this resentment of the new but would have been heartened by these new cultural congregations that seemed to be emerging, sweeping up lively and eccentric personalities, individual talents. It could only offer her more opportunity for writing. Little magazines flourished throughout the 1940s in Australia, and drew from a pool of writers whose names at least were now familiar to Astley. She read as much as possible: *Poetry*, edited by Flexmore Hudson; *A Comment*, edited by Cecily Crozier; *Angry Penguins*, edited by Max Harris and John Reed (who with his wife, Sunday Reed, was the patron of the artistic community at Heide, on the eastern outskirts of Melbourne). Both Harris and Reed would later become entangled in the Ern Malley poems hoax.

The next event in Astley's life would have far-reaching ramifications. She had become aware of a writing group for young people called Barjai, from an Aboriginal word meaning 'meeting place for youth'. This had metamorphosed from *Senior Tabloid*, a school magazine of Brisbane State High. Its contributors, like Astley, were now out of school and interested in writing and literature. The original schoolboy editors, Barrett (Barrie) Reid and his friend

Laurie Collinson, were now university students interested in the group as a meeting circle. Between 1943 and 1947 they continued to edit their little magazine *Barjai*, named after the group, with Reid as the editorial commentator on literature and society. The magazine declared its youthful edict: 'All published writers must be under twenty-one.'

This was the moment Astley had been waiting for and she wasted no time in joining the group. Barjai lived up to its name for her: it was the meeting place where she formed many of the literary friendships she valued for life. And many of Barjai's members, especially Thea herself and Barrett Reid, went on to become distinguished and vital members of the Australian literary community. Reid's influence, in particular, is notable. He was a published poet; he had a long involvement with Heide and its support of contemporary art; he was involved in the major initiatives to promote Australian books (National Book Council, *Australian Book Review*); and he edited the influential Australian literary journal *Overland.*

Socially, Barjai provided a vital network. Astley had to confront the fact that many of its members already knew each other and that she was something of an outsider. Her confidence was tested but she seemed to fit in, was accepted. This affirmation was all-important to her. The interests of the group were liberal in the true sense and Astley could express her views on literature and on creativity. Among friends she could start to enjoy words that did not fit with the academy, a crucial new freedom she immediately embraced.

Barjai helped Astley to find and begin to develop her own voice. It built a social bridge between the CWM, her Catholic background and the larger world and hinted at a creative future. The group was serious and seriously fun, though not especially bohemian and certainly not dissolute. Barbara Patterson, who had not yet met her artist husband Charles Blackman, was one of Barjai's younger members (she had attended Brisbane State High with Reid and knew him well). At the fortnightly meetings in the ladylike Lyceum Club near the city centre of Brisbane she couldn't help being rather impressed by the 'well dressed, well spoken, very couth' sophisticates of the Barjai gang.[23]

Now twenty, good-looking in an angular way, Astley read her poetry to her fellow Barjai members in the crackling and acrid style that became so distinctive in the world of Australian writing, deepened twenty years later by her constant smoking. This younger version was slightly high-pitched with just a hint of the Queensland drawl. She changed her natural vocal rhythms with sudden pauses for effect which would one day turn into her trademark timing. It was almost sex.

The young intellectuals and artists of Barjai were a formidable bunch in some ways. Barrett Reid was the 'essential romantic hero – but with a rascally wit'; Laurie Collinson 'personified avant-garde subversion'; artist Cecil Knopke was 'swaggeringly serious with a drawing-room lisp'.[24] Astley gloried in their company; no longer just a 'marked out' schoolgirl, she had fought her way to literary comradeship of a high order. Astley thrilled to hear Judith Wright read her first book of poetry, then unpublished, at one of the evening soirees. She was intrigued by Wright's philosopher husband J. P. McKinney's compelling papers of a non-academic nature, highly sympathetic as he publicly staked a claim to an independent viewpoint about social and philosophical ideas. She valued this because her father, Cecil, had passed down to her an egalitarian sense of the right to free speech.

The CWM no longer seemed completely separate either: Paul Grano floated through the Barjai meetings and mingled with the Barjai set, as did Clem Christesen. Astley's friendships with women were based on intelligent rapport. She became close to the writer Vida Smith (later Horn) and Thelma Forshaw, later a prominent journalist, short story writer and book reviewer in Sydney. Here, too, were opportunities to mix socially with men, even if behaviour was still conservative. Astley later remarked: 'When a male hand brushed against your arm or, even more thrillingly, a waist or hip … did you know it!'[25]

Astley's literary circles were broad enough yet sufficiently safe to accommodate homosexuality. She became close to Collinson and

Reid, both openly gay. For the first time she was given an insight into differences that perhaps she had intuited from living with her brother, Phil, now studying philosophy with the Jesuits and still in Melbourne. She at least had a social context within which to think of men who were not lovers of women or husbands or fathers.

Barjai also provided a connection to her artist grandfather, since Collinson was a painter of watercolours, as well as being interested in psychology and writing, and so brought along some of the artists of the Miya studio, a group closely associated with Barjai from the outset. The Miya group had formed as a separate young artists' collective, away from the Royal Queensland Art Society's Younger Artists' Group. Laurence Hope is thought to have painted the Barjai group in his 1945 artwork *Literary Circle*.

Ambitious as they were, all were vulnerable young artists and writers; the most important aspect of Barjai meetings for Astley was the supportive atmosphere. Nobody needed to fear ridicule. Years later, the students in Astley's university creative writing courses would benefit from her experience. Barjai gave Astley all-important focus, recognition, and esteem; here she felt she could trust in a measure of objectivity without inviting anything like the 'scathing' critique she had requested from the poet Paul Grano only a few years before.

The Miya studio artists and Barjai writers enjoyed mutual social interaction and publishing opportunities in the *Barjai* magazine but they also shared a wish to challenge the conservatism of the local audience. At this stage in her life Astley was not really prepared to identify publicly with the competing issues of nationalism and modernism raised by Barjai. She was still living at home and felt keenly the debt owed to Cecil and Eileen, and all these new experiences and relative freedoms did not erase the fundamental conservatism of her upbringing. She had befriended openly homosexual men in the group and might have wondered about Phil's sexuality, as well as her parents' views about that. What might they think of a radicalised daughter? The need for change that energised the group would have been at odds with her personal reticence. Astley was different, too, in her particular fascination with language; creativity was not to be sidetracked by activism. One day she would attempt to bring the two together in fiction.

4

We've Freud and Nietzsche at our finger-tips

Is meant to represent a breadth of vision
Such as all these great Bohemians have …
You wonder that the artist called it 'Life'?
Then note the hand that clasps a little dust
(Of bone, no doubt.) It's clear that you must read;
We've Freud and Nietzsche at our finger-tips,
And all that sort of thing.

'Culture, 1945' by Thea Astley, 1945[1]

Astley was alert to the heady mixture of art and politics that membership of Barjai represented. The group's credo was becoming known: 'The poet must become a politician in the cause of culture.'[2] Given the times, Astley's Barjai was infused with literary modernism, the philosophies of youth for a new world, and a whole generation's response to World War II. CWM, on the other hand, believed that the poet should become a politician in the cause of Christ. It was a worldwide organisation preoccupied with 'a positive programme to restore Christ to culture'.[3] However, politics and art – let alone religion, politics and art – sat uncomfortably with Astley's still developing views on such things. Her own 'faith', if she'd been asked to name it, was simply in the vigour of the creative life. Self-belief was the 'belief' fundamental to her membership of two such different organisations.

Barjai and the CWM were similar in reflecting the mood of the times. The war was almost over, a new order beginning. And Barrett Reid and others like him thought the talents of artists and writers should play a part in this new Australia. He expressed this 'call to arms' in his poem 'These Leaden Weights':

> We can no more allow the warped will of old men
> to fashion for us the future. It is ours.
> Cast off the leaden weights that make the drab decrees.
> Climb the high heart's wall and cry out Action.[4]

Astley was no activist. She was more at peace with her own inwardness, that tendency noted in her even at school to be 'possessed of her own internal world'.[5] However, she naturally shared the sense of expectation that the war's end would bring about extraordinary change. High spirits bound together the cultural hopes of that generation. As the poet Judith Wright would recall: 'If the end of the war was not far off, they implied, a new wave of art and literature might cross the continent and sweep before it all the old conventions and imitations of European nineteenth-century writing and Georgian shibboleths.'[6]

Barjai preached cultural salvation: war had sidelined culture. ('Most people lay aside their books, store their musical instruments, forget their art shows.')[7] Reid did not want their group to seem frivolous but at the same time he knew it was not a political organisation. Astley certainly did not want it to be seen that way either: she always inclined to the human, the people behind the politics. The writer in Astley would have been fascinated by the interplay of personalities and she had a way of stepping sideways, to see more – she hated being *forced* to believe anything. Astley was hugely fond of Reid, not for his stirring views on what the future could be but because he was an irrepressible young man, a humanist with a great flair for living. His discussions in the pages of *Barjai* about social order and democracy were youthfully zestful but Astley liked it best when he tired of fighting the dour spirits of wartime and asked the question more to her liking: 'What time, then, is left for living?'[8]

Arguments about life and art, beauty and art, did engage Astley. Modernism had come to Australia, was embraced by many in her circle like a long-awaited lover, but the fervour made her uneasy. A lot seemed to be claimed in its name that had little to do with soaking up the poetry of Eliot, Spender and Auden. Australian artists and writers wanted to affirm their relationship with the culture of other places. Wasn't there a risk, Astley would have wondered, that the valuing of Australian writing (old and new) might be at stake?

Astley inserted herself with gusto into all-out debate about the traditional forms of literature and those emerging. Reid tried to defend what he saw as literary experimentation: it was not a desertion of cultural tradition and nationhood. He was committed to the 'reforming impetus of youth', an energetic *agent provocateur* for a postwar 'blueprint for happiness'. When working by instinct, as a poet, making his own images of the country he loved – or as an editor of *Barjai* – he felt a responsibility to encourage innovation, assuring his readers that 'although there are many classical forms and metres in which the elder BARJAI writers could excel, a little experimentation would not be out of place'.[9] At this time Astley was struggling with questions of value, craft and form. Her education helped her in this: she had encountered Edgar Allan Poe's essays 'The Poetic Principle' and 'The Philosophy of Composition' and Poe's views that the 'Poetry of words [is] the Rhythmical Creation of Beauty'.[10] Poe debunked 'aesthetic intuition' in favour of process towards an effect ('like a mathematical problem'), a view that appealed enormously to the young writer-in-the-making who loved logic and maths.[11] 'An appreciation of beauty', with its olde worlde colourations of truth and order in art was to come under increasing pressure from modernism.

Astley began to take a personal interest in these issues – the mixed messages often embedded in discussion – subjecting them to a scarifying logic. Reid pilloried the Anglocentric Australian book trade (demanding that bookshops carry at least twenty-five per cent of Australian titles) while lecturing on the pitfalls of clinging to Australia's colonial past. Astley, for her part, saw how the value of her own work might be threatened by Reid's advice to writers: 'Twentieth century ideas simply can't be expressed in 18th and 19th century language. "Thee", "thou" and "thy" sound hollow and forced in most contexts; epithets such as "stilly" are now near-extinct; and if the writer does feel about nature the way Tennyson did, it's no use writing about it in a Tennysonian manner because (1) Tennyson has already done so, and (2) written to-day it is artificial and stilted.'[12]

From the time Astley was a teenager she had enjoyed imitating the traditional metres and forms of classical poetry. She loved to match her poetic skills to those Elizabethan and Victorian metres. As she would boast, 'At eighteen I could turn out a Petrarchian sonnet easy as winking.'[13] Greek legend, Anglicisms, classical allusion and dramatic mannerisms and punctuation are all here in this poem:

From Troy

Sing of the sunset sky, the strange, chill plains
Of pallid evening; the wings
That passing make a music murmuring low,
Sing of the golden love
That mocked the night of woods,
Where Ida sang the love of woman's heart.

Sing of the flashing trees, the star-lit night,
With wonder from the shrouded years

Up shooting through the liquid centuries,
Sing of the golden flame
That mocked the night of woods,
Where Ida cursed the love of woman's heart.[14]

Love, love lost, loneliness; (however self-consciously interested in form) many of Astley's poems are directly emotional, such as 'Saturday Night':

O aching sear!
I sit and long for life—
And pen a sick love poem, to a star ...[15]

These autobiographical pieces were reflective and melancholic in the Romantic tradition, rather than being experimental in form in any way, so Astley was slightly uncomfortable with the arguments in favour of experimentation.[16] She decided she would have none of it.

Astley was beginning to do something that would become characteristic of her from time to time: she wrote against the trend, using satire. Hints of dogma, like the smell of incense, always brought her fighting spirit to the surface. Using references to Poe, Astley denounced the avant-garde. She was anti-elitist about literature but desperately interested in creativity and in writing, a difficult standpoint to reconcile with her formal stylistic preferences. Her *Barjai* essay 'Poetic Fire' tells a story about a 'butter magnate whose sonnets were found hobnobbing with butter consignments and quotas', revealing Astley's penchant for cryptic titles.[17] This exotic placement of sensitivity among the mundane would become a trademark of her novels, which often deal with characters caught out being gifted in unlikely places, such as a pineapple plantation. It was a reaction to modernism tainted by cultural insecurities she had breathed in first as an Australian, then as a Queenslander. Astley was well on the way to inventing an angry persona out of parochial defensiveness, outbursts that eventually became affectionately known as 'Thea being a professional Queenslander'.

Astley really did want to support the view that anyone anywhere is capable of creating Art; this suited her own determination to write from what she knew. Even poetry, she insisted, arose from nothing more glamorous than the need to express 'emotions suppressed by the monotony of habit'. Nor were those emotions to be taken for granted as the springboard: technique, process, craft were all. ('I always commence a sonnet thinking out a fine first line,' she said.)[18]

Was Astley simply being difficult?

She had the final word in her poem, published in the university magazine *Galmahra* – not *Barjai* – suggesting that she needed to go outside of her group's influence to exercise her brand of satire:

Culture, 1945

It's symbolistic, dear, that's what it is!
You'd never guess at first, I know. But see,
It's merely self-expression. What? My dear!
Of course there's no repression these days. Art
Is what the artist cares to give us. Look—
That eye behind the swan's wing on the right
Is meant to represent a breadth of vision
Such as all these great Bohemians have …
You wonder that the artist called it 'Life'?
Then note the hand that clasps a little dust
(Of bone, no doubt.) It's clear that you must read;
We've Freud and Nietzsche at our finger-tips,
And all that sort of thing. O darling, stop
Gaping at the Holbein! Here's the finest—
And that ghastly 'Sunset on a Hill'—
Picasso right behind you, *and* Matisse.
Must you, dear?—da Vinci makes me ill![19]

Astley was now utterly disaffected by what she increasingly saw as the abstraction 'culture'. As far as she could see, modernism was removed from a felt sense of being human, of people's inconsistencies; it was too removed from the local. For her this was also déjà vu. Just as Catholicism set itself above the human and the vulnerable, here was another '-ism' that seemed to be doing the same thing. She felt this keenly because the poetry she was writing, and the writing she was thinking about, came directly from her own life and her own emotional reading of experience. Pushing to the surface, always, was an urgency to reveal the essence of the human, the truth of things.

This is why she loved Gerard Manley Hopkins, his auditory particularity, and the sound-sense of French symbolist poets like Charles Baudelaire and Stéphane Mallarmé. When it came to Australian poets, what one critic described as Kenneth Slessor's 'exceptional gift for creating sound patterns' would have appealed to her. She and Slessor were alike, too, in being vitally connected to musical forms; Slessor was also known to have possessed a 'deeply responsive but sceptical mind'.[20] Her quest to produce poetry of the 'flesh and blood' kind even in her best work was obscured by intellectual abstraction. Astley's challenge was what to save and what to give up in the interests of her quest for an authentic voice.

Artists and writers responded to the enormous changes in society in the first half of the twentieth century by moving from representations of external 'real' life to a fascination with the inner life. They were exploring feelings of alienation and despair in a new way, often doing so in a new language. Astley responded to the emotional heart and simplicity of some of this new writing but she was still obsessed with finding her own style. Writing could not – no contemporary writer could – afford to stay working in one style. This openness to creative change, which she first confronted here in the 1940s, probably added many years to Astley's writing life.

Slowly Astley's poetry did reflect these cultural shifts. The imagistic satisfied her aesthetic preferences but she added her own version of the modern. There is a little of T. S. Eliot's 'Rhapsody on a Windy Night' in the following poem by Astley, revealing a susceptibility to the modernism she liked to satirise.

I.

Boringly repetitive the night
Takes up the tale, and streets reveal,
Lamp-posts polished by the moon to steel,
Elms of ebony and fences white—
Gaspingly unreal.

Eyes and lips, and lips and hair become
Ash-grey daubings. Breath and bone
Chilled, magic-killed, can now disown
The sun's disquietudes, and moon-mad-numb,
Repress day with a groan.[21]

The wordiness, the clutter! This would become the chant of many a critic of Astley's writing. The auditory effect is strong but the odd disjunctive word ('disquietudes') is too elaborate; then there are the fierce image-struck invented compound phrases (like 'moon-mad-numb'); and climbing scales of adjectives ('Boringly repetitive', 'Gaspingly unreal'), the alliterative listing of the sensory ('Eyes and lips, lips and hair') seem obsessive, as if something uncontainable needed expression. The poem and others like it were virtually prose experiments.

Was this a kind of emotional subterfuge? Twenty years later Astley herself answered that question. 'Can you imagine reading your poetry to a live audience? It would be like exposing yourself in public,' she said.[22] She was uncomfortable about personal self-revelation in a public confessional sense: there could never be enough mannerisms to hide behind. But in these early poems she was satisfying an urge to dramatise. Later she read poetry as 'a stimulus to write prose' but now she had no sense that prose would be the form that offered more space to explore her emotional and psychological self.[23]

The aura of the Barjai group was not infected by modernism's preoccupation with bleakness – they wanted life too much. Astley empathised with Reid when he wrote '… to us who are still young the experiences of living, eating and loving and sleeping, are sharp and important, more important than subtle speculations about the nature of death'.[24] In Australia there was 'little sense of modernity being an issue other than on the grounds of stylistic decadence'; there was still 'the essential belief in something'.[25]

At the tail end of her time with the group, in 1944, there was the Ern Malley hoax – a spoof against modernism now legendary in Australian literature. Well-known Australian poets James McAuley and Harold Stewart invented the 'undiscovered' genius Ern Malley, creating poems for him in a surrealist style. The hoax was supposed to fool the modernist *Angry Penguins* editor, Max Harris, and did so – as well as many other respected writers and critics of the time. Barjai felt the ripple effect since Reid and Collinson had connections to this fiasco: Collinson's own work had been in the same issue of *Angry Penguins*, and Reid had been the magazine's Queensland representative from 1943 to 1947. It was a savage time. Years later Reid recalled just how personal the whole issue became: 'Immediately friends, relatives became not so much agin the poems as agin the kind of person who could read such poetry or believe in it, the kind of experimental mind that wasn't conformist.'[26] A radical taint had attached itself to the Barjai group; the hoax would prove to be a fissure in its demise.

Astley's own life was removed from all of this because of her teaching commitments, which involved her working during the day most days. She was being affected by quite different experiences – was open to such experiences – some that meant a lot to her emotionally: 'I have stirring memories of my teaching career … teaching at Shorncliffe primary school. A state string quartet came down and played a movement from Dvorak – American Quartet – to fourth grade – superb playing.'[27] This was the memory that popped up fifty years later when she was asked about culture – classical music for kids in bayside Brisbane.

Some Barjai poets were personally affected by the talk of styles and hoaxes; some became 'cagey about emotions in their writing'.[28] Perhaps to soothe such spirits, Reid discussed other things: the progressive educational theories of A. S. Neill or transactional analysis (reflecting Collinson's interests). Collinson, however, became more radical and would join the Communist Party in 1947. Socialism and communism were endorsed in print and there was a transparent anti-Catholic sentiment in Reid's quoting of Thomas Hardy's post-World War I poem as part of his scathing review of a new Catholic journal (*View*):

Christmas: 1924

'Peace upon earth!' was said. We sing it,
And pay a million priests to bring it.
After two thousand years of mass
We've got as far as poison-gas.[29]

If Astley secretly wished that she had written this she could never have publicly owned it; in any case her own anger against the Church had not become fully realised in her own mind. She also had Cecil and Eileen to consider and didn't want to hurt them, nor Phil, who was still interstate studying with the Jesuits. What would her family make of her affiliation with a group that publicly declaimed Catholicism? Astley distanced herself a little, knowing that many would understand her personal reasons. She was not alone, as her friend Vida Horn later summed up: 'Some – but not all – of our fathers worried, [was Barjai] left-wing? Poetry readings might lead to communism. Most of our mothers would worry. Poetry readings might lead to sex – though they never said so bluntly.'[30]

There is no way of knowing whether Astley had any sexual relationship at this time but it seems unlikely. In any case, 1946 brought these Brisbane Barjai days to an end. How would she remember them? She penned her farewell thoughts with a prescient sense of how such times do pass:

Juvenilia

All we regret, we singers in the sun
Is the long age coming after, wasted days,
Senility of withered mind. No ways
Lead to avoidance save the mortal one—
And we have no thought of death, and death is done
With, but for that regret—the sixties' haze
Of graveyard gossip, harmless teas, and praise—
Fruit bitter for the fact youth gave us none.
We are afraid of age—not for its lack
Of physical advantage, like a flower
Wrinkled and sapless; not that we must track
Into a place of pain; but just because
We may forget ideals, as in an hour
Even the rose forgets what once it was.[31]

Members of 'The Barjai Gang' were all still very young and bound to take different paths. *Meanjin Papers*, with Clem Christesen, had moved to Melbourne University in 1944, joining 'what amount[ed] to a Queensland colony – writers, artists, musicians, sculptors, scholars …'[32] Reid followed. Within a decade he would hold a key position in the public library system; Collinson went overseas. After the war Astley was obliged to resist these pilgrimages. She lived in a vast rural state and had already committed herself to the lottery of teaching posts.

In the city, many Brisbanites longed for a return to sanity and peace. But not all: in one of his last *Barjai* pieces Reid lamented the return of the sleepy prewar town: 'The Americans have left ... the prevailing influence is one of inertia. Brisbane has had culture.'[33] In the next few years Astley's life would be very different from the lives of her Barjai comrades: she, as well as 'culture', would be relocated. It was something she never quite forgave.

PART 2

DREAM COUNTRY

5

Dream Country

Actually I don't like the heat, but I like that do-it-tomorrow feeling. And I like the plants, the rainforest, the water cobalt off the shore, the tropicana. It's my dream country. And you know – the dream country is always where you aren't!

Thea Astley, interview with Graeme Kinross-Smith, 1982[1]

Astley's time at university was at an end. She was now a graduate with a Bachelor of Arts degree and a teaching diploma. Gone were the lively Barjai evenings, a shared comradeship in letters. All of that belonged to time past and she was left to contemplate facing the next part of her life completely alone. Teaching as her future career had made Astley very conscious that her situation was quite different from many in the Barjai set. She was now twenty-one, bonded to the Queensland Education Department; unless she paid back the entire cost of her tuition and left the profession, she had no choice but to go wherever she was sent. It was common then, and for years, for government education departments to require graduates to work regionally within their state. It was a tense time in the Astley household while they waited for what seemed like a life sentence to be handed down to the new graduate. The letter finally arrived and Astley faced Cecil and Eileen with the news: 1947 would take her away to a full-time teaching appointment in Townsville, north Queensland. It could have been worse: Townsville was a regional metropolis compared with other towns she might have been allocated. When Astley much later recalled her younger self as being 'too sanguine to be filled with despair', she must have felt optimistic in the last moments of her life in Brisbane.[2]

Townsville was a shock, both visual and physical. Much of rural Australia was ramshackle but the Queensland variation was several degrees more dilapidated than 1940s Brisbane. Astley could never have imagined the tourist development that was to blight the region, mercilessly satirised some forty years later in her novels. In 1947 'old Queensland' seemed to be in a state of permanent rot. Vegetation clambered all over buildings painted decades before. Houses little better than shacks, although some large and rambling, were on flimsy stilt supports and everything was perennially attacked by humidity and heat. Townsville provided Astley's first compelling experience of what she later called being 'outmanoeuvred by weather'.[3]

Then there was the rain, which was tropical and heavy. As roads in many isolated areas were still dirt, this meant mud and lots of it. There was no sewerage. Schools were mostly sheds without electrical power, telephones, typewriters or copying machines; pot belly stoves and later kerosene heaters provided warmth if necessary. Petrol was still rationed, even though the war was over; farmers grew and fermented tobacco for fuel. Townsville, like other remote and isolated places, seemed to exist in its own space and time. In her novels Astley would re-create the makeshift quality of these towns in caustic tribute to them. In her early twenties, however, she simply missed the city.

There is no point in resenting the physical character of a place, and in any case Astley had other preoccupations. Her first salary was close to two pounds weekly. She had little to spend it on – accommodation accounted for about thirty shillings of it – and it irritated her to be paid less than men in the same situation. Towns needed teachers and socially they were regarded as assets, so lower pay for women seemed like inexplicable exploitation. The local community was obliged to find a suitable place for her to stay, under threat of the department withdrawing her. Astley was eventually forced to take one room in the Railway Hotel. This was not a good start: teachers, she discovered, 'were treated with suspicion … had to behave very well – couldn't be seen in a bar' – not that Astley was a drinker.[4]

The room in the local pub was a stage-set copy of all such rooms Astley would re-create for her novels, including this one based on her Shorncliffe, Brisbane, boarding house Villa Marina, described more than forty years later in *Reaching Tin River*: 'My narrow bedroom. Eight by ten by twelve. The twelve's the height. One window and a Holland blind, a stretcher, a clothes cupboard, a dressing-table drunk with seventy years of salt air.'[5]

At the Railway Hotel Astley huddled in bed at night, listening to steps on the verandah passing her room, with just a bolted door between her and possible danger (reflected in the menacing versions of pubs that recur throughout her novels). She was a young and naïve city girl thrust into rough company and it was the first time she had felt physically threatened. Twenty-one was old enough, perhaps, to enter the classroom but perhaps too young to be drafted to an isolation for which her education and upbringing had not prepared her. Astley never forgot the fear and vulnerability she had felt in these places.

Anxiety pressed in on her. She was not yet the young novelist who could examine with detachment the impression she might have given the locals, a 'somewhat priggish city girl' forced into their midst.[6] As she wrote years later, 'The only social life seemed to be in the pub, which would throb until ten at night, when they would lock the policeman inside because that was the official closing time. He would go on drinking with them until everyone fell outward. I found it ugly because I was young and intolerant. I was discovering books, and poetry and good music, and nothing cultural like that was happening in the small towns.'[7]

One day walking home from work she heard a piano being played quite well and stopped to listen outside the house. The owners saw her and came out to wave. This buoyed her spirits, but these were rare moments.[8] Townsville was a world away from poetry prizes and Barjai and the belief that culture and writing were important to life: loneliness was turning her time in the tropics into an ice age.

As Astley would later reflect, 'It was chilling to be flung out into the world – your own controller – and you're timorous. You become an observer, not an integrator.' How, she might have wondered, does one even become an integrator?[9] What Astley saw as the narrow-mindedness and conformity of the town life grated on her nerves and she did not see much kinship on offer. But then she was not feeling much like joining. She played tennis but was not a member of the tennis club. She saw this community as dispiritingly familiar, involving a slavish following of customs and social practices, a version of orthodoxy, though not necessarily religious. These views could cause her capricious mood swings that might well have tainted relationships with possible congenial companions. Astley still struggled to be accepted, while at the same time asserting her individuality. It would be difficult to balance those needs in Townsville.

She was forced back to the interests she could enjoy out of town, in Brisbane, and was building up a healthy resentment about being the sole representative of city civilisation in 'enemy territory'. The feeling stayed with Astley. Thirty years later she gave these feelings to the character of Tom Dorahy in *A Kindness Cup*:

> It all seemed so useless, as foolish as trying to put 'Tintern Abbey' into iambic hexameters. He had come with a zealot's earnestness, believing a place such as this might need him. And there was, after all, only loneliness: he was cut off from the pulse of town, although he insisted to himself, rationalising furiously, he had been

> regularly to meetings of the Separation League and had blown only occasional cold air on their hot.[10]

But Astley didn't attend any meetings and her small Townsville Central School was devoid of like-minded souls. The school, which catered for very young first-graders through to early adolescents, was run by a petty and officious headmaster with whom Astley fell naturally into disagreement. Apart from teaching, her duties were disconcertingly trivial – she spent a part of each week making the school glue. An Arts degree, published poetry, her membership of Barjai – and glue making. What a trajectory! She was developing a habit of making lists, counting, and luxuriating in the absurdity of the humdrum, and this would stay with her: there are few Astley characters who don't indulge themselves in making such lists.

She tried to rally herself but she was genuinely disillusioned and unhappy. She wrote to Martin Haley, her old friend from the Catholic Writers' Movement, threatening a novel about 'the lovely rut', as she now referred to her teaching job.[11] The thought of writing prose was becoming attractive: perhaps she might become a north Queensland version of that 'butter magnate' from her *Barjai* essay, whose sonnets could be found 'hobnobbing with butter consignments and quotas'.[12]

Haley had guessed how things might be for Astley in such a remote place and before she left Brisbane had given her the names of some of his friends in Townsville. Astley was surprisingly diffident about approaching strangers; she longed for the informalities of the 'Aquinas gang' (CWM) and Barjai. Eventually, she wrote a note to one of the suggested contacts but with such obsequiousness – for having to '[force her] presence upon him' – that it hardly augured well for friendship.[13]

This over-diffidence went hand in hand with a jerky forcefulness, making Astley seem odd to others. Haley, for his part, was a good friend. She valued his friendship, all the more because he did not ply her with 'dogma or doctrine'.[14] She didn't know it but she was speaking too soon: in the end their differing degrees of allegiance to Catholicism would cause them to fall out. For now, Haley was a life-saver. Astley looked forward to her favourite walk each week, to the little local post office where she knew she would find the *John O'London's Weekly* magazine sent to her by Haley. The English literary magazine featured a mix of established and lesser-known writers, something that would have appealed to a young writer such as Astley.

Astley was becoming depressed. It was difficult to know who best to talk to and she was missing home and family. Phil, who would also soon go on to teach, was at this stage engaged by full-time Jesuit studies in Melbourne. She had missed him now for years. When he left, Astley was just finishing school and had written a tender poetic dedication:

To My Brother

Sunlight and spires are strangely tangled
With plane trees and elms in a Monday memory
Of fat brown horses, listless waiting,
And laughter waltzing from a woman's lips.

You were the serious one, who gravely
Listened to snatches of dreamy Debussy
And arrow-like echoes from old Lamartine,
Smiling the moments away in a prayer;

Fathomless, even. But this day remembers
Your feet on the pavement of three people's hearts,
Strangely confused with a cold rain and elms,
And a red-headed child in a sunlit street.[15]

Phil would have his own problems with teaching, but for now reports of his progress floated back via a proud Eileen and Cecil. Astley's parents were not only a long way away in Brisbane; their conservatism meant that they didn't talk openly about feelings with their daughter, nor would they have wished to worry her about her brother. What they communicated of Phil's life conveniently excluded the events and experiences that were troubling him. Astley, who had flirted with the idea of becoming a nun when she was a child, knew she could never have endured life in any enclosed religious order. However, in the 1940s, Phil's choice of vocation was not as uncommon as it is today, which also would have tempered Astley's view of it. She could see that at least Phil was part of a social, even intimate, society *chosen* by him, that he was not a misfit in a rural town, as she was.

Astley had great respect for Phil's sacrifice, just as she had for the nuns at All Hallows', but she was looking for some less extreme version of giving to others, to life. She found it herself years later by inventing a breakaway order of nuns in the late novella 'Inventing the Weather', expressing a combination of self-sacrifice and non-conformity that she came to find irresistible.

Away from the city, Catholicism wasn't a prominent feature of Astley's daily life but its legacy held fast, quietly circumscribing her behaviour. Had Phil known of his sister's loneliness, his own similar plight might have been a sympathetic echo, but actual contact between them was limited. They had more in common than they could know: Phil was also being forced to make adjustments that proved very taxing for him. Already, he had been observed as not the usual type of novice.[16] He displayed no interest whatsoever in sport and made his fervent nature known in prayer and in endless walks conducted at high speed across the grounds. His superiors watched, concerned.

As Thea battled heat, humidity and the tropical skin conditions of irritable schoolchildren, Phil suffered painful chilblains in the unaccustomed cold of Melbourne. Brother and sister were both beset by anxiety, Phil more so at this stage. From the start he suffered self-doubt about his calling, which made him feel less worthy before his God, and his was a very exacting God. These inward troubles only underlined that his was a disposition unsuited to social interactions (especially the schoolteaching he would agree to try), whereas his sister's instincts for teaching were healthily intact. Tucked away as she was in the far north missing city culture and yearning for people, she did not know that a cloud had well and truly settled over her brother's life. Later she discovered the extent of this, and would capture such agonies in her novels with whimsy; a character at a low ebb could be at risk of 'committing sideways' ('Inventing the Weather') or perhaps just watching his own 'personal weather' sink to temperatures ever closer to zero.

Astley was psychologically stronger than her brother but she did not have his social protection. If Phil stood out among his peers he was not ostracised for it, whereas Astley was discovering that in small country towns people like her were considered outsiders in every sense.

In 1948, after one year in Townsville, she was moved to Imbil, near Pomona, a quaint Mary Valley town 140 kilometres north of Brisbane, but she was still alone.

Despondency coloured her thoughts and she wrote poetry of her days filled in too-familiar ways: 'As today, and hours more empty/ And a lovelessness, and the little town.'[17] Her thoughts had nowhere to turn except upon themselves, or to find their place in her writing. She wrote disconsolately to her old friend Martin Haley:

> I'm commencing to hate this forced introspection that seems to descend on one in the country. Time here floats lazily by, and the slow music of the trains – and I feel useless and defeated. If I could think that at the end of this brief time I could go out assured of one thing well done I'd be content. As it is Martin I view my shortcomings and mediocrity with horror. The confidence I possessed at nineteen has been leaped over by an accumulation of loneliness, country hotels, with all their paraphernalia of potted gumtips, symbolic of mealtime, smells, of the sound of feet following upon the dinner gong. Sorry, I shouldn't mope. It's not that I dislike the

> country, it's just that I miss people and books, and music, and the interchange of ideas.[18]

Astley had foreseen that she might lose the vitality of those old days she had written about in 'Juvenilia', her final poem in *Barjai* magazine. She wasn't summoning the requisite Astley family 'stickability' of Cecil's cheery ditty 'Comin' into Work' – not that she minded hard work. As there was no immediate prospect of escape (much as she fantasised about it), she knew she must survive somehow.

Her mind focused on what escape there could be within the prison itself. In this small town she would let her powers of observation roam free, at the school, in the dining room of the town pub, in the streets. Practising the 'art of self-containment' the locals so disliked, the self-described 'priggish' city girl could behave according to their rules, knowing that there were no rules in the house of the mind. It was like daydreaming in Latin Mass at school, years where the hum of ritual nurtured her secret, separate self.

In her life now the lazy, predictable routines in the little country hotel gave Astley an unexpected opportunity. She found herself in a world of ideas for writing about her current life. She gleefully faced tedium with irony and became obsessed with the 'paraphernalia' of mealtimes, partly a reflection of her own nervous habits. Drawn in detail from this period are the exact conditions of the dining room, taken from her second novel, *A Descant for Gossips*:

> The repetition of the cottage pie drove Helen from the green cave of the dining-room earlier than usual … the six permanent boarders had sat tense in their dislike of each other's eating habits … The sucking action of one mouth dreaded and fought back the clicking dentures of another. One pair of hands chopped all the food into prissy segments, another forked in clumsy gobbets, angry plugs. Conversation was sterile for two meals a day, seven days a week, four weeks a month, curving its full cycle through weather and

> politics and local scandals back through weather and scandals and local politics. Mouths minced or pursed or dogmatised or vanished altogether in refined outrage and jaws became prognathous over unimportant points of view.[19]

Later in life Astley's views softened; she would see warmth, friendship, kindness and intelligent society in the towns of regional and remote Australia but in the Pomona of 1948 the young teacher cut adrift from the fellowship of intellect was shuttered in as much as she was shut out.

Being on the outer was something Astley had already embraced. From the time she had been the pupil who read out loud perfectly to a resentful peer group, she had been prepared to form a set against her circumstances, even if it precluded the warmth of inclusion. Her fascination with the lives and conversations of the people she met meant she could be privy without necessarily being party. It was the perfect insider-outsider role, the twin modes of existence that by now were habitual to her.

At the same time she was pleasantly surprised to find that the chat of ordinary people appealed to her enormously. She was moving a step closer to the life she wanted to capture in her writing. Her egalitarian instincts drew her to the larger canvas. She now knew that her impulse to listen was intimately tied to creative freedom, that gossip gave her the oxygen for invention.

Until this point Astley had experienced gossip as an expression of powerful moral censure, one largely conducted by and against women. In these small towns it still played a part in the relationship between men and women. Her own life as a single female was an object of curiosity. Astley felt under constant idle surveillance by bored, disapproving local inhabitants who were 'small, nosy'. As she later remarked, 'You didn't dare put a foot out of line. They knew everything you did.'[20] Conducting any sort of private life under these conditions would be, she knew, extremely fraught. She disliked intensely the usual rituals of courtship and marriage, critiquing them in a poem written about this time:

Love in Our Time

Always, and reasonably, it is sad
That one should so impersonalise
Question and answer in the flesh,
Reducing to a brief schedule
Form-to-be-filled-relationship
Woman with man

The woman questing in the truth
Acts out the essence of a lie
To please the partner who must see
Himself more willing than she wills,
While both behind their guarded eyes
Know truth for lies.[21]

Love in her time was subject to caveats. A woman could not live a life like a man, with sexual freedom and freedom from negative social consequences. Her early autobiographical novels (*Girl with a Monkey* and *A Descant for Gossips*) dramatise her views about this. Both have young female characters who suffer because of an affair keenly observed by town gossips. In her first novel Astley has the young woman character casting off her male suitor against stereotype. Even in her later work, with the novelist's voice disguised in male narration, a character marvels at the marriage contract and women's acceptance of the poor bargain: 'Loneliness and a carefully organised social stigma that applied most heavily to single females.'[22]

This was not in fact a new sentiment for Astley. She was not quite twenty when she had written about 'love' with what seems like preternatural melancholy:

Revelation

Enter – harshness
The facing of the world.
And you who say you love me, Wanton, hurled
Your pretty little love-arts to the air
And said – 'There –
'Love is cheap, and I have little money,
'Buy me a brazen word or two
'And dip in honey.
'Press
'With a caress
'My sweetened offerings of bliss,
'And swear eternally
'To one'
Meanwhile between this and thou kiss
You boast of other women you have caught,
Then come to me
And swear with eager eyes
That you are the ardent seeker
I, the only prize![23]

What the gossips did not realise, and what Astley did not broadcast in her letters to family and friends, was that she had recently met the man she would go on to marry. 'I'm missing your mouth,' she wrote in the first line of her poem to him.[24] If love was a kind of self-delusion ('My subject is self-delusion and the pity of self-delusion … the point … of all my books'), then for a certain young woman stuck alone in rural Queensland it was one worth having.[25] Even in love Astley was a doubting believer, the kind of romantic who can be lost in the moment of love, while distrusting the shape she suspects that ordinary living might give to it. The same tendency can be seen in the 'watching the self' role she gives to her early female characters, even 'in love'.

A perfect example of this is Helen Striebel in *Descant*, who believes, 'Loving should not be so sad … nor seek in the inevitably cruel way it does a sort of nostalgia in fine weather, in days of irresistible blueness and greenness, as if the rain that was not visible in the physical world were gently falling within the mind. Nothing, not even the most pellucid of moments, was ever recalled without a certain misting in the effect, a regret for loss, for the impossibility of repetition.'[26]

As Astley, the self-described 'stickybeak' and 'people freak', watched this enclosed society from which she herself felt alienated (and perhaps a little superior), she was storing away mannerisms of personality and the social dynamics of groups. This was synchronous with the writing: 'Gossip is the creative process in action,' she would say. 'It's just like making up jazz on the piano, it's improvisation.'[27]

This social claustrophobia of the boarding house was liberating Astley creatively while her own social self was on hold. All she could do was make mental notes, keep writing, trying to keep alive the vivacious Thea the Barjai set had known. She still needed to see herself in relation to intellectual and literary life. She was desperate to hang on to a sense of being a writer, not someone with a dilettantish interest in the arts, and Barjai had been and remained an important part of that.

Once again, it was Martin Haley of the CWM who came to the rescue. Astley picked up a copy of *The Bulletin* he had sent and a letter of good wishes. This issue, she said in reply, reminded her of 'the warm camaraderie of the magazine's early days' and she daydreamed about those old times: 'Do you think that special quality the writers of the 1890s and early in the century possessed of being able to dramatise situations, weaving a little magic into the commonplace, was a fault? I often wonder about it, and the lack in the modern realists like Auden and Spender.'[28]

There was comfort yet to be found in the old arguments about modernism and nationalism in literature. The days of the Dawn and Dusk Club of the old *Bulletin* – reminding her of her maternal grandfather, Con Lindsay – reignited her interest. She was toying with the possibilities of 'weaving a little magic into the commonplace' in her own writing. She had promised herself late in 1946 that, whatever the demands of her job, the following year she would begin writing a novel. She stuck to her plan and in 1947 started 'Moontower'.[29]

Each night Astley removed herself purposefully from the downstairs noise of the dining room. Alone in the quiet of her own room she pondered, imagined the whispering behind her back. None of that mattered once she sat down to write. She was also listening to herself: writing did not come at all easily. It seemed to her a rough apprenticeship when she wrote to Haley of 'the infinite erasings and scratchings needed to obtain a glimmer of style' and the burden of having to deal with 'the ritual difference between the true and the false'.[30]

Eventually she would go on to use real places strongly connected to her own life but with altered names: Reeftown in *It's Raining in Mango* (Cairns); Sugarville in *Girl with a Monkey* (Townsville); Condamine in *The Slow Natives* (Warwick); Allbut in *An Item from the Late News* (Cairns tableland); Kristi in *Beachmasters* (Port Vila); and Doebin Island in *The Multiple Effects of Rainshadow* (Palm Island). She was starting to fashion her own community where what was true or false would be under her control. She did not mind working during the day and writing at night: this was a discipline she would retain for over thirty years, whatever her other full-time occupation. Writing her novel, her satirical comedy of manners away from prying eyes, Astley found herself relaxing more than she had imagined. Her work had the allure of distraction with a purpose.

6

Jack

Such sweet compulsion doth in music lie.

'Arcades' by John Milton, 1645[1]

People who are lonely and wish for love but doubt its existence often despair of finding it. This was true in Astley's case, but she was about to have her doubts cast aside. Her escapes to Brisbane were convivial as well as necessary – and one of them turned out to be more than surprising. Sometime in 1947 Astley set off to see a chamber music concert in Brisbane. She had been looking forward to it, not least because such events provided a rare chance to be among folk talking her kind of talk. She was now twenty-two and in some ways more confident than before: she was in her second year as a qualified teacher and had survived both isolation and the rigours of her profession.

That evening she noticed a man approaching (definitely a 'man'), strongly built but not tall at five feet nine inches and evidently older than she. He spoke to her about the music in an engaged way Astley had not previously encountered: his passion and knowledge were surely rare. Whenever people asked Astley about her husband in years to come she would always recall this moment, as pure romance, the way they had met – talked at interval – and had coffee afterwards: apart from her brother Phil, she said, 'He was the only person I'd ever met who knew anything about music!' Music would forever be their bond. But now this man was interested in this woman. Jack Gregson had been formally discharged from the army in January 1946, recording his marital status on that certificate as 'Married'. This official record would not necessarily have reflected a marital estrangement had it existed. What did he see in the twenty-two-year-old Thea Astley at a chamber music concert in Brisbane?

He might not have seen a potential wife: he was married, ten years older than Astley and had seen considerably more of life. Jack had married before the war, in 1937, and had been living in Sydney at beachside Clovelly with his wife, Marion Eileen (known as Eileen). They had one daughter. He had enlisted in the army in February 1942 and at the age of twenty-seven had been 'demobbed' at the rank of private. Much of Jack's war had been spent in Higgins Field, a large airstrip near the tip of Cape York in far north Queensland, but he had not been posted overseas. Like Thea, he knew a great deal about small-town ennui.

Ten years into their marriage Thea and Jack remembered their early days fondly. In 1958, when Hal Porter published his first novel, *A Handful of Pennies*, drawing partly on his army experiences, Astley wrote her first fan letter, lauding his rendition of 'life in the army mess' and 'all that shallow … brainless authority'.[2] She and Jack bonded in their enjoyment of the farce of officialdom. Astley later said that she was naturally 'agin the government' being half Irish.[3]

As a Protestant and a married one at that, Jack Gregson was out of bounds to any Catholic, a difficulty that loomed large for Astley. However, neither she nor Jack intended to let this get in the way of their developing relationship. Jack was with this attractive, lithe, assured, apparently independent, educated, clearly single (but not outwardly sexually confident) young woman. Astley was intoxicated by this man who knew more about music than she did and who had evidently lived more. Jack had a sly wit to match hers; he was calm if on the cynical side, and apparently a man of few words. An unsuccessful first marriage might have sobered him, as probably had the Depression, giving gravitas to his presence.

His family background was different from Astley's too. When Jack was small his mother had been hospitalised for serious post-natal depression, which at that time could mean a lifetime away from the family home as sufferers were often institutionalised. Jack had grown up largely under the care of his father, helping bring up his three younger brothers. Clearly his had not been an easy life, with difficulties that were not easy to speak of in those days. Was Astley already sensing Jack's strength and stoicism? If one day there was leaning to be done, might he be the rock?

After so much isolation and life endlessly deferred to the occasional forays to Brisbane, Astley was thrilling to the possibility of romance with velocity and surprisingly little fear. She fell passionately in love with Jack, knowing full well the vocal disapproval that would be heaped upon such a marriage in the eyes of the Catholic Church. What mattered now was the freedom to pursue a sexual relationship, and in a small town that meant marriage.

Jack's divorce appears to have been a very efficient one for the times. A year or so after their concert meeting Astley reorganised her teaching commitments so she could attend a registry office ceremony in nearby Gympie. Without fuss or ceremony Edmund (John) Gregson married Thea Astley on 27 August 1948, just two days after her twenty-third birthday and with none of her family present. It was not an elopement, but it must have felt like it. It would be eight years, and after the birth of her son, before Astley resumed regular contact with her parents.

The newlyweds headed straight for the honeymoon hotel they had booked. On the wedding night, as Thea later joked to her women friends, the mystic and the spiritual aspects of marriage were absent.

In the morning she and Jack discovered large bloodstains on the counterpane. Mortified, they tried to wash them out. The attempt was hopeless; they started to laugh. They quickly bundled up the counterpane and took it to the nearest rubbish tip, a gaily hysterical pair of co-conspirators.[4]

In many respects the marriage really was the beginning of new freedoms for Astley. Not the least of these was her freedom to express herself sexually. Twenty years later in very different circumstances she shared memories of these special early days of physical abandon with Tom Keneally, a fellow writer and former seminarian who she knew understood her Catholic background. 'When we first met we used to make love like crazy … total abandon,' she said. Keneally understood the 'emotional dwarfism' the Church tended to inflict on its followers, had seen the kind of euphoria Astley expressed in other Catholics; he had seen how repression, once lifted, led to an almost compulsive temptation to sample pleasures in abundance. As he said to Astley, the trick was 'not in leaving the Church, but in making the Church leave you'. But even in the 1960s, twenty years later, Astley was a long way from quite managing that and she seemed to Keneally 'Godstruck and Hellstruck'.[5]

In her relationship with Jack, however, Astley was free and exuberant. Marriage had put her outside parental control. With Jack she could say anything, however unconventional: that bond was strong from the start, made stronger because they knew that theirs was an unconventional marriage. Their partnership was illuminated by jazz, which Jack was rapidly introducing to his new wife. Together they thrilled to the sounds of Duke Ellington, Count Basie, Ella Fitzgerald, Sarah Vaughan. Johnny Hodges's 'Star-Crossed Lovers' became a favourite.

The energy and freedom of new love, sex and jazz became inseparable in Astley's mind for the rest of her life. This new sense of aliveness would have the most profound effect on her writing, introducing a physical tension, a need for perpetual inventiveness, a certain largesse. The lushness was music's equivalent of Queensland's 'overblown quality'.[6] Classical music had played its part in her early striving for technique in poetry; now this new kind of music attuned her to words and mannerisms in a quite different way. This affinity with jazz was opening up a new form of auditory imagination for her, the very kind that might lead to a fiction of the 'flesh and blood' she so wanted to create. It was a way of being able to hear the full range of sounds in the world, then being able to reproduce them in a fresh composition.

In her fiction Astley used musical references to model characters or to shift them psychologically. A character's mind might be full of classical music – to show an evolved intellect – but jazz was better to bring out a character's exuberance and refusal to follow convention (for example, the drum-playing Bonnie in *Reaching Tin River*). Likewise, she compares the appreciation of genuine 'improvised music' with 'musical pretension' (especially in her favourite novel, *The Acolyte*, about a musical genius and his followers).

Characters who use musical knowledge as a form of snobbery, 'merely as a dividing line between themselves and the hicks' – as do the Talbots in *A Descant for Gossips* – do not fare well in Astley's fiction. This seems a kind of projection on Astley's part, since she herself had a tendency to slip the odd musically obscure reference into a conversation. Those on the receiving end were supposed to assume passion and pure motive on her part, but this could also seem curious, if not spiteful, behaviour. A former colleague recalls such conversations:

> Astley: 'You do know jazz musicians are serious musicians?'
> Colleague: 'Yes, I do.'
> Astley: '"Knoxville 1915" op. 24 – cantata for voice and orchestra by Samuel Barber – ever heard of it?'
> Colleague: 'Well, yes, in fact I have.'

The colleague added, 'She assumed I would never have heard of it and that she was the only one in Sydney who knew of this glorious work. She was very disappointed when I knew.'[7]

Jazz provided another opportunity for Astley to be 'agin': classical music lovers widely considered it a threat to the aesthetics of musical composition and an inferior form of music generally. The fact that she and Jack thought the opposite was another co-conspiratorial act against convention: two serious music lovers bonded in a defiant gesture. It was the kind of gesture upon which the marriage more or less permanently settled. Thirty years later, in the 1970s, when Astley gave a speech on behalf of the Sydney Conservatorium's Big Band (then being wound up) she reminded the audience of how jazz came into its own, quoting Henry Pleasant's *Serious Music and All That Jazz*, explaining that jazz was the only satisfactory exit from the technical cul-de-sac recognised by composers everywhere.[8] Her defence of jazz thus lasted well beyond its rapid rise as a popular form; in her mind it remained entwined with her own emancipation.

Thea and Jack spent their early time together at Jack's place in Rome Street, Yeronga, a southern suburb of Brisbane leading down to the river. It was here that they spent their last few months of living in Brisbane. Jack's support of his former family seems not to have been discussed openly ever, but Thea's own independent nature meant she was happy to see things being shared, especially the finances. Jack was marrying a professional teacher: they would be a team. Both were disgusted by the Department of Education's view that once married and pregnant, a woman should give up her teaching position. Thea deferred to Jack in many things, but she also liked the fact that this was not always necessary.

The hunt for jobs, money, houses became urgent and Jack began applying for clerical and accountancy positions in Sydney. Jack's father and brothers were there, and he would be nearer to his daughter, though there is no record of any formal arrangements for visitation being made. A move away from Astley's parents would have seemed wise, at least for the time being. Jack soon accepted an accounts job, firstly at Elder Smith and then the Mitchell Library in the city while Thea applied for a teaching transfer. It would be their next adventure.

The suburbs that became the sprawl of Sydney were barely starting to form and there were few rentable properties that would allow Jack to get to the city on public transport. Difficult as it was in the late 1940s to find affordable accommodation, they found one floor of a large Victorian mansion at Ellesmere Avenue, Hunters Hill. Perched magnificently high on a hillside overlooking one of the many Sydney waterways leading into the harbour, it gave them more space than either had ever dreamed of.

They were now Mr and Mrs Gregson, one couple among others. When Jack's friends, usually army mates, passed through town Thea held the floor, providing a new kind of theatre in which Jack was to be forever cast as a background character. He had become used to her outspokenness and was happy to be less vocal in company than she was. When Thea took the floor he enjoyed watching.

At the time, and into the 1950s, Astley's outspokenness attracted silent disapproval and discreetly raised eyebrows. Jack remained a loyal support, while Thea became ever more expansive. She must have felt lucky that she had such an equal partnership herself, but was troubled by the unequal nature of marriage itself. She began to watch other couples like a hawk.

The lot of the married woman was tied up with Astley's own sense of loss, which included, to her surprise, the loss of Queensland. Having spent the last few years there looking and feeling every bit the town outsider, here she was an outsider again, in Sydney. Nothing had changed the long-standing interstate rivalries and snobberies that bound her to parochial defensiveness. She found plenty to resent in the so-called sophisticated capital of New South Wales: Astley's new teaching job with the New South Wales Department of Education began on a pay scale that officially erased her previous years of teaching in Queensland, and she was being paid less than her male counterparts too. The metropolis could be, she realised, its own kind of prison.

As always in such times, she turned to poetry. If she could write about routine and banality from Pomona in Queensland, she could write about banality from Hunters Hill in Sydney: '"Clerk; eight fifty; family; office". Feeling homesick, her feet craved "familiar floors".'[9]

Money was an extremely pressing matter for the couple. Neither had brought capital to the marriage and their savings had been eaten up in the interstate move. They really were watching pennies and they never forgot arriving in Sydney with less than two shillings to their name. Their financial struggles became part of the mythology of Jack and Thea, in stories endlessly retold: 'Almost like the time that …', 'Not as bad as when …', 'Try arriving with …'

Perhaps for this reason one of the earliest decisions in the marriage was that Thea and Jack would maintain separate bank accounts and would carefully tot up and divide everyday expenses. It helped that Jack was an accountant but Thea was no fool with maths and figures either. Money changed hands according to what each agreed was owed the other – receipts held as proof – a habit that would stick throughout their lives together. In years to come this division of money would perplex their son and it was certainly unconventional for the times. But Jack and Thea both knew that even with two incomes they would need to be careful with money if they were ever to think of owning their own home. There was little to do but work.

Jack began his city-to-suburb commute while Astley calculated for amusement, as was her habit: '3,482 train trips as of …' Astley started full-time teaching. As the years passed, family and friends would wonder at Jack and Thea's perverse respect for each other's ability to 'slog it out'.[10] As they did not own a car, they had some serious daily travel in a city whose public transport systems were yet to be fully established.

Astley went first to the secondary Drummoyne Boys' School, not far from the Hunters Hill flat. After that she was moved to outer west Homebush, an Intermediate Girls' High School that was still also part of the primary system (taking girls up to the early years of high school while Strathfield Girls' High was being completed). Astley's experience of teaching was about to change dramatically but it was in these busy suburban schools during the 1950s that her natural gifts as a teacher found genuine expression. Toughness of all kinds had been required in the small Queensland schools, but now she was dealing with city adolescents, not primary school children as she had in her first teaching positions. Teenagers had other sometimes challenging ways of behaving and the grown-up-sounding married title of Mrs Gregson might not offer much protection.

At Homebush Astley was teaching large groups of girls in what could be a rough outer suburb. Any camaraderie between staff members was based on survival, and in this school the most difficult class was '2K', known as the 'hound dogs'. This academically and behaviourally challenged group of thirteen- or fourteen-year-olds met Astley for English. Colleagues were often amused by Astley's off-the-cuff commentaries on dullness and dullards, and they couldn't wait to see what Mrs High and Mighty would make of the infamous 2K.

But 2K mattered just as much to Astley as the bright girls did, for reasons her colleagues couldn't guess. She did not see them as a job-lot of human nuisance; Astley saw young, vulnerable girls who already believed they were somehow 'not worth the effort'. The scholarship girl from All Hallows' who had been humbled by good fortune still had egalitarian instincts. To Astley the girls in 2K were like the Fortitude Valley girls who used to wait on her table.

The young teacher walked quietly into the rowdy group, who largely ignored her. She just stood there, she did not raise her voice. This was a simple, human act that made Astley different from other staff members and it had the effect of uniting the group in silent curiosity. She immediately capitalised on her advantage and moved slowly but athletically into a cross-legged yoga pose on top of her desk. She then began speaking quietly and respectfully, waving her arms expressively, as if she naturally assumed they would be interested.[11] The 'hound dogs', by now, were in a state of rapt attention.

Staff members took turns to look in on the famously raucous 2K, now quiet, and its new English teacher: the taming of 2K became staff-room legend. As one colleague put it, Astley had been so successful with the students because she related to them, they to her, and the girls felt that at last someone was being 'real' with them.[12] Astley had chanced herself on being herself and they loved her for it. Even Mrs Gregson's chalk throwing – her aim was deadly – they could accept as serious because it was done without rancour. Astley's carrying voice helped, trained for an audience from her Barjai days.

Working with Astley made a difference to some of the other teachers too. Mary Sainty remembers the day she started at the new Strathfield Girls' High, where Astley was now settled teaching French as well as English. Thea was collecting material for class when Sainty heard her remark: 'If I had any more safety pins in my skirt it would be chainmail.'[13] It was a style of approach Astley would perfect: when she wanted to make a connection with someone she would often try to make them laugh. She also liked to puncture the pomposity she saw in some of the more conservative teachers.

Mary, for her part, decided that this unconventional woman might just save her from the occasional dreariness of work. The two became firm friends; they had the kind of woman-to-woman friendship Astley had lacked up until now. Both convent-educated, they could communicate with just a wry phrase or a look, and both were aware of the possibilities of ambiguity in language. Mary was someone Astley could talk to about Phil, who was still in Melbourne and now close to being ordained, and about her own anxieties regarding her Catholic faith and the expectations of her parents.

Astley was being candid in a way she badly needed to be; her colleague understood implicitly her need for the self-protection of irony. The two young teachers would whisper with amusement and self-knowledge. Mary came to think of Astley as having helped her discover irony – she had grown up with it but hadn't recognised it in herself before. Astley knew how to treat 'everything serious as a joke', playing the Queenslander to the hilt, sending up pretension.[14] This sometimes offended people: they were not quite sure of her tone and something in her delivery could make them suspect personal insult.

Astley took her teaching responsibilities extremely seriously; her anxiety guaranteed more than due diligence. Teaching was a satisfying if exhausting occupation capable of attacking the nerves, something she would one day discover to her cost. In these early years of their marriage she and Jack were both working long days, travelling long distances, and spending the evenings recovering with quiet talk and music.

Astley's colleagues knew that she was 'writing something fictional' because she had started to talk openly about her experiences of teaching up north, but she didn't want to be seen as 'one of those intellectuals who wrote'.[15] She continued her habit from early teaching days, satisfied to write a little each evening. Poe's idea of creativity as a process, in increments, still appealed. It was also the only way circumstances allowed her to write.

Within three years Jack and Thea began looking to buy an affordable property in Sydney. This meant moving further out of the city to the newer subdivisions of land where there were settled homes, usually on large blocks of land. Thea and Jack had come to value the spaciousness of the streets in their current neighbourhood and the long wide avenues of suburbs to the north, but house and land on such a scale would have been much too expensive.

As luck would have it, a family living on one of these large acreages on the outskirts of Epping, eighteen kilometres northwest of Sydney's centre, was considering subdividing their land. What had originally been a tennis court could become a small house-sized piece of land in an established street. Jack and Thea could secure land relatively cheaply and could build their own house themselves. They acted quickly and began an exciting joint project designing a new home from scratch at 44a Dorset Street, Epping. From this address Astley would write and publish eight books over the next twenty years.

Astley was the creative energy behind Dorset Street. She could have studied architecture at university and now she could indulge her interest in building with a purpose. The inside covers of her favourite orange-covered writing exercise books became host to sketches and plans of the new house, a habit she kept up for future house purchases. The sketches show Astley was playful with spaces in a simple way, breaking them up idiosyncratically. She was determined that their house would be different from the standard suburban home. Their limited means would not stand in the way of creating something distinct, expressing their own way of being and living.

When the house was completed, Thea's efforts expressed a simple dictum: 'Whatever you do,' she would say, 'if you build a house, even if it's just one room, make it a beautiful room.'[16] Visitors would look around at what seemed a modest dwelling yet the expression of this sentiment was evident both outside and within: sparse furniture, an unusual fireplace, furnishings carefully chosen.

There were immediate construction problems. Bricks were still expensive and hard to come by. Fibro was cheaper and more commonly used, but for a girl from Queensland timber was the only choice as a building material. Their next obstacle was officialdom. There were many heated consultations with the conservative local council about this 'exercise in the modern'. The building was compliant with regulations but considered rather too boxy, and the use of timber set it apart from the more typical brick and tile of the area. Thea and Jack enjoyed 'talking up' the narrow-mindedness of these Visigoths, pledging to take them on. It was home theatre, a 'we'll show you' attitude they loved to adopt together, but in reality it never ended in actual confrontation.[17] They were not lawbreakers; a few years later Barry Humphries would satirise mercilessly the attitudes and mentality they so disliked. They were suburban anti-suburbanites.

In time an unusual two-storey dwelling emerged, with a side (not front) door entrance. The separations and divisions of space were a natural and agreed extension of their union: Jack needed a good space to listen to music properly and Thea a private space to organise herself and her thoughts for writing. The fact that few married couples planned a house on quite these terms was of no interest to them: neither would have thought that they were doing anything other than carving out a living environment for two individuals. And now a third person had entered the calculations. At thirty, Astley was pregnant. Life needed to speed up and building issues preoccupied Jack and Thea in the little time they had outside work. Thea was to continue teaching as close to the birth as possible, even if some of the women on staff looked askance at her decision.

Sensing the enormity of change ahead, Astley felt that writing at night seemed the way to meld all the changes in her life, the way to keep the writer Thea moving forward, not just the half of Mr and Mrs Gregson, not just a woman with a house and baby on the way. Of course Cecil and Eileen had to be told, the beginning of a rapprochement. They were delighted that they were about to be grandparents, but after some frosty years they were still unhappy about 'that marriage business', as Cecil liked to refer to it. In their minds this had remained unresolved for eight years and now the coming birth had raised all the earlier concerns, plus the question of baptism within the Catholic Church.

The move to Sydney had made the impasse easier to ignore but the impending birth ensured that this would not continue. Astley knew from her upbringing the punishment in store for them: the Catholic Church did not regard Jack and Thea as married, the child would be born in sin, could not be baptised, could not be buried according to the rites of the Church and would be spiritually doomed to limbo. Astley was restless and anxious by this renewed fervour about her life choices. It went beyond trying to please her parents: she was still emotionally involved with Catholicism, not because she was devout but because she was inclined to be self-doubting. Pregnancy had made her feel vulnerable too. She was not ready to denounce her faith, but nor was she any more inclined to be bullied by those she saw as bigots.

In such a situation, it was impossible for Phil – ordained in the previous year – not to be involved. He had not yet settled all of his own misgivings about life in the Church; he was shortly to start teaching at Burke Hall, a junior Catholic boys' school in Melbourne. Phil's shyness and natural deference were anything but assets for a teacher and he would find himself seriously undermined, cowering in the face of the thoughtless cruelty and irascibility of young boys. Phil, who was immensely fond of his sister, was the unlucky negotiator on the question of Thea's marriage and the Church, since Cecil and Eileen naturally turned to him for expertise.

Astley also began to field regular 'mission' visits from clergy informing her of her spiritual wrong-footedness. These visits did not go well. During one of them, the option of a Pauline Privilege was suggested, which dissolves an actual marriage (different from an annulment, which declares a marriage invalid from the beginning). The Pope could be petitioned to allow this, and it would be satisfactory within the Church if she and Jack remained as 'living companions' – though not in a sexual relationship. Jack and Thea enjoyed the absurdity of this – but it still left Astley genuinely distressed. She leaned on her good friend Mary Sainty and Mary laughed with her. But the situation was clearly costing her, as seen in this poem, named after an ancient Roman female poet and written around this time, but published the following year in 1957 in *The Sydney Morning Herald*:

Sulpicia III

Half of my kith and less of my kin
Have long passed me over,
Pursuing no plan but to counteract sin
Of love with lover.

I ask me why years should beacon like this
In diminishing torches

Long galleries of loving that should point to a kiss
And some passionate matches.

Of laughter, perhaps; but the truth is it matters
Far less than the pleading
That thread sighs to thread when the day's fabric tatters,
While half the heart's bleeding.[18]

The title is significant. There are thought to have been two such ancient Roman poets of prominence, so by making herself the third (Sulpicia III), Astley was casting herself within a tradition of poetry about marital devotion and love dating back centuries.

It would take a few more years before 'kith and kin' would become a regular part of Astley's life again. She continued teaching until the winter term of 1955: money as always was an issue. She couldn't know how she would find her way back to work but hoped there would still be a shortage of teachers. Four months later, on 18 November, Edmund John (after Jack) Gregson was born.

Jack, Thea and baby moved into the just-completed 44a Dorset Street. Disapproval from the Church about the marriage no longer dominated amid the concerns an infant brought into the new house. In the background, however, Phil had advanced the various paper machinations that would at least enable a marriage to take place. What was termed a 'Validation' of the civil marriage meant that the couple would go into the sacristy and sign the register and not sign in the church itself, in front of the people. Jack did not have to convert to Catholicism, but it would all take some time. Godparents for Ed had already been settled: Mary Sainty and her husband, Frank.[19]

It was an emotionally battle-scarred and weary woman who began life as a new mother in this northern suburb of Sydney. Busy as she was with a newborn, Astley was for the first time away from full-time employment and she had time to think. Recent events had been a poignant reminder of her past in Queensland, and her family. She was becoming increasingly reflective about 'home' and the ten years since she had been alone and single in Queensland's north seemed suddenly close in memory. She found herself recalling her Townsville days, her first teaching appointment. Nor had she forgotten her abandoned novel manuscript 'Moontower'; she had been writing prose now for about eight of those ten years.

As she looked back on her previous life Astley was thinking about a new character, a young woman teaching in remote Queensland towns whom she would call Elsie Ford. It was a plain name for a character who would be naïve and a little self-absorbed, and perhaps painfully self-conscious. There would be room for a little cryptic wordplay and some compassion for this young woman, the central character, for whom 'the very emptiness of the future gave a sorrowful pleasure' and whose only self-protection from the menacing townsfolk is the 'complete isolation of the mind'.[20] Elsie was a girl with a monkey on her back.

Astley asked herself who these townsfolk might be, sweating in isolation, with their flaws, doubts and fears. She already knew, as she said, that, 'Any sort of person can be interesting in circumstances that create antagonism with other people, circumscribing them so that something breaks out.' She now wanted to understand people differently, to see their complexity, not as much as an exercise of satire. She seemed to know already something she would only articulate a decade later: that 'true emotional adventure lies in the geography of other people's minds; as long as a writer has that it doesn't matter where he is'.[21] Astley was safe in the geography of time: a world away from the remote lushness and beauty of the tropical north, in suburban Sydney, she entered her Dream Country.[22]

7

The Gorgon of Epping North

The neighbours think I'm the Gorgon of Epping North.

Thea Astley to her editor Beatrice Davis[1]

The care of a newborn was a bigger challenge for Astley than writing, and it brought up the question of her social identity. Her roles in life were multiplying fast: Thea of Barjai days, Thea and Jack, Mrs Gregson, and now mother. To this she added one more, a writing pseudonym named after her brother, Phil: Phillip Cressy. She was convinced that signing a woman's name to a poem was a distinct disadvantage in getting it published, and Astley needed confirmation that her poetry was of publishable quality. She had always taken risks with inviting appraisal and this would be no different: she was prepared to stake a name on it. To her delight a clutch of poems were published over the next two years in *The Sydney Morning Herald*.

She enjoyed the freedom that a male persona gave her. In 1956, when the bank cheque for her latest poem didn't arrive, Astley rang *The Sydney Morning Herald* demanding payment. The literary editor, Sidney Baker, was forced to write to a 'Mr Cressy': 'If indeed, you are not at [Croydon] as you say in your letter of July 26 this may be less the fault of an unsympathetic commercial world than you imply.'[2]

Baker's sarcastic response was because staff at the paper had innocently sent the payment cheque to the address Astley herself had put on the back of the submission envelope. The Croydon address was the home she and Jack had rented just prior to the move to the new Epping house.

Astley was caught up in her own game of hide and seek: she wanted recognition but wished to be incognito. Now she was left wondering: had the poems worked, or had the male name led to their acceptance? Writing as a man, writing as a woman, and the relative value accorded in each case would become an enduring struggle for Astley. It would be many years (not until *An Item from the Late News* in 1982) before she chanced the first-person female narrative perspective. For now, the only way to assuage that self-doubt was to use another name: Thea Astley.

These were things to mull over amid radically unfamiliar domestic routines. There was little time to look for advice on baby care, so that Astley was as lost as any new mother. The days were long. She felt unprepared, much as she had as a young single woman thrust into teaching in far north Queensland. And in a way new motherhood felt like the same kind of betrayal: nothing in her life had warned her what motherhood might be like. Astley knew that motherhood was seen as central to the domestic ideal of femininity.[3] It was assumed women wanted to be, and would become, mothers, and young mothers at that: Astley at thirty was out of step because of her age, and she had spent almost a decade as a professional in the workforce. None of this made her feel more competent or suited to the realities of motherhood. At the same time, Ed the baby was perfect. Their relationship was like a second love affair.

Astley's nerves were not ideally suited to the care of a vulnerable infant and she compensated by doing everything meticulously and to a schedule. As she had with the Latin Mass during her school days,

Astley found ritual a comfort. Thirty-five years later when she was old enough to be a grandmother, Astley still remembered her confusion: 'When Edmund was born I had no sisters around me, I'd never had the experience of looking after children. I found motherhood a terrible moral burden. I had no idea babies stayed awake twenty-six hours a day. I used to boil everything he ate and drank, even his orange juice, until a nurse told me I was boiling all the vitamins out of it.'[4]

Life at 44a Dorset Street was uneventful and isolating. Astley had taken little interest in the street or her neighbours when she had been working full-time. She was preoccupied by her own family now and her parents were back in touch with her from Brisbane, and she wrote weekly to her mother. Phil wrote often (though worryingly) of his life in training for the priesthood. Devout as he was, his letters made her think he was perennially anxious about performing his liturgical duties. Astley knew her parents were becoming concerned for Phil, and now she was able to help: what better distraction than to share little stories in letters about a grandson?

Astley plunged headfirst into the 'horror domestica' of 1950s suburban life in the conservative suburb of Epping. A familiar sense of entrapment, of surveillance, pressed in on her: 'It was all about pavlova – I wasn't interested in making pavlova successfully – this branded me an unsuccessful mother in the area where I lived …'[5]

She had to get out of the house. Ed was soon old enough to be pushed in a stroller and Astley began another ritual: long walks around the wide streets of Epping. Even though there were a lot of young mothers in the area, she cut a strange figure. Betty Judd was at home one day with her two young children on the other side of Dorset Street when she noticed a slightly built young woman pushing a stroller at high speed. Betty laughed out loud: this woman looked so desperate. So, Betty realised, she was not the only one who felt stuck. A meeting between the two women seemed inevitable. This happened when Thea, en route, turned to shout to her: 'Don't you just *have* to get out of there?'[6]

Astley was distracted, but her earthy casualness surprised and appealed to her neighbour. The two women soon found they had a lot more in common than being housebound. Betty had avoided needing to leave her job setting up libraries by marrying late. She then had to move to be close to her ailing parents. Like Astley, she intensely disliked the postwar pressure to get women back into the home.

A firm friendship began, with a candour that surprised Astley. Before long she felt she could talk about her writing seriously, even when she and Betty were in the mess of young children. Betty was a good listener and she knew that Astley was 'someone different'.[7] Life in Dorset Street would now be different for both of them.

Astley warmed to the new possibilities of this friendship. She had enjoyed some of her women teacher colleagues but this experience was different. Gradually she met other women who lived nearby, and Dorset Street became 'quite a little island of people getting to know each other'.[8] Astley soon met another kindred spirit in Yvonne Wyndham, also a teacher (whose sister, the writer Gwen Kelly, corresponded with Astley over the years). Before long Astley found herself in a group of women who mixed freely, while the children played together in the safety of the wide streets or at each other's homes. There were quite a few parties where couples had the chance to be couples; Astley even played tennis with her neighbours. She somehow managed to be inside the situation while she maintained her listening-observer perspective of old. She could see other marriages close up and was fascinated, though she was naturally drawn to the wives who either had, or had wanted, careers outside the home.

Astley did appear to the other inhabitants of Dorset Street as quite eccentric. This wasn't necessarily obvious in her behaviour; Yvonne had already noticed that Thea was not aloof as much as seeming to want to set herself apart. The women of the street, in fact, thought of her as generous, always willing to help. But Astley's tongue got in the way too often. She was frequently unable to control her desire to shatter the cosiness of life in Dorset Street. She held back a lot from others. 'You never knew what she was thinking,' Yvonne commented, meaning that an essential part of her didn't seem to be present in the moment. And besides she was often 'outspoken and cruel in her assessment of other people'.[9]

Astley chose to be close to those who did not judge or take offence. This was not always successful: some neighbours decided to keep their distance as whispers got around about the 'writer at number 44a' who intruded into people's lives, asking questions, collecting material. It is easy to see why some thought her prurient, though good friends who knew Astley were aware that she enjoyed playing with words, that her 'fascination was as much with words and particular phrases' as it was with people.[10] The cleverness of a phrase was in some ways overwhelming in the moment for her, to the point where she could be genuinely surprised by the effect of her words, if negative. The more conservative couples began to distance themselves; the men claimed to be 'terrified'. To them a sharp-witted woman openly speaking her mind made Astley the 'Gorgon of Epping North', as she later dubbed herself.[11]

The quiet times with the Dorset Street women and children did contradict something fierce happening in the background of Astley's life. She was still preoccupied with Catholicism and its effect on her for she and Jack were still not yet married in the eyes of the Church. Betty Judd, who was not a Catholic, thought the strength of Astley's loyalty to Jack was admirable, despite all the religious objections to their union.

But Astley was struggling with guilt, not from a rational sense of acknowledging wrongdoing – she didn't really think that – but the culture of conscience she had known from childhood had permeated her psyche.

But she was also writing. When she managed to get Ed to sleep Astley was immersed in her notebooks, in the world of her Dream Country. She had continued with the same writing methods she had already established: phrases and notes of significance jotted down (sometimes anywhere – back of a postcard, a shopping list – which only she could decipher as part of an idea). Sketches, plots and character lists would then emerge all over and inside the covers of her favoured lined exercise books, which she would fill with careful, handwritten prose. Most of this could then be transferred almost unaltered to the 'typer'.

This way, without sitting formally at a desk, Astley knew she could secure time for writing – even for fifteen minutes a night – because the words inevitably added up. It was a story of writing that she kept telling for her entire life, encouraging beginner writers to write in such a way, regardless of their current work circumstances, to believe that it was possible for a novel to emerge thus. She had moved far beyond the safety nets of home and convent, yet it was all still so near, and writing brought it even closer.

She was shaping a novel that would explore the exercise of will, and her mind went back to the time when her view of sexuality had parted way with the Church's. Astley did not want this first book to be merely a critique of the Church; it was her own consciousness she wanted to navigate. She would base this on her first teaching appointment in Townsville.

She chose to condense this first autobiographical narrative into a twenty-four-hour time frame, describing the young teacher Elsie Ford's last day in the town, with her farewells almost entirely described through the prism of her own self-absorption. This could be balanced by a third-person narration exposing the shortcomings of the townsfolk and the misery of Elsie's half-hearted romantic mishap with the unsuitable roughneck Harry.

Astley re-created all the details of her life back then: the shock of the hot, wet, ramshackle world; the mundane realities of the job. Elsie feels lonely and the 'false heartiness' of the people in the boarding house where she has lived appals her. There is a brief affair with a town road-worker, and she is ogled by the prying townsfolk, much as Astley had felt herself to be when she and Jack first courted. Elsie is 'held in the still centre of egotism', and gains 'pleasure from the process of her ego'. In some ways *Girl with a Monkey* seems a guilt-laden portrait of the author when young.

Astley wrote the novel to give expression to the battle with herself and with the beliefs she had grown up with. She would often speak of writing as 'a selfish way of writing out things that worried me'.[12] She found it easier to dramatise this dialogue between inner and outer self in prose rather than poetry, but it was difficult for her to abandon the highly stylised rhetoric of poetry she loved and was technically good at. She found dialogue difficult too, and would later defend criticism of her characters' rather stylised dialogue, saying it was better 'to have characters talking and not sounding totally trivial'.[13] She read poetry as a writing stimulus but she no longer wanted its emotional nakedness; she was carving out new creative freedoms for herself.

Astley had not tried her hand at a novel for about eight years. What she needed was a response she could trust. She knew very few people in Sydney literary or publishing circles and she didn't want to send any part of the novel to anyone who would easily recognise its factual basis, including her old friend Martin Haley. The writing had been hard work, building slowly from the fifteen minutes a night she had been able to spend on it. She knew there was a literary competition in *The Sydney Morning Herald*. The only way forward was to test the waters and enter just a section of the novel, which she called 'Tropic', under a *nom de plume*. It didn't win. Astley turned immediately to the judges' commendation. It was on the strength of their praise, without any idea whose desk it might land on, that she sent the full manuscript of her first novel to 'the Editor' at the Sydney offices of the publishers Angus & Robertson.

This time she used her own name.[14] There would be no pseudonym for this manuscript in what was really a tentative new reckoning of self. Although subsequent correspondence for years was addressed to 'Thea Gregson', Astley would within a few years become consistent in use of her unmarried name.

She could hardly have known from these first steps how blessed her foray into the world of literary publishing was to be. *Girl with a Monkey* attracted the attention of renowned literary editor Beatrice Davis, who exerted a strong editorial influence over the publishing house Angus & Robertson. The firm had originally established itself as a huge outlet for bookselling as well as a publisher of local titles. It was known for publishing many early Australian authors of the early 1900s. By the late 1930s the firm had opened offices in London, in a bid to expand internationally. This tended to concentrate decision-making overseas, and in 1956 A&R was still struggling with the conditions of an Anglicised book culture: management was inclined to dismiss Australian literature as a poor sales proposition. Davis persisted in a belief that the 'auld firm', as it was affectionately known, should publish quality Australian fiction.

In fact, she was eager to expand the list. She knew she could only break through these negative ideas if she could find 'fiction writers with imagination' and she was not blind to problems: too often, she felt, 'Australian novelists were documentary rather than creative writers'.[15] Davis suspected this new author was one of those commended in the *Herald* competition but she couldn't guess that she was about to find exactly the kind of imaginative fiction she'd been looking for. Publishing a first novel was always a big decision in-house, so Davis waited until after the readers' reports were in before writing to Astley. She delicately deleted the readers' references to 'obscure wordiness', perhaps already assuming a protective role towards this potential new author.

Six weeks can be a long time for an author to wait in such circumstances but that was how long it took before the letter from A&R arrived at Dorset Street. Certain phrases lit up the page: 'quality of the writing', 'evocative and individual'. Then came the crash: 'rather too slight' for publication. It was disappointing but when Astley read down to the last statement she was transfixed: 'I think you could become a very good novelist indeed.'[16]

Davis had suggested a meeting. Surely this was better, almost, than publication? A week later Astley made her way into the A&R offices at 89 Castlereagh Street, Sydney. Once there she found a petite, carefully groomed and very reserved Davis, working from a tiny and most unglamorous attic-sized space.

To say the two women got on extremely well is an understatement. They were *simpatico* despite a fifteen-year age difference (Davis was then in her late forties). In no time they were exchanging likes and dislikes: their similar university studies in English and French, their shared ironic sense of humour and, even more compelling, their passion for music bordering on devotion. Both women played the piano with skill; each regretted she had not been able to pursue a career in music.[17]

Astley observed Davis's constant smoking with the curiosity of the non-smoker and thought it a great signature of personal style, forming an extension of natural expressiveness.[18] More than twenty years later, when Davis was leaving A&R, Astley would write a tribute to her editor's skill and their time spent together, and how 'she has, indirectly, and simply by being Beatrice, taught me ... much about living'.[19]

Astley came to appreciate Davis's contradictions, which in some ways mirrored her own. Davis sometimes displayed 'Anglophile gentility, even pretension, at other times uninhibitedly doing as she pleased without apparently giving a damn for anyone's opinion'.[20] The way this behaviour seemed almost scripted when so much else was left unsaid would have been very appealing to a young writer. Davis had a fully fledged career, engaged in flirtation on a grand scale with her male authors – as she did with Hal Porter – and took lovers. It wouldn't be an exaggeration to say that it was Davis who in the years to come would most influence Astley in some of these ways of 'living'.

Davis knew about duty and obligation too. Before she had married (a doctor many years her senior) she, like Astley, had taken on a teaching bursary largely as a means of getting to university. Davis was also unfaltering in her commitments and loyalties to those who were close to her.[21] But it was the *style* of Davis that impressed – so unlike anyone in Astley's orbit. She was, in the parlance of the time, a classy dame.

Davis didn't appeal to everyone but Astley didn't know that yet, nor did she care. Years later she would learn that Patrick White had little time for the editor's 'most artificial – refaned' way of speaking.[22] The quiet young author in front of the renowned book editor loved the theatricality, the Sydney North Shore *hauteur* that would always be such a feature of Davis's personality, both personally and professionally. Davis also entertained elegantly, was a good hostess, knew all the right things to eat and say and serve. In this way, she was in effect teaching Astley lessons in being a successful social person.

Astley might have been enchanted but Davis must have been equally impressed by her 'find'. Her misgivings about *Girl with a Monkey* evaporated less than two weeks after their meeting. Astley had made no revisions when Davis wrote 'pleased to advise' that the manuscript had been accepted for publication.[23]

Not one inclined to dwell on good fortune, Astley set about correcting what had slightly peeved her in all of this. She got out Davis's original letter and homed in on the word 'slight', which she took to mean too short to be a 'proper' novel, then scribbled some careful calculations of figures on the back. Nobody, she must have thought, should ever underestimate writers (well, not her anyway) on the subject of numbers. She estimated her manuscript to be about 35,000 words. By the time Davis wrote the in-house memo the word 'slightness' had disappeared from the description. Publication was to be of a 'short novel' of 'about 45,000 words'.[24] Astley had not added those extra words, but what might seem petty – the totting up of words – enabled her to make her first strike, nor would it be the last time she would take an editor or publisher to task. Her editor was merely being conciliatory: she had no idea that this new author intended to take the writing business as seriously as the business of writing itself.

On 14 March 1957 'Mr and Mrs Gregson' went into the A&R office to sign the contract: Astley was determined that Jack, especially given his expertise in bookkeeping, would always be on hand for these occasions. She enthusiastically signed her contract as 'Mrs Thea Gregson', with Jack as witness. At home in Dorset Street they celebrated quietly. This was a huge step forward, yet both suspected it would make little practical difference to two busy working lives, with a young child to support. Money was still tight. Jack, who was very proud of his wife and wanted to show his faith in her, splashed out on a surprise present of a brand new Green Hermes 'Baby' typewriter, and Astley would use it for the next twenty years. This was a substantial cost, beyond their means.

Davis made it clear that even well-known writers could not expect to make much money from their work: it was a privilege to be published. The new author could not see why this should be so, or why it was such an accepted part of publishing life, and she simply never accepted it. One day Astley would be proven right. Making a living out of writing fiction was, perhaps, not likely but it was possible to achieve commercial respect in small but not insignificant sums. Her attitude would become a thorn in the side of her publishers.

For the moment, Astley decided these issues were best left alone in what was already a blooming friendship with an influential editor. Davis thought they should address each other by their first names in letters. Astley was undoubtedly flattered to be so invited, replying that she did '*want* to' but 'thought it seemed a bit "fresh".'[25]

Compared with Astley's day-to-day life, her persona as an author was odd. Wasn't she still just a teacher who had written a book, a mother with a toddler who would need her regular job back? Was she a teacher or a writer? These questions brought self-doubt, which shadowed her success. Astley was not comfortable with the concept of 'being a writer'; she hated what she saw as its pretension. She found it hard to resolve these conflicting ideas about herself, as if something she had longed for had suddenly arrived too soon.

She was certainly taking writing seriously. The question of a writing persona was difficult because it brought together roles she was used to keeping separate: woman, wife, mother, writer. Creatively, too, she struggled with 'voice' – was she writing as a man or a woman or, as she would later say, 'a neuter'? She was defensive about the possibility of being typecast as a 'women's writer', which she felt meant being robbed of due recognition.

Beatrice understood the concerns women authors had about being valued; she was already known for her support of women writers. Astley had counted – as she would – eleven out of the thirty contributors in the anthology Davis had edited were women. Davis was the force behind reissues of out-of-print titles by several women authors including Christina Stead. She championed women writers of intellect: being recognised in *that* company was what mattered the most to Astley – struck the most 'sympathetic chord'.[26]

Davis found little to change when editing *Girl with a Monkey* and quickly became 'an urger'.[27] Astley was excited by this, but also extremely anxious about how to meet such expectations. It was a mixture of exhilaration and compulsion; this sense Astley gave to some friends, of 'having a huge burden to shoulder' and it was often inexplicable to others.[28] Astley confided to Betty Judd that she felt nurtured but a bit 'pushed' by Davis, who was already talking about a deadline for a second novel. Where would she find new material? How could she complete it in time, with Ed still so young?

Astley was suffering from second-novel nerves. Success was now tied up with liking but also pleasing Davis, who had managed to give Astley the not-altogether-welcome idea that Davis was depending on her author. Astley knew she could not afford to write her second novel without some assistance, and applied for a Commonwealth Literary Fund grant. She was not successful, as she wrote to Davis. In the first of many such letters, Astley also wondered whether there might be a further advance on *Girl with a Monkey* so that she could buy air tickets to visit Cecil and Eileen in Brisbane.

Astley loved being literal in this way, deliberately flagging the trivial and the domestic in the face of important-sounding talk of 'the work'. It became her way of shining a torch on what she considered the petty and venal practices of publishing. By insisting on the ordinariness of such a transaction, she hoped to expose the extraordinary penuriousness of publishers when it came to literary fiction. It was also a deflection, part of her complex about 'being a writer'. She also had other questions that needed answering, when she wrote to Davis in June of 1958:

> Dear Beatrice,
>
> Can you bear this question? I know how pestered publishers are by writers, but could you give me, please, a definite publication date for *Girl with a Monkey*? I know you think I'm over-anxious about the book – but it does seem an awfully long time.
>
> I have started something else – very slowly. I want this one to be good – as good as I can make it. So far I can't feel really satisfied with anything I've written. It's a fearful thing to have de luxe standards and be limited by technique and self. I know the country I want to explore but I only seem able to chart its coasts.[29]

She could express herself like this because she trusted her rapport with Beatrice Davis, knew that her editor was sensitive to how much authors needed care and encouragement. Years later in her retirement tribute to her editor, Astley observed that Davis's skill was to 'advise without hurt, to correct without making the author feel ashamed or inadequate'.[30] She also knew how and when to be firm, correcting Astley's hyphens and inconsistent use of 'which' and 'that' pronouncing, pen in air: 'I think we'll have a teeny piece of comma *just there*!'[31]

Davis did not hold back from mentioning some of her reservations about her new author's prose style, which Astley acknowledged: 'Have written 1,000 words of the new opus – only 79,000 more to go! However, long before that goal is achieved I will be only too thankful to come to discuss it with you. My prose style seems to be the same as in "G with a M". Is that all right? Or should I strive for something a little different?'[32]

Davis picked up Astley's anxiety straightaway, and responded: 'Can think of no especial fault to find with your style – which is imaginative and vivid; except perhaps to warn you against preciousness. And if you do have a crack at some arty people, please let them be merely noises off to some real and likable character.'[33]

Astley placed enormous confidence in Davis's judgement. At this time she couldn't have changed her 'prose style' if she'd wanted to – it had been enough to leave poetry behind. Yet having no children herself, Davis did not understand the very real struggle entailed in writing anything while caring for a child aged two. Even so, Astley liked the company of this independent woman who had lived a full life inside and outside her marriage, feeling that her own life was staid by comparison. She had been married for more than ten years; she and Jack were less close now that they had a child. Marriage forced arrangements on people that made it seem routine, leading often to dullness, and Thea wondered whether this was the fault of the state of marriage itself, or the individuals within it.

Astley was making progress with the second novel and had once again returned to her experiences as a teacher, this time in the Mary Valley towns of Queensland. The title *A Descant for Gossips*, she decided, would be an apt reminder of those small-town eyes looking at and judging the self-contained young woman in their midst. That tight social world she had known, and her outsider status in it, came flooding back. She pencilled a map of Pomona (a town close to Queensland's Sunshine Coast) at the back of her orange-covered writing exercise book. In it she added possible teachers' names and grades. Here, words fought for space with numbers: long lists of words (crossed off when used) and regular morale-boosting word counts vied with each other.

It all seemed so laborious and dispiriting. Might it all lead nowhere after all? Astley quickly scribbled a gibe to herself on the back leaf: 'A portrait of the artist's wife in middle-age.' Astley was thirty-three years old. She would always see herself as older than she actually was – by about a decade. It was a deflection of a very complex kind: she never quite inhabited the present. When she was in her late sixties her view of herself as 'aged' caught one radio interviewer off guard. It came as a surprise that 'this vital women in her sixties thinks of herself as elderly' – but Astley did.[34] A year before, she had said, 'I didn't think I was mortal for years. I'm sixty-eight. I feel the tumbrels rolling more closely.'[35]

This backwards-forwards perspective of her writing was proving to be (and would always be) for Astley a sobering lesson in the work of Time. She added to herself in her notebook: 'Time, the great heel!'[36] The pun shows how the ephemeral nature of life was continually present in her mind. It meant that she imagined the future as a version of the past, in itself an extraordinary in-the-moment layering of human experience. It seemed so odd in one so young.

Astley's acute self-consciousness about action and guilt now returned with vigour. The story she was writing about Helen Striebel, another alter ego, involved visiting the origins of her own neuroses. Astley was remembering censure in the context of her own upbringing. She had been angry at having being controlled, then guilty for being angry, then resentful for being made to feel guilty, then ashamed for feeling this way, as she was also grateful for many aspects of her schooling and childhood. Talk of Phil and the Jesuits, the fact of Jack being a divorced man not accepted to marry within the Church, the fuss over Ed's baptism, made it difficult not to dwell on such things.

Phil's concerns were radically different: his problems were about his own disposition, with himself, not with his faith. The writer Michael McGirr, who was for a time a Jesuit, came to know both Phil and Thea, and remembers thinking of them as being subject to a kind of 'big soul and little soul' view of faith: here, he thought, are a brother and sister whose souls had been 'bonsaied'.[37]

When Astley wrote in the quiet of her Epping home study, this was the emotional legacy that unrolled in her mind, now shaped and controlled by her imagination. Writing about it gave her a cathartic sense of relief perhaps, but nothing would make it go away.

While she continued with the new novel *Descant*, Astley was annoyed that it was had taken until past mid-year in 1958 for *Girl with a Monkey* to be released. She was especially keen for this first novel to do well. She lost her reservations about the autobiographical nature of the book and sent an advance copy to Martin Haley. Astley also suggested to Davis that her former teacher Dr Robinson at Queensland University might help publicise the book. A bemused Davis replied that she could not 'imagine the dear good man doing anyone any great service as a publicity agent'.[38]

While Astley was wondering about the first novel's publicity and, as she wrote, becoming 'sordidly interested' in sales, she was also more conscious of how her next novel would fare.[39] Davis politely reminded her of the limitations of literary publishing:

> … we find it [*A Descant for Gossips*] perfectly acceptable as to standard plus sensitive and imaginative, though no bookseller's dream of a best-seller. If only we could find that a first-rate talent like yours was also a spinner of beautiful money – for you and for the firm (not for *us*).[40]

Her words fell on deaf ears: Astley never accepted that writing fiction and money-making did not coincide. She had finished the manuscript of *Descant* – what more could an author do? Davis, of course, didn't want to mislead authors about the possible financial gains. It would take the better part of thirty years but Astley would prove Davis wrong: money would be made by the writing and publishing of Australian literature, if not always in the grand sums Astley hoped for.

Davis was herself a product of a set of attitudes towards publishing that had existed in Australia for generations. It was hard to interest that market in Australian titles. Many writers tried to get published overseas, for these reasons. Attitudes towards being published were different too, with less emphasis on the commercial transaction. This suited the conservative style and tastes of Davis and then poetry editor Douglas Stewart.[41] The close author–editor relationship it engendered was exactly what Astley was enjoying and directly benefiting from. It was years before she would reconsider the virtues of such a dependent relationship between publisher and author. For now it was clear there were few alternatives: there were no 'bidding wars' between rival commercial publishers. It mattered who you spoke to and once a manuscript was declared 'out of favour' you had little chance of resuscitating it.

In the meantime, reassurance was what Astley longed for. Letters and critiques came via Davis's office – with her circle of influence she knew they would be from important figures in the local literary scene – and so passed them on to Astley.

> Congratulations on Thea Astley's little novel. It is the promise that strikes one: there is not much solid substance in the people other than 'I', but she can write. And how few can! (Vance Palmer)

> A recent publication that interested me greatly was *Girl with a Monkey*, by Thea Astley; a remarkable short novel, beautifully sculptured, and with the final impact of a short story, or a theatre curtain. It had a few faults but they were minor and superficial, a tendency to the unnecessary use of the sort of words that set ordinary people like myself reaching for the dictionary; perhaps a little bit culture-conscious – but they are of small account set beside the author's real achievement. There is human insight as well as great skill in handling narrative, and that tight final chapter is like the swift and correct totalling of a sum whose respective items have excited interest. (Frank Dalby Davison)[42]

Palmer was an influential writer and critic, which was flattering interest perhaps, but his remarks smacked of faint, even patronising praise of the kind Astley had feared for years. Dalby Davison warned of 'preciousness' that had also concerned Beatrice from the beginning, but his review was otherwise very positive.

In August 1958 a letter arrived from Douglas Stewart, literary editor of *The Bulletin*, saying much the same thing. He was influential in this role at the magazine for over ten years, between 1950 and 1961, and his advice was worth noting. Writing to her about *Girl with a Monkey*, he urged Astley 'to simplify, since I feel your whole intellectual drive goes the other way', 'moderate stylism' to make the words more 'natural', more 'her own'.[43]

Astley now waited to hear from Martin Haley, who was reviewing the novel for *The Catholic Leader*. She wondered whether he would include the criticisms he had sent to her shortly after receiving his advance copy. She had written detailed responses, so she hoped not. Astley was particularly sensitive to criticism but because *Girl with a Monkey* was so closely based on her life – something Haley knew better than anyone – she had taken his response as an oblique personal slight. In years to come, interpreting criticism as personal abuse would become *de rigueur* for her.

In his review Haley quibbled over which elements were factual and which were invented. He thought the characters lacked depth, but his most hurtful objection was to what he saw as Astley's uncharitable toughness. Hedge as he might, the conflict that lurked in the shadows of their friendship stepped into view: he objected to her negative attitude towards Irish Catholicism (had even said she was only hard on characters with Irish names!).[44] Astley did not think she had been 'uncharitable', protesting to him: 'Do you mean graceless, or disgraceful? I wrote about my social life as a teacher, as I saw it. I thought I was being honest – a little bitter perhaps. I can't say I ever found scores of polite, generous, friendly people opening their doors to me. Still, the fault was probably mine.'[45]

It was a disingenuous remark: she was 'sticking her ground' in repeating her claim not to have found 'scores' of 'friendly' people and she did not think the fault was hers. Revisiting the 'material' in this way only proved to her how easily she could still be wounded by the very memory of her experience. It would be late in life before Astley could control this reaction. Wanting the last word, she attached favourable comments about her sympathetic 'handling of the Catholic moments' made by the literary editor of an overseas Catholic paper.[46]

In these private exchanges Astley was able to own her story but she still felt uncomfortably 'outed' in the public domain. Despite Vance Palmer's remarks and the fact that any experienced reader would expect a first novel to be based on the writer's experience at least to some extent, Astley was inclined to blame Haley for introducing the personal into the situation. She took him to task for a betrayal of trust, for what she saw as his insensitive retailing in public, through his review, matters she had revealed to him in private. Another friend from Barjai days, Laurie Collinson, had been far more subtle in his review.

Astley was becoming increasingly defensive, answering these criticisms and aware that her second novel was also closely based on this same period of her life. She wrote to Davis that in her third novel there would not be 'a teacher in sight'. In the meantime, Astley decided to take another good look at *Descant* while she could. She quickly changed characters' names and the original (and real) setting for the published version, so that they would be harder to recognise.

Her struggle with the 'ritual difference between real and false' was not over yet. Knowing how much she was drawing on her own life, she became aware of another problem: all this talk about real or accurate details was obscuring the emotional nature of her Dream Country. She tried to make Martin Haley understand:

> [*Girl with a Monkey*] wasn't meant to be a novel in the strict sense, more a landscape with figures. It was a study in emotions.

> Technique interests me far more than characters, or plot, just at the moment. And until I find a style that I feel happy about, I shall probably go on labouring with insipid people performing routine tasks. You know, to be perfectly honest with you, I've looked at that book myself lately, and I feel rather ashamed of the whole thing: the style, the dialogue.[47]

By the time Astley returned to teaching, she would be a published writer, with her first novel having appeared in 1958, and her next due to be published in 1960. She was nervously anticipating staffroom gossip. Davis understood and appreciated her talents, but that did not mean others did. Astley felt self-conscious about her persona as a writer, worried that her colleagues would judge her because of that. However, she was not the odd one out in her own group of friends: Yvonne Wyndham was also about to return to teaching and Betty Judd was looking forward to returning to her career as a librarian.

Because Astley knew she could expect no financial reward for her writing, she was in fact glad that the teacher shortages had continued. She had heard that the brand-new Cheltenham Girls' High School in her area was almost ready for its first student intake, and that the school's foundation headmistress in 1958, Bessie Mitchell, was a very unusual woman. Word got out that she was actively drafting teachers who were highly regarded and recommended to her, and the staffroom was starting to fill with highly qualified, experienced, mainly mature women. Astley applied and was accepted. When she joined this select group she was in for a very different teaching experience from her last appointment.

The difficulty was finding someone to look after Ed, who was not quite four. In Dorset Street most of the young mums were homemakers and Astley did not feel comfortable leaving Ed in their care, nor were they necessarily interested in caring for the children of women who returned to work. However, the school principal and the new teachers, some of whom had young children, got together and worked out a way to make use of the kindergarten on the corner of school's site. A gate was cut into the fence, giving the mothers easy access to their children without having to leave the school grounds. Timetabling was then organised so that teaching commitments for these women ended in time for the 3pm pick-up.

Astley could hardly believe her luck: she could pop down in her breaks to spend time with Ed. Cheltenham GHS in the late 1950s became a charmed place, somewhere her teaching abilities – especially in her main subject area of English – were appreciated and where she could express her feelings about things, including the lot of women, and be heard rather than resented.

The warm atmosphere at Cheltenham Girls' made it possible to overlook the austere physical conditions. New buildings and facilities were emerging very slowly; Barbara Abouchar, a young convent-educated music teacher, remembers having to use her cello to teach in the absence of a piano. She also recalls the kindness of this extraordinary staffroom full of older women. 'We were all together in a close-knit group. The school was being built around us. There was virtually nothing there.'[48]

One day Barbara noticed Astley, known in the staffroom for her wisecracks, eating a cream bun (a second was lined up) with ferocious intent. Astley had trouble gaining weight, a condition bound to draw mock-envious remarks from the other female teachers. Over the cream buns, Barbara and Astley became friends. A convent education and love of music made it inevitable that Astley would share a special bond with this young teacher: before long they were sharing thoughts on Catholicism, the struggles with conscience that still engaged Astley. Barbara and her French husband, Claude Abouchar, would visit Jack and Thea. On the way home, they would discuss their hostess. 'She was unsophisticated – a Queensland girl with a Queenslander's view of things.'[49] It was difficult to see where Astley thought her writing fitted in – she didn't seem self-assured about it. Everyone at school knew

Astley had published a novel, but there was no sense of her being part of the 'literary scene'.

Astley met and befriended Joan Levick (who wrote under the pseudonym Amy Witting), who was also on staff. One day she noticed that Joan always carried a lot of cash in her purse. Joan explained that during the Depression she had not been able to afford shoes and so was determined to have enough money at the ready to buy them, whatever happened. It was the kind of character-in-a-gesture that Astley loved. Witting was also writing a novel, which Astley immediately read.

Astley knew that, like her, Joan was also trying to fit her writing around job, husband and children. Watching Astley and Joan Levick become close was interesting for the young Abouchar, who observed: 'Thea admired Joan. She knew she was a strong woman who would leave a man if she wanted to. I felt Thea was more dependent, fearful of being alone. Joan's husband was very much like Jack, a non-intellectual partner. The way that Joan managed her "happy" relationship and marriage intrigued Thea.'[50]

It was a balancing act that did not seem to be part of what Astley could manage. For her, everything seemed to exist at the edge: she had to push to achieve what she wanted with her writing, she was increasingly anxious as a parent, even her marriage had developed a sparring quality she couldn't quite control. Astley's life seemed like two distinct worlds moving alongside each other, accompanied by the percussion of routine.

Her only links with other writers socially came through Beatrice Davis, and she grabbed them with both hands.[51] Davis had a vast literary network, and a linchpin of it was the poet and fiction writer Hal Porter, whom she introduced to Astley. Astley wrote him her first fan letter, praising his work, though she was probably as impressed that he worked full-time as a librarian in Shepparton, Victoria, while also writing himself. Perhaps Davis passed on some of the generally unfavourable critical chorus about Astley's 'style' – which Astley may even have guessed at the time – but she must have been flattered by Porter's comments on *Girl with a Monkey*: 'I've bought three copies of your novel for the library and read it twice with admiration and delight. For one who lives in an eternal slipstream of the latest books this is no gesture – it was for my own pleasure.'[52]

Such events formed a welcome bridge to the world beyond the classroom. Astley was the staffroom wit but her colleagues did not particularly take notice of her burgeoning career as a novelist, though they paid her more attention after her second novel was published.[53] While Astley waited for *Descant* to appear in print in 1960, she returned to thinking about her own family's attitude towards her writing. Barbara Abouchar found herself the confidant of a woman who seemed increasingly persecuted, and who particularly wanted the approval of her father. Abouchar noticed that Astley often spoke about her father, but never about her mother.

And Jack's status as a previously married and divorced man was still causing entanglements with Church bureaucracy.[54]

None of this appeared to affect Astley's energy for writing. Early in 1959, before *Descant* had been published, Astley embarked on a third novel. She wanted to be recognised as a writer not simply by Davis: Australia's leading literary figures and opinion-makers were men. So far, almost all of her correspondence about her writing had been with male literary editors of newspapers; the leading figures in academic study of Australian literature – including those who had sent appraisals of her work so far – were also men. The list from as far back as Barjai included Martin Haley and Paul Grano from the Catholic writing groups, her male lecturers at university, more recently Vance Palmer, Frank Dalby Davison, Douglas Stewart. So were the senior publishing house editors and managers. The Australian writers Astley had read and admired were also mostly male; it would be a long time before Astley could clearly identify herself with an Australian literary female tradition, which existed historically but even so had not yet been fully appreciated publicly.

Astley's need for male approval was complex: in these new intellectual and literary friendships there was a sexual frisson. For a woman of Astley's conservative background, one who had been sexually inexperienced before marriage and was now settled with a family and domestic commitments, this was extremely appealing. She was very much enjoying her 'enchanted' and regular correspondence with Hal Porter, whose letters came to Angus & Robertson and were redirected to Dorset Street. There was something exotic in receiving these epistolary literary attentions on the domestic doorstep. Marriage, work and motherhood sent Astley, often compulsively, chasing esteem. She was prone to infatuation; partial to praise. Theatrical in gratitude and defensively modest, she was learning to adjust socially to being a 'writer'.

An intense period of contradictory drives and anxieties was just beginning for her. The past would remain troublingly present. She had sent a signed copy of *Girl with a Monkey* to Cecil and Eileen, who had made no comment. A friend later sent her this same copy, inscribed 'To Mum and Dad', having discovered it languishing in the library of the Toowong seminary in Brisbane.[55]

Astley also sent an advance copy of *Descant* to her parents. One day she received a parcel from her parents' Ashgrove address, containing her novel. Eileen had fiercely crossed out passages and phrases she considered sacrilegious. Astley understood her mother's attitudes towards sex and other matters, and constantly reminded her about her marriage outside the faith, but her reaction was still a shock.

Astley said nothing. Cecil and Eileen were shortly to visit Sydney, and Eileen wrote afterwards of how the visit had been 'a real tonic'.[56] Thea had written to Cecil asking for some information as a resource for the novel she was now writing – *The Well Dressed Explorer* – with a journalist as a central character. His reply seemed a bit blunt, and she didn't care for his remarks on playing with 'fact and fiction'. In a letter addressed to her and John (Jack) he wrote: 'I wish Thea would NOT use actual place names; Condamine is … on the Downs or near west, only 30 miles from Chinchilla.'[57]

Cecil said he was 'rather in the dark' about what she was writing, and after the return of the marked-up copy of *Descant* Astley hoped to keep things that way. Still, it was pleasing that the letter was signed affectionately: 'Daddy'. Cecil also wrote, 'I'm personally looking forward to hearing that you've got that old marriage business firmly settled.' Official news from the Church via Phil had come through that made a marriage possible, and Jack and Thea began to plan a simple wedding; Cecil's health was deteriorating – he had inoperable cancer – but would at least have this satisfaction even if he couldn't attend. Astley was aware, too, that there were equally pressing anxieties for her parents in the trials of her brother. He was nearing the end of his Tertianship at Sevenhill in South Australia and worried about his future. Eileen had scribbled ominously at the bottom of Cecil's letter: Phil was still 'waiting to hear from his superiors'.[58]

8

An armed neutrality

These days, Bernard decided during the few seconds a perfunctory wave took to his wife, we are an armed neutrality.

The Slow Natives by Thea Astley, 1965[1]

In the new decade of the 1960s, people believed that life for women would be changed, largely due to the introduction of the contraceptive pill in 1961. Not much else was different, or so it must have seemed to Astley. Like others of her generation, she would not be part of a counterculture when it did arrive almost a decade later. She was thirty-five, married for more than ten years, a mother and in a responsible professional job with a duty of care to young people.

Women like Astley were already halfway to following the life patterns of their parents. In Dorset Street Astley watched some of the women silently – and vocally – question their personal choices. How much choice had they really had? To these wary souls, to Astley herself, new social freedoms lacked credibility, looked more like a selfish escape from the shackles of maturity.

Social change as it is lived will always be slower than history remembers it. The so-called sexual revolution of the 1960s did not take place with the rise of the women's movement in Australia, which came later. Initially, 'feminism' tended to be greeted as an overseas phenomenon. Another decade would pass before Germaine Greer's *The Female Eunuch* was published.

For fun, Astley, assuming a fruity voice higher than her own, would read aloud the current social pages at get-togethers with the Dorset Street women. The popular press was full of advice for them all, and Astley found particularly amusing the *Pix* magazine advertisements and advertorials such as 'Doctors Tell How to Stay Happily Married'.[2]

These gatherings of women in each other's homes offered a rare chance to share private things they wouldn't tell even family. The women were all 'stayers' in marriage, but full of rueful whimsy about its monotony, in contrast to the idealistic women's-magazine portrayal of the marital state. Astley, who tended to push things in this setting, was provocative; although she was a member of the group she liked to offer the commentary of the outsider, often sending up popular culture. She was enthusiastic about the daily TV soap operas from America (*The Bold and the Beautiful* became a favourite). When Australia began producing its local versions Astley could be found every day, on cue, sitting in front of *Home and Away*. Years later, neighbours Bryan and Jennifer Bruty – just retired from the ABC – were bemused by what seemed to them her inexplicable taste.[3]

Yet these dramas were full of highly exotic sexual liaisons and the outrageous plots had the overblown quality Astley loved. Watching them was not only fun, it provided material for her own writing. She loved 'rubbish' for being just that. At the same time Astley was capable of intellectual snobbery, too, which made her attitudes perplexing to some: she would blurt out something about a particular school class being stupid.[4]

Astley scoffed at the hypocrisy of most social attitudes but as a writer she knew it was important to tackle the social agenda. At the same time, she knew she needed a new direction; she couldn't go on writing about north Queensland schoolteachers forever. Where to from there, in terms of social commentary?

Past writers did not prove much of a signpost. In the 1930s and 1940s Katharine Susannah Prichard and Henrietta Drake-Brockman had described the plight of Aboriginals; later Dymphna Cusack and Kylie Tennant had written with compassion about the aged. Much as each of these writers had developed a prose style to suit their purpose, Astley was more self-conscious about that aspect of her work in a way that for the moment put her aesthetically out of kinship with these social realist writers: she would have to find her own way.

A Descant for Gossips would be the last of Astley's self-when-young novels. She now wanted to write about relationships of dependence and inter-dependence, about marriage and family: her life now. The canvas had to be life itself; that set of perennial dynamics of need and power – the world divided, as she would one day say, into 'feet, and boots and mats'. This was what really fascinated and appalled her. She was convinced by now that her Catholic background had handed her the ultimate prototype.[5] Her creative animus came from this very personal confrontation, and nostalgia gave way to anger.

A third novel was emerging. Astley was very aware that she had been handpicked by the doyenne of Australian literary publishing and did not want to disappoint Beatrice Davis. She was especially grateful to her mentor for helping her develop literary friendships. Not since the university days of Barjai had Astley felt among such kindred spirits. Here she could mingle with writers and poets such as Hugh McCrae, Kenneth Slessor, Hal Porter, Xavier Herbert, Ion Idriess, Kylie Tennant and Douglas Stewart. The social gatherings at Beatrice's house would have seemed a bit risqué – with a more relaxed and daring use of language and behaviour than was common in the 'couples' socialising she was used to. Unlike most of those at Beatrice's parties, Astley was not a 'drinker' (nor yet a smoker). She drank as occasional smokers smoke: only when the occasion demanded it – except for one rare session drinking late afternoon vodka with tired mothers, when she had to be carried home.[6] Her very slight frame was not equipped to handle excess alcohol but she could manage an elegant wine or two. Astley must have wondered how on earth she would fit into the literary world.

Her own vulnerabilities she kept well masked. Sometimes, however, Astley's confidence played destabilising tricks on her. She could muster a surprising degree of front but it could collapse suddenly under strain, turning into a radical pessimism about herself, about her life, about her writing. Davis saw this tendency when she requested a brief biography from her new author. Astley's brutal self-assessment came rocketing back: 'Apart from a few poems in *Australian Poetry* and some in *The Herald* and other lesser places, I've made no impact on Australia's literary life … I assumed you wouldn't just want a list of my friends. It wouldn't be very long either.'[7] Davis could tell it would take this writer a long time to feel confident in owning the title of author.

In years to come, Astley's self-deprecation would take other forms, twisting and turning around a sense of persecution about reputation. Was she or wasn't she making an 'impact on Australia's literary life'? 'I've never had many reviews from the literary people,' she was fond of saying, even when it wasn't true.[8] Astley's anxiety could also make her shy and nervously awkward in company. As such, she developed a life-long habit of bursting in on friendship (presumably so she could slam the door in its face when she chose). She developed the habit of fronting people she wanted to get to know.

Astley continued not to know where she fitted into the literary world. In late 1959 she began planning an approach to none other than Patrick White for advice, feeling that he at least would understand her dedication to style. White was to her – to many writers of the time – the ultimate prose poet, so she knew she would be seeking advice from the best. A few years later, when Tom Keneally moved into the Epping neighbourhood and became close to Astley, he realised the enormity of White's influence on both of them. White already had an international reputation as a novelist and playwright. In Australia his fifth novel, *Voss*, had won the inaugural Miles Franklin Award in 1957; in 1961 *Riders in the Chariot* would win him another. White's prose, Keneally recalled, seemed to them like this 'gorgeous jungle you had to penetrate – a sort of veil – in front of the characters, but a delightful veil, undergrowth – you knew you'd been on a hunt but a fulfilling kind'.[9]

As Keneally reflected years later, 'it was as if [Australian writers] were writing flash prose in attempt to show the world that we weren't a debased race – not convict-class'. But he also understood Astley's 'cultural yearning'. Like her, he had grown up in Queensland, where there had been few high schools and a single university. 'If Australia had cultural envy and yearning, it was easy to see how it would be multiplied in places like the Queensland of Thea's youth. It was powerful stuff.'[10]

Astley set off for Patrick White's Castle Hill property, 'Dogwoods', hoping to have a cup of tea with him. His partner, Manoly Lascaris, answered the door and told her that White was working, as he always did between nine and five, and she would have to come back another time. Colleagues at Cheltenham Girls' watched amused as a furious Astley stomped into the staffroom cursing in her frustration. Finally, in the New Year she was able to visit, and she left White with a signed copy of *Girl with a Monkey*.

White wrote back a few months later. He had 'too, too enjoyed' the visit, and though he could not immediately read her novel, 'From thumbing through it, I feel it looks like the real thing, not just another novel by an "Australian writer". That terrible phenomenon!'

He advised her to 'ignore other people's books' and to 'write more and more'. He added: 'In fact, after the age of thirty, the less one looks at fiction the better, if one happens to be a novelist. But perhaps you have some years of pleasure before you.'[11]

This was not exactly praise but perhaps something better: a possible friendship, though evidently not one on equal terms. Astley treasured the present of a book – *Selected Writings of Gérard de Nerval* – that

White sent to her in September 1960, inscribed playfully: 'For Thea Astley Gregson the Dropper-in from the Dropped-in on'.[12] She also treasured his letter's all-important phrase: 'if one happens to be a novelist'. Their friendship would always be close to idolatry on Astley's part, but she was hardly in a position to mind.

Astley noticed, too, the worryingly negative use of the term 'Australian writer': White's disparaging tone was not unique. Eight months later she received a letter from Hal Porter, also disdainful of the 'Australian writer' tag: 'There's very little quality in 97% of Australian writing – it's good that your Quality is receiving its meed.'[13] These were rather defensive gestures from writers she admired, especially given the talk in literary circles about recognising 'Australian writing'.

The assumption that only a select few could discern this elusive 'quality' was no problem, of course, if you happened to be considered one of them. Astley was lucky to be hearing that she was one of the chosen. She had her own ambivalent attitudes towards such things: she loved White's deep aestheticism but she was also the girl who had satirised modernism in Australia in her poem 'Culture, 1945'.

It was a confusing time. Astley's relationship with writing was fundamentally emotional: intellectual debates about art were not and would never be for her. In any case, she risked looking conservative when she argued for hierarchies of value in literature. Writers needed encouragement as well as being valued. Astley privately craved both and in sympathy was often supportive of anyone trying to get their work published.

She found literary life convivial. She enjoyed going to literary soirées by herself and was glad that Jack was happy about this. Porter's 1960 Sydney farewell party had been fun and it had been a thrill to meet the poet Kenneth Slessor, introduced to her by Porter. But she found Beatrice Davis's literary parties useful too. Writers might hear something about their chances with this or that publication, or how a grant might be coming their way. Astley had applied for a Commonwealth Literary Fund grant. Slessor, who had some inside information, approached with the news: her CLF grant had come through. She probably assumed this would help restore dignity to her sense of how she should be viewed as a writer, after her 'run-in' with the A&R publicity department. Astley had written to complain about the review list they had concocted: she'd expected, she said, that they'd send her books somewhere better than the *Women's Weekly*!

Astley was becoming increasingly resentful that issues of domesticity, juggling commitments to family, holding down a responsible job, finding time to write, were not, by and large, faced by male writers. She was cautious about seeking sympathy from other women, especially if they thought she was trying to be all things: wife, teacher, writer, mother. She hadn't forgotten the offhand gibe from one of her female neighbours: 'Still scribbling, are you?' And so the CLF grant was enormously important. Sympathy came, for Porter had heard of Astley's CLF grant and wanted to congratulate her: 'The grant should be wonderfully useful to you – though, of course, it's rather different for women with kiddies (oops!) I was able to cut-and-run ... Will you be able to do the feminine form of cut-and-run?'[14]

The phrase 'cut and run' would always remind Astley of this exchange with Porter: it impressed her that a bachelor knew how different the literary life of a woman was compared to that of a man. No, she was unable to 'cut and run', but the fantasy of escape appealed enormously to her imagination: she would write many such escapes into her novels. The fantasy was made more exquisite because she knew she could never do such a thing herself.

Bohemia came across as a very masculine domain. Astley and Amy Witting had many staffroom conversations about the libertarian ideals of the 'Sydney Push' of the 1950s and how such ideals seemed to be 'off duty' when it came to gender.[15] The group, which met regularly in inner city pubs, included a wide range of well-known intellectuals and artists, including at times Clive James and Germaine Greer – and others outside the academy committed to social and sexual freedom. There were many philosophical arguments conducted by interested heavy drinkers, amid lively all-night parties. None of it was consistent with the kind of domestic circumstances Witting and Astley understood as the lot of women. Astley's own quiet married life and the despondency arising from it drove her view that there was a set of ancient and unchangeable contracts of sexual and social inequality, which no one is ever going to change'.[16] The novel she was now writing, on the subject of adultery, found her considering her own choices.

As Porter had said, one did need to be mindful of the 'kiddies'. Love dictated this as much as any diligence or sense of responsibility. Porter had intuited that the emotional responsibility in Astley's family (as for so many women) had fallen on her shoulders. There were problems: Cecil's cancer was advancing and nobody was talking cures. Astley did not speak about her father's ill-health, and since her mother had briskly returned that acidly marked-up copy of *A Descant for Gossips* Astley had said little to her about writing or the literary life. Eileen was beyond pleasing on matters of value and faith and it was no time to broach such subjects with Cecil. Perhaps Astley quietly resolved to stop trying to please either of them quite so much, but in her mind the gloves were off. In her writing she was beginning to give vent to deep anger and anxieties.

The widespread reviews of *Descant* in 1960 provided a welcome distraction. There were notices in all major Australian broadsheets and Australian literary journals, and notices in Astley's old favourite magazine *John O'London's* and the *Times Literary Supplement*. Overseas reviewers did not miss the 'caustic and convincing satire' but thought *Descant* an otherwise 'workaday novel'.[17] Locally, too, her imagistic style was reprimanded as 'overwriting'. In *The Sydney Morning Herald*, Sidney Baker was more generous but still patronising: 'With discipline, and a sense of direction, Miss Astley could go a long way.'[18] It was more than twenty years later before a reviewer would capture Astley's own feelings at the time of writing the novel, seeing that 'though carefully constructed, it is sad'.[19] Buried in the passion of the prose was a sense of loss, not just nostalgia for Queensland: Cecil was close to the end of his illness and Eileen had been telephoning every few days with regular updates.

At the same time Astley had no doubt been relieved to report that an important service, conducted simply and behind the altar of her local church, had finally taken place. The 1948 civil marriage of Thea Astley and Jack Gregson was validated at Our Lady Help of Christians Church, Epping, on 1 March 1961, with Claude and Barbara Abouchar as witnesses.

The year 1961 would be one of the most eventful and difficult in Astley's life. Perhaps it was inevitable that some of her frustrations would spill over into her relationship with her publishers, despite the relative success of *Descant*. Even Davis's support, Astley was about to discover, had limits. The previous year Astley's third manuscript, 'The Little Lie', had been turned down for publication.

This story of a female university researcher falling in love with an insane and dangerous fortune-telling shyster who takes off for America with her sounds like the kind of 'cut and run' situation Astley loved. But according to A&R readers' reports the novel was 'a pretty far-fetched melodrama with too many foreign names and too little credible action'. Astley suspected correctly that Beatrice Davis agreed. The clues were there: after minimal editing, Davis wanted major revisions and Astley had simply refused to make them. She was absorbed in a new novel about a philandering journalist (*The Well Dressed Explorer*).

Astley was very annoyed about having her novel rejected and sent it to none other than Patrick White. In the last year they had become friends through phone calls and occasional dinner parties but it was a brave, if not reckless, thing to do. White held on to the manuscript for what must have been tense months for Astley. Eventually, in late March and from the safety of New Zealand, he sent his reply to Dorset Street.

Astley could hardly have been prepared for what she read. Slowly, she absorbed the blows, one after another. 'It is rather difficult to write about that book, because I did not like it, but imagine you had gathered that already. It was very disappointing, as I had expected this to be the book, and it seems to me such a falling off from *A Descant for Gossips*.' Astley's characters, said White, were 'flimsy' or 'repulsive', 'throw-offs' from an 'impatient ego'. He added: 'You have no spiritual values. Even in *A Descant for Gossips*, moral indignation was as far as you could go, but that was not enough. Spiritual values should have carried you just that extra distance ...'

There was even worse to come:

> You must just wrestle with yourself I suppose and stop being that bright girl who has escaped from the stuffed lounge suites to a rackety career of novel writing and sitting on the floor. (By this time you will have regretted bringing me the [manuscript] and yet another literary friendship will have been broken.) I think you should write nothing for a bit. Read. Have you read *Recherche* etc, *Le Grand Meaulnes*, Dostoevsky, Tolstoy, Pasternak, Ibsen, Chekhov, The Bible? You should read them all and many others ... Read, and think, and listen to silence, shell the peas, not racing to begin the next chapter, but concentrating on the work in hand until you know what it is to be a pea – and drudge at the school, sleep with your husband, bring up your child. That is what I mean when I say 'Living', not going to parties and taking lovers. (I don't suggest you have taken any!) Then, when you have become solid, you will write the kind of book you ought to write. You may even find you've come to believe in God – in spite of the fact that you are a Lapsed Catholic Soul – which I personally believe to be the root of all matters.[20]

For a Catholic girl, convent educated, and deeply absorbed in moral and ethical dilemmas since childhood, this was a devastating letter to receive. Astley knew that White could be difficult, and severe in his opinions, a forbidding personage if the mood took him. The poet Robert Gray described being greeted by White with pursed lips, a 'mouth … like a folded warrant for someone's arrest'.[21] Worst for Astley was White's linking of the faults in the writing to matters of belief and soul – the very nexus in which she was already trapped within her own family. The acid of the words etched themselves into her memory. This was one letter that Astley kept but refused to make public. The manuscript itself was the only one Astley ever burned.

White had taken some care to anticipate his friend's hurt: 'I hope you are all well and that you don't take the criticism too hard. (One always does though), Yrs, Patrick.' She liked the way White regarded her as a comrade-in-arms in the 'rackety career of novel writing' and she liked it enough to overlook a lot – for now. This is an excruciating example of how Astley was prepared to risk herself personally in the pursuit of critical validation.

Three months after White's letter, in late June, came more distressing news: her father was close to death. Up until this point, Astley's mother had reassured her that the 'Blue Sisters', Catholic home nursing nuns, had been calling in daily to help with his care, but Eileen gradually found managing at home nearly impossible. Cecil had taken a sharp downward turn: could Thea come to Brisbane urgently? Astley did, but she was too late to see him before he died on 24 June 1961, aged sixty-four.

The day after Astley arrived in Brisbane she and her mother went together to a 6.30 am Mass for Cecil. Both quietly attended the prayer before the formal funeral and later watched as the four pallbearers, Cecil's colleagues, followed the other mourners to the graveside. Dark-suited men from 'the profession' chatted quietly in groups; Thea and Eileen were astonished by the large number of journalists who had come to pay their respects. Thea shook hands with Theodore Bray (later Sir Theodore), Cecil's editor at *The Courier-Mail*. When they were dealing with the condolences, they found a telegram from Sir John Williams, who had been managing director of *The Courier-Mail* in Cecil's time, and was now managing director of the Murdoch-owned

Herald and Weekly Times Ltd, saying how much he had appreciated Cecil's work for Queensland journalists. It was pleasing recognition for her father and his lifetime of 'the daily grind'.

Phil had not come to the funeral: he was in England. He had been struggling with his mental state and had written to his superiors about this earlier in the year. Before Cecil died Philip had received an obliging reply telling him not to worry so much about his duties or the opinions of others.[22] Thea sent him a cable announcing their father's death.

Eileen was not one to spare her children the details of Cecil's final days: when she wrote to Phil some days after Cecil's death, she described the final 'collapse of his bowels' and his pain, without adequate relief, which had caused him 'extreme distress'. Phil would have understood how Eileen's reactions had affected Thea, in situ and forced to bear witness, but he himself hadn't escaped.[23] By November Phil was in an 'enhanced emotional and nervous state'.[24]

Astley read her father's public obituaries over the next couple of months. One was particularly important: in *The Journalist*, the house magazine of Cecil's union, the Australian Journalists' Association, Cecil was mourned as 'one of the last eye-shade journalists', with his death marking the end of an era. The article mentioned the newsroom in Warwick where Cecil had first worked at seventeen; he had sketched these same newsrooms for his daughter in his most recent letter, details that went into the novel he would never see. At the end of the obituary was a reference to herself and her books. Cecil had died 'just five days too early to know that film actress Anne Baxter wants to make a film of one of Mrs Gregson's novels, *Descant for Gossips*'.[25] (An hour-long telemovie of the novel directed by Tim Burstall was made more than twenty years later, in 1983.)

Astley had a hunch Cecil would have appreciated *The Well Dressed Explorer*, alive as it was with the old-time routines and the hierarchies of the old press. In its way the novel was a tribute to the life of journalism Astley had known as a child. Cecil would no doubt have been awkward about her writing of an adulterous journalist, but would certainly have known men like him. But pride in his daughter's achievements had been denied to Cecil. His death, coupled with Astley's letter from Patrick White, were omens of vanishing approval from two men who greatly mattered to Astley.

When Astley plucked up courage to look at White's letter again she remembered how the tone at the end had been rather practical and friendly in its way. He wrote as a 'fellow writer', when he suggested that she hang on with A&R, but be wary of signing up for the next book. Astley had come to suspect he was probably right about the faults of her rejected manuscript too – the votes were already in on that – and sending it to him had been a chance to see what he really thought of her. Hadn't he taken the trouble – a lot of trouble – to consider her writing? She decided to be flattered.[26]

Astley drew strength from her own knowledge: she knew White was wrong about where she stood with her writing. She'd never been more certain of what she wanted to write about, even as she troubled over the *lingua franca* that she was fashioning. The deep domesticity White advocated did not seem to her the best path to a life of literature and the mind. Well, it was and it wasn't. She knew what he meant: good writing can come from engaging with and describing the ordinary things of life. Yet Astley was still conscious of a gendered aspect to such remarks, could see the way women writers slipped awkwardly between mutually exclusive zones, being accorded a status as 'less complex' or of 'less value'.

White had not seen that she intended to write about precisely this kind of compromise, yet she couldn't see herself as a member of a vocal political movement about women. The 'women's movement', as such, was yet to gain ground – it did not become forceful until later in the decade. In Australia, women were still not even allowed to drink in pubs. It was thirty years later before Astley openly acknowledged what still bothered her about feminism and writing, even though she was in a profession where she received about sixty-five per cent of the male rate for the same job. 'I dislike the dichotomies – bringing out anthologies of women writers – nobody brings out anthologies of male writers,' she declared.[27]

Astley's novels were drawing their intensity from the conditions of her own life – they always had. She could no longer write about that single female figure stranded in inhospitable small Queensland towns because she was now fully engaged with the issues of middle life: child-rearing, earning a living, marriage. She had an endless internal debate about the place and value of marriage and family, the genealogy of character and human patterning, the drive to social conformity versus the will to break away from it. She wanted to write about the possibilities for human companionship in the search for love beyond the 'hinterland of childhood'.[28]

Was marriage the most prized bond, or was there something else? Astley claimed that marriage – not necessarily her own marriage – was an 'economic necessity' for women. It was a subject for tart remarks, perhaps, but was infinitely more complex than that, as her next two novels, *The Well Dressed Explorer* and *The Slow Natives*, would prove. Still, Astley's novels about 'marriage alternatives', the kind that would appeal to feminists, were years away. In 1961, her conservative married life in the suburbs did not make her gravitate to the emerging liberalism of the social climate that was becoming noticeable in other parts of the Western world.

How then can one explain the extremes in her writing, her tendency to typecast her characters' morality almost to the point of caricature? It came from a deeper source than newly raised consciousness about the lot of women. Astley might have personally identified with her beloved misfit characters, but she couldn't see anything of herself in the next generation of young people who saw themselves as outcasts. *Her* misfits were characters whose individuality – eccentricity – was threatened by the forces of social conservatism, the status quo and the powerful. The next generation – 'hippies' – were to Astley either lazy or egocentric 'self-seekers'.[29] She was happiest when 'agin'.

The question of self-seeking was certainly on Astley's mind but she struggled with the terms of such thinking: there had been no such thing as healthy self-interest in her own upbringing. Astley was simultaneously repelled and fascinated by the very concept. Self-interest in one form or another drives most of her characters' behaviour.

Much of this apparently selfish behaviour was visible to Astley personally, as she watched infidelities and the subsequent demise of several long marriages in the tightly knit Dorset Street group. The women were usually left with the responsibility of the children – not much time for healthy self-interest there. Astley thought about the old questions: Did love and responsibility ever meet on equal terms? Was love self-sacrifice, the kind her mother talked about? With Cecil now gone, she could think about her parents' marriage. Had that been an exercise in Eileen's self-sacrifice? Still in her thirties, Astley wasn't yet convinced, but it would be this single idea of Eileen's that she expressed throughout her life.[30]

She knew that self-sacrifice hadn't got Phil anywhere much. He was not managing his teaching easily at St Ignatius in Norwood, Adelaide, during what had been a dreadful year for him. There was talk of a move to Sydney and he was becoming deeply depressed. God, self-sacrifice, need, self-interest, sex, freedom, relationships – all now constantly preoccupied Philip's sister too.

At the same time Astley found herself enjoying a new sexual frankness, entertaining others with dramatic outbursts about men and women. Ten years later the poet Fay Zwicky, who by then knew Astley well, could sense how a degree of what she termed 'word starvation' drove her. She was 'satisfying her hunger for words in writing what she could [not] get in life'. Astley, Zwicky knew, could be 'invasive in her studies of people … frightful about men sometimes … with an obsessive need to observe their worlds before they imploded'. Zwicky could see how Thea was 'so sharp but didn't want to appear sharp'.[31]

But Astley did sometimes 'appear sharp'. 'When Thea … called in for coffee,' recalled a neighbour, 'she would burst forth with the bluntest of statements about men being unable to cope with "women's needs",' and even about [her] and Jack. 'He's dried up,' she said one day.[32] Not long after, at a party one night Jack (after many whiskies) confessed to a troubled physical side to the marriage.

If it was Freud who commented in as many words that 'in the world of sexuality the weather is always bad', then it is a style of remark Astley would have loved. Yet for her and Jack, married for almost fifteen years, the sexual weather had often been good. A new cooler air stream that had begun to drift through the marriage threatened only a cold spell. Then and for many years to come, Jack and Thea seemed very wedded but estranged. Their relationship could seem abrasive, with full and frank disclosure the order of the day.

The 'Jack and Thea' show was not to everyone's taste and could be quite confronting. Ed, their son, took almost a lifetime to understand this marriage organism and how it survived. He said: 'By the time I was old enough to understand, their relationship seemed fairly prickly; they bickered a lot. In the early1960s they were fighting a lot, especially on holidays … mostly about petty irritants … but you got the sense that was not really what it was about.'[33]

Ed grew to see that both his parents were short-tempered, with Jack particularly 'irritable and goading Thea, who would flare up, boiling over without caring what she was saying or of the consequences'.[34] Did Jack provoke Thea because he knew she needed a safety valve? It is unclear. Thea and Jack were not openly physically affectionate with one another and maybe both understood, certainly better than a child could, that antagonism can be a form of sexual intimacy.

Long marriage is about more than years; buried within it is the accumulated understanding of the unsaid. Thea and Jack went in for a peculiar kind of bickering, an armed neutrality that they both understood. In antagonism they could be the co-conspirators of old. When Edward Albee's *Who's Afraid of Virginia Woolf?* became a hit stage show in the mid-1960s, Thea and Jack rejoiced in the version of themselves they saw in George and Martha's volatile sniping. They saw their best chance of survival as a couple in a naked, if excoriating, honesty. Thea liked to think that Jack gave as good as he got.

For Astley, the only kind of marriage to countenance was between equals, conducted by negotiation and agreement, as theirs had always been. While they argued over money, there was no argument about their equal contributions, and they were meticulous about this. It was certainly unusual for onlookers: Astley would return from shopping with an itemised list, precise calculations of 'owings' for Jack. Around the house, on the kitchen bench, tucked away in drawers, at the back of Thea's notebooks, were similar running tallies. Ed began to notice that his parents always referred to objects, and even houses, as individual possessions: 'that's Jack's' or that's 'Thea's house'.[35] It was odd, but like the division of upstairs/downstairs into Jack's and Thea's spaces, it was absolutely mutual.

In the early 1960s Astley began to seek out something of the same uncompromising candour in other friendships. It was hard to find and it might have been a strange pathway to a reappraisal of her bond with Jack.

In *The Paper Chase* Hal Porter had described 'the versions of self compelled into existence by others': Astley already understood the social falsehoods enacted in the name of friendship.[36] What Astley craved was escape from her own life routines, yet she disliked the pretension of the literary 'game of the writer-taking-himself-seriously seriously'.[37]

Astley was now very comfortable with female friendship; being a mother and at home had made that possible. Men mattered equally to her but only certain kinds of men, as with women. Even Beatrice Davis was not 'a writer' nor a creative person in that sense, and talk with thinkers and writers was what Astley most needed. Even as she clung to the stability of her marriage she was fascinated, even obsessed, by partnerships, particularly how intellectual or creative women managed marriage. Colleagues at Cheltenham became used to Thea nudging conversation towards what they assumed were her own neurotic concerns. A caustic remark about men and women was enough to set things off. Astley's colleagues saw how intrigued she was by Witting's apparently happy marriage to a non-intellectual partner; it was hard for those listening not to draw inferences about the Astley marriage.[38]

Behaviour is always fashioned by present needs, and sexuality and sexual freedom were never far from Astley's thoughts. However, though she openly spoke of such things she certainly didn't want to write in an explicit way about sex, not about the 'calisthenics' of sex but of 'what is in the heart' and about 'the corroding effect that sexual relationships have'.[39] It gave Astley a necessary distance from which to view the sexual mores of her own upbringing. Sexuality in her writing is ever-present, but as a drive (and a foil) to character. Privately, Astley was in the grip of her own scepticism: she wrote sombrely to Porter (whom she felt at least understood these things) about how the age-old and virtually unchangeable contracts of sexual inequality were a 'constant in society'.[40]

That inequality, Astley knew, was expressed in hypocritical double standards about female sexuality. Women of her generation had been infected by the same views; she had grown up seeing that women with ideas were a social curiosity, not feminine, not perhaps quite female. Even Miles Franklin believed in sexual continence as the source of intellectual energy and had been amazed by Dymphna Cusack's female characters with sex drives the equal of men's.[11] Astley knew she had not shaken this particular monkey off her back: it was impossible for her to think of sex without revisiting those restrictive edicts about sex that had been part of her young adult life and her Catholic upbringing. This left her in her late thirties struggling with her own feminine identity, complicated by her emerging social identity as a writer. Astley would remember the extraordinary power of this confusion: '[If women] did express any thoughts then either no attention was paid to them or they were considered brash and aggressive … women writers were ignored, or whatever women did was ignored … I don't even know how women think. I've been neutered by society so I write as a neuter.'[42]

Astley had spent the last two years thinking obsessively about marriage and infidelity while writing *The Well Dressed Explorer*. Being 'neutered' as a writer was the last thing she planned for herself when she asked important questions of her novel: Was there an ethical way to commit adultery within a marriage and avoid deceit? Is discretion really secrecy? There was no way around the fact that women with children were not free in the way that men were: single parenthood was becoming more common but she could see the enormous post-divorce burdens for women, even when the women made the decision to leave. If she did that herself, she knew it would be difficult to write.

9

I merely crave an intelligent buddy

I merely crave an intelligent buddy. Can't talk Vogue *patterns and ninety ways with a meringue.*

Thea Astley to Thelma Forshaw, 1963[1]

Astley saw herself as trapped; dissatisfactions bled into each other. Jack's strength and stability did little to ward off her unhappiness. She still felt let down by Beatrice Davis and A&R over 'The Little Lie' and White's drubbing was hard to entirely forget; there was Cecil's death and anxiety about her continuing relationship with Eileen. At least this fourth book, *The Well Dressed Explorer*, was to be published in the New Year, so 1962 could be a good year. Davis had given her every reason to believe in herself as a writer but Astley started to grumble about the 'unbusinesslike' treatment by management at A&R. There was just the whiff, it seemed to her, of writers coming last in the list of priorities – especially with the forward planning of publishing timelines and publicity. Astley also resented that the important decisions in planning and marketing books were made by men.

Astley wrote a detailed letter of complaint to A&R's managing director George Ferguson before the publication of *The Well Dressed Explorer*. As a relative newcomer to authorship, with two short novels that had received good reviews but had not been great marketing successes, Astley's letter must have been startling, for despite adding to numerous complaints, it set out the issues with confronting acuity. Publishers, let alone male publishers, were not so accustomed to demands from a 'literary' writer asking them to respect the commercial contract of publication. Astley was sick of the lowly commercial status accorded to all literary fiction and try as she might, Beatrice Davis had not reconciled her to this in any way. Astley thought A&R's 'poor sales treatment' was deliberate and believed that publishers did not reward authors adequately for their work, while at the same time – paradoxically – they failed to exploit it commercially.[2] These unhappy arrangements between publisher and writer seemed to her another version of what she called 'the tacit war between men and women'.[3]

Within five years, in November of 1967, she was saying all of this to a live television audience. An ABC panel, which included publisher Sam Ure Smith and George Ferguson, then regarded as the doyen of Australian publishers, joined Thea and Tom Keneally, representing writers. Interviewer Bill Peach was enquiring about Australian books and the publishing industry; he asked Astley, 'Are you blaming publishers for what is really a small public demand?' Astley replied, 'Well, I'm not sure about this. It's sort of a love-hate relationship I have with my publisher. I find publishers like husbands – whenever you ask about money they become cagey, you know, rather evasive, you know. I feel I have a certain indebtedness to my publisher because they took a risk on me in the beginning.'[4]

It was a fair retrospective assessment of the mixed feelings she had developed by the early 1960s, which represented what many writers also felt. In publishing male power was entrenched at senior level with few staff changes. Astley wondered whether what she saw as A&R's lack of serious commitment to her as a writer was because of some attitudes about men in her novels. And the division she saw between the literary and commercial aspects of publishing became a lifelong irritation. It made for awkward moments in her relationship with Davis when those things were on her mind. Instead, she wrote of the restraint in expressing dissatisfaction: 'Knowing you and liking you makes it extremely difficult for me to ring up and go crazy or write and go crazy, both manifestations which seem to be a natural part of the publisher-author relationship.'[5]

When Astley began announcing that she had 'never had many critical reviews from the literary people' – not true then or ever – she was thinking of A&R's lacklustre approach to the promotion of literary titles.[6]

A&R were, in fact, convinced that Astley's next novel was a considerable advance in maturity and technique. Davis had already been at pains to point this out and would later tell Astley that *The Well Dressed Explorer* was the novelist's 'first big break'.[7] But Astley was still vulnerable and moody. She was dangerously tempted to compare her achievements with others – something that never worked for her. In 1957, when she had been rejected for a first Commonwealth Literary Fund fellowship grant, she said she was 'embarrassed' to be competing alongside Xavier Herbert.[8] Later, when Amy Witting 'cracked the *New Yorker*' with her short stories, Astley wondered whether she, too, should concentrate on short stories for a while.[9]

This volatility was now very much part of Astley's response to life. The publication of *The Well Dressed Explorer* would bring out the best and the worst of it. The novel, with George Brewster as the male protagonist, was described by one reviewer as 'a scarifying and richly amusing portrait of a completely selfish lover' and would establish her as a satirist of sexual mores, but not without cost.[10]

Jessica Anderson's novel *An Ordinary Lunacy* was published only a year later and dealt with many of the same themes, but was more concerned with female vulnerability – especially of one of its main characters, the beautiful Isobel, doomed to male disrespect. In Astley's case, her view of men attracted negative commentary. Even favourable reviews by writers Kylie Tennant and Thelma Forshaw saw the book in similar terms. Tennant observed that Astley 'gives a woman's view of the life of the Australian man, sweeping over his small and feeble pretences like a crown-fire, exploding and crackling in a withering, twisting verbiage, and leaving a devastated area which was once a comfortable, philandering journalist'.[11]

Tennant's brilliant turns of phrase must have pleased Astley. Male reviewers, unsurprisingly, saw the novel very differently; the main character's behaviour was 'quite comprehensible in terms of class, occupation and upbringing'; her writing was 'grey puritanism' devised purely 'in order to condemn'.[12] It had the ring of a very personal public censure. Astley took it to heart. This transported her back to a crucial problem she had always had with her writing: people misread the compassionate spirit of the work. Astley always argued that she felt enormously for her characters, and expected readers and critics to intuit this. Like Miles Franklin, she often felt that critics '[didn't] see the underside or the innerness' of what she was attempting.[13]

This reaction was particularly stinging to Astley since the novel was the extension of one of her first short stories ('Cubby'), one that meant a lot to her emotionally, the story of a teenage boy who is lonely, lost beyond 'the hinterland of childhood'. He tries to recapture the 'primary magic' of his first love. This was the child-in-the-man who became George Brewster, her unlikeable philanderer in the novel. Casting him as such put Astley in the way of being labelled a 'man-hater', as some women writers were then. In fact, an adversarial vision of all human relationships now had her in its grip.

In *The Well Dressed Explorer* relationships are cannibalistic, formed in dependence, a fusion of unhealthy selflessness and cowardly abuse. If the novel reveals an unrewarding coupling of men and women, it expresses exactly how Astley was feeling herself. Power in relationships fascinated her – that world of 'feet, boots and mats'.

The relationship between Patrick White and his partner, Manoly Lascaris, intrigued Astley. At dinner one night, trying and failing to be arch, she blurted to Manoly: 'If you had married, what sort of woman would you choose?' Astley got an answer to appease and disguise: 'I would have married her for her brains and lived happily thereafter.'[14] The words left unsaid – love, self-sacrifice, service – were distilled into the stunned silence.

Her relationship with Jack had deteriorated. Astley now talked openly – more hypothetically than directly – about what she might do about this. She had heard from Eileen about being the child of a single parent, and she did not wish to inflict this on Ed, so she was not considering divorce. Nevertheless, visitors to 44a Dorset Street were treated to a startling monologue about her marriage. Jack kept his distance by listening to music upstairs, or was outside raking leaves in silence. Astley would say – just loud enough for Jack to hear – 'There's no way we can divorce because our lives are too complicated, our assets are too complicated.'[15] Jack, used to these utterances, said nothing.

All distractions became a blessing to Astley. She had been impressed with some articles written about depression by a New Zealand journalist, who then sent her a letter admiring her work. Jack declared, 'Oh, that's one of Thea's fantasy love affairs', 'a figment of her imagination'.[16] When the admirer wrote of coming to 'Sydney the sin city', Astley's friend Barbara Abouchar couldn't help thinking how naïve Thea was in failing to see sexual intent in this, but she knew her friend lacked that kind of experience. Astley had never really seen herself as especially sexually attractive to men, but she liked to invest something sexual in her intellectual engagement with them.

The marriage of George and Alice Brewster in *The Well Dressed Explorer* is similarly stalled, but any sexual liaison outside the marriage is short-lived and generally no more satisfying. Sexual unfaithfulness is accepted with resignation or bemusement. When all around her marriages were falling apart amid jealousy, hurt, fights, and tears, it was perverse of Astley to write in this way. Her work became a lifelong dialectic about the mythology of romance, love and marriage and the delusions that sustain them, and by this stage nobody was more troubled by them than she was.

Testing things to the extreme, playing with reversals, was a freedom she could enjoy in fiction. In *The Well Dressed Explorer* Astley creates a wife so resigned to her husband's sexual forays that she gives her blessing in a letter; the husband of another of his conquests comforts his unfaithful wife. Sex displaces the mind in a disturbing way; Astley was interested in this 'antithesis between the violence of sexual communication' and 'this other intimacy required by love'.[17] Thinking of the early days of her own marriage, that need for intimacy was really the one that interested her now; it was like looking for 'primary magic'. There was no going back, or was there?

Her writing was energised by this despair, possessed a dark exuberance. Astley was following her emotional journey, giving it shape in a protean prose that moved as she moved, from anger to compassion, and back to anger. In a few years a similar 'not-niceness' would make the poet Sylvia Plath a feminist icon.

In fact, Astley was developing an emotional *lingua franca:* hurricanes of adjectives whipped into tumultuous fury, then dumped into silence. Boredom – always a subject that attracted her – could be delivered *furioso*. In this she was like Christina Stead, who in answer to the question of why she wrote once said: 'My own life is too calm for my energy.'[18]

Life at 44a Dorset Street was anything but calm, but it was predictable. Beatrice Davis had told Astley that she could be a confronting person to meet, making Astley self-conscious as well as defensive. She had challenged: 'Do I terrify people?'[19] She knew she seemed brash to some people, but candour, she would have argued, was not aggression. She was underestimating her effect on others. Her theatrics were for her about a special form of 'being' in friendship, with women and men of like mind, of being herself with others. Patrick White saw these internal struggles surface:

he had picked up quickly the sense that here was a woman craving intellectual and social ease beyond marriage and suburban ritual yet anchored to much of it.[20] Invisibility was more than a matter of being female and 'writing as a neuter' – as Astley would term it: despite her socialising with writers at times, she was still capable of feeling left out of the hub of literary and cultural life.

In 1962 Astley repeated the social manoeuvre she had used with White, this time making an impromptu visit to the home of Thelma Forshaw who had written a positive review of *The Well Dressed Explorer* for *The Sydney Morning Herald.* They had known each other as young writers in Barjai and now Forshaw was also writing short stories Astley admired.[21] This would be a more equal meeting of fellow writers than her approach to White. It would be a literary friendship begun in excited sympathy. For Astley, Forshaw was a perfect friend of the moment: a woman of letters but, like her, living a settled married life. She was also a caustic wit who bemoaned literature's peripheral role in Australian culture. Given the attention Astley had been receiving in the press, a persistent nerviness in her demeanour made Forshaw eventually wonder what did lie ahead.

Astley had much to be hopeful about. Writing and publishing circles were small, which meant the networks of influence affecting the fate of books in the public domain were also tight. Beatrice Davis was the chair of the Miles Franklin Award committee for 1963 and *The Well Dressed Explorer* was shortlisted. It was a mere six years since Astley had received that first letter from Davis telling her she might be a 'very good novelist indeed'.

The announcement came: she had won the award, to be shared equally with George Turner for *The Cupboard under the Stairs.* Later he became known for writing science fiction, but at this stage Turner was well known as a writer of literary fiction, producing a string of novels in the 1960s.

Astley climbed the stairs of the Rural Bank Building in Sydney to collect 250 pounds and a plaque. It was, perhaps, a moment in which to think about how the judges came to be split in their decision; it was natural to look around for her fellow recipient so she was disappointed not to see George Turner. She knew she would write to congratulate him – the only decent thing to do. The 'after party', she reassured him in her letter, was 'dull' – a nice gesture since Turner had been unable to afford to come.[22] What she didn't say (it would have sounded ungracious) was how dull the actual Miles Franklin Award plaque was, dowdy in its plain wood – a sombre memorial plate.

Some of the press coverage for the award had been disturbing. Astley had been compared to Grace Metalious, the American author of the popular novel *Peyton Place*. Much was being made of her married status and the fact that she was local and *The Epping Roundabout* was now claiming her as an 'Epping writer'. Astley felt she was being publicly undermined; it was a kind of backlash to her success and she would spend much of 1963 feeling this way. She wrote to her friend Thelma Forshaw: 'Still have not begun next book. I sit and brood and lay obsessional eggs all over the house … Since the reviews I find the neighbours icier than ever – or do I imagine this? Not that I need them – or do I?'[23]

The friendship with Forshaw was a good antidote to such feelings. Or was it? Astley's general demeanour often made men uncomfortable and Thelma had reported that her husband, George, found Thea quite odd and a bit threatening, wondering of course whether they might find themselves rather thinly disguised in a novel. Astley wrote in her defence:

> Thelma Chum, I laughed till I literally wept over this latest. Thank you, you silly chump for making a manic depressive laugh. Tell George he is bloody wrong and I observe you no more closely than I observe anyone and certainly have not the slightest intention of using you in a novel. So there. Doesn't he approve of me. I am not a grand seducer and do not intend for you to deceive him, me, us, all pronouns, objective case … I merely crave an intelligent buddy.

> Can't talk *Vogue* patterns and ninety ways with a meringue (That's Patrick's joke) all the time.[24]

The phrase an 'intelligent buddy', the put-down quip about domesticated femininity and the inclusion (with a nervy familiarity) of Patrick White's name all show how much Astley needed to feel she was accepted. It was not only Forshaw whose friendship she could not be entirely sure of; the friendship with White was now also strained, if only in a mute sense. There were still phone calls and letters throughout 1962 and 1963. Even so, the anxiety and effort the friendship cost Astley comes through in this description of a dinner party not long after the publication of *The Well Dressed Explorer*:

> The dinner at Saint Patrick's was yummy. But felt Manoly slightly effer so slightly antagonistic. To punish him I helped Saint P do up the zipper on his windbreaker. Wow! (My dear, any time you need it renewed simply ask ...) There was cold soup in cups and I disgraced everyone by prolettishly attempting to use a spoon instead of quaffing the muck like tea.
>
> ... He and Manoly have been losing thousands on the stocks and shares poker machines so should be bitter, but P was the most genial I have seen for a long time. And suddenly, tho I love him dearly, I DON'T CARE ANY MORE. I mean the friendship suddenly seems easy-pleasant. I don't have mental post mortems, duzze want to be pals or duzznt he. Nice this way. [25]

The business of 'that letter' from White of nearly two years prior stayed in the background, for there did seem to Astley a generosity in the friendship. She and White enjoyed each other and had a rapport. Dinners would end with Astley cross-legged on the floor, a quirk White and Manoly celebrated with a gift of a huge red and white striped drugget on their first visit to 44a. It was a kindness Astley found 'melting'.[26] White was overseas for most of 1963 and wrote her superb long letters describing his travels or sent a card virtually every month.

Astley was particularly pleased with White's letter after she had won the Miles Franklin Award. He had picked up *The Sydney Morning Herald* at the office of the Australian consulate in Greece and wrote to say, 'I'm glad you won some of it, even though it made you look sour – I'm sure it was only officially sour.' White had, of course, been the first recipient in 1957. He and Manoly had been to a house in Kavala full of rugs and commented to each other, 'Wouldn't this be just the thing for Thea. No chairs, only rugs, so that you could start sitting on the floor right at the beginning.'[27]

Later in the year, when his play *A Season at Sarsaparilla* was running, he made sure that there were tickets waiting for her at the box office. Astley loved the performance but White was frank about its commercial loss: 'It looks as though the lousy Australian public won't leave their television sets for anything but *My Fair Lady*.'[28] They shared a disillusionment with Australian cultural life. There was a certain kind of frisson to be had from bemoaning this – together as fellow sufferers – which both probably understood, a resigned repartee about the writing life in Australia.

The most important thing for Astley about White was now more personal. They had had many conversations about love, marriage, and selfishness. White shared his thoughts with her, including his thoughts about his Anglo-Saxon emotional repression, and knew she would understand. He had left Greece amid emotional farewells from Manoly's family and had been forced to reflect on how different he was – he couldn't join in. 'Perhaps,' he wrote, 'that is what turned me into a writer – to get rid of my feeling through the bodies of other people.'[29] No remark could have been more simpatico with Astley.

This did not mean White had abandoned the issue of her Catholicism and her writing that he had raised in his earlier letter about 'The Little Lie'. He and Astley discussed Graham Greene – White found *Brighton Rock* 'horrifyingly evil' – and wrote that he was 'not a buyer of these Catholic conflicts'. White could really tease; it was better not to react. He was now regularly referring to her as 'a lapsed Catholic lass', but taken the right way, the phrase could sound like an endearment, couldn't it? The fact that White hated 'any kind of pretending, avoidance of the realities' brought him and Astley closer together. But she was always and forever sensitive to perceived or imagined slights, and there was still the sense that some of these were slipping through.

Laurie Collinson, her old friend from Barjai, copped his own drubbing from White for his criticism of the painter Sidney Nolan. White dismissed Collinson in a letter to Astley.[30] Astley must have wondered if the end of her own friendship with White was also nigh, so easy did it seem for White to be critical in this way. White was not quite right about how 'lapsed' the Catholic lass really was; Astley still attended local Mass with Ed, though he attended the local non-Catholic state primary school and would later go to Epping Boys' High. In the late 1960s Ed would also be confirmed, with Tom Keneally acting as his sponsor. Jack, officially accepted in 'the flock' but not having had to convert, never attended. Phil's personal trials had led to another mission overseas: his love of the Church's liturgy, music and ceremony made him fit for Benedictine life, or so it was thought. In 1963 the letterbox at 44a could be an oddly contested space as anti-Catholic postcards and letters from White mingled with those from someone questioning his vocation as a priest.

Astley was always mindful of Eileen's reactions, especially concerning her writing career. In April Jack had waited nearby, tense, as Thea opened the envelope with the familiar handwriting. It contained a huge surprise: her mother congratulating her on the Miles Franklin win, 'I expect you are feeling very pleased with yourself.'[31] It was, perhaps, still one step away from a frank congratulation but as Eileen had been fielding various media enquiries herself, and seen the announcement on the ABC and a paragraph in *The Courier-Mail*, she was immersed in her daughter's success. In the flush of this public favour, the earlier marked-up copy of *Descant* became unmentionable. Eileen had other things to worry about. Phil was becoming ill with depression again.

The seriousness of Phil's situation was of great concern to Thea and satirical writing was her own way of clearing her mind. In this spirit she wrote to Forshaw about a 'convent novel' the two of them might write:

> … How's about a series of notes exhangee [*sic*] by two convent school girls, Thellie and Theie, (other names, of course) just busting out all over with gamps and coifs and throbbing inuendoes [*sic*] going on under the veils. Could be a gimmick. Don't think any one has tackled that line. Maybe we could be in separate convents, parted for the semester, smuggling some letters through and some not. Faint story line, developing hinted at scandals of appointment, dominance of horsey nuns and so on. We could work out details and then work roughly to a plan, actually sending each other the letters, waiting for replies, and getting spontaneity that way. Do I hear you throwing up? Is this crummy? Think it has possibilities myself. Nothing like it done here or elsewhere as far as I know. Then we will rush gloriously neck and neck into print with Faber and Secker and Warburg who love off-beat thingos. No illustrations by request and it will sell like *Franny and Zooey*, I know it.
>
> Listen, Forshaw, I read your letters and they are literally flashing opal mines of wit. You are seriously one of the funniest, no. THE funniest women I have ever met. All I could do would be the stodgy chummo who sparks off the old unpredictable. Think it over, shook [*sic*]. Could be therapeutic as well.
>
> Love, you old clot,
> Thea.[32]

Astley was, in fact, busily writing a novel (*The Slow Natives*) into which she would pour scenes just like this. In that novel, set in a convent, Sister Matthew and Sister Celestine confront each other with their 'inappropriate' fantasies about the novel's principal character, Bernard, a music examiner who is visiting the convent.

To Thelma Forshaw all of it was beginning to seem a little more than the search for an 'intelligent buddy'. Astley may have sensed disapproval in the air, for on her next visit she declared: 'Forshaw, you are a militarist and a fascist.' The attack seemed without provocation – some forgotten offhand remark? But Forshaw later reflected she and Astley were 'never really simpatico'.[33] Was Astley poor at reading emotional signals? Did she need something of others that they did not necessarily need as badly as she did? Her compulsiveness and the inability to deal with the consequences would yet cost her dearly.

People were still attracted to Astley as a vital conversationalist, finding her attractive with a great sense of fun. This was rather at odds with a perception of her in press articles as hard-bitten and anti-men. Some men, such as Thelma Forshaw's husband, found her hard to take, but plenty didn't. In fact, Astley liked men. At thirty-seven she was still very conscious of her looks and naturally flirtatious. Astley was attractive; her hair was full, had a natural soft wave and was a rich brown. She seemed to need almost no make-up and for a long time looked younger than she was. Her sense of dress was fresh, in so far as she preferred a casual look, plain or checked shirts and pants, but the style suited her easy way of movement and her slim figure. Astley could be disarmingly candid about the renaissance of her social and sexual self beyond her marriage and the suburbs.

Life at 44a Dorset Street was now schismatic: domestic routines harboured unquiet energies. Astley still felt the eyes of the neighbours on her but cared less and less about that. In fact, this reaction only made her want to be more outrageous. The house was divided by silence, between the early morning typewriter tapping and the evening music.

When a neighbour mentioned to Astley one day that it was a shame Jack was sitting alone at night, she found herself 'cut off' for months.[34]

Astley was now utterly preoccupied with writing her new novel, *The Slow Natives*, which would be published in 1965. She'd taken a joke of Ed's for the title: 'What's that black stuff between elephants' toes? Slow natives.' As always, the ideas in the new book were exaggerated – 'overblown' – versions of what she was feeling. She was writing about the 'silence of long marriage' and it was absorbing a great deal of her disillusionment.[35] She still badgered A&R about the ill-fated 'The Little Lie' but as *Explorer* had won the Miles Franklin, Davis could argue more convincingly that it was not 'particularly good tactics' to follow that success with what she saw as a lesser book. Astley let it go.[36]

Friends and literary acquaintances were treated to more frivolous asides. A publicity photo arrived at A&R with the quip: 'Glorious photos of me with my wrinkles smoothed out and my ego trimmed en brosse ...' Astley was already (as if to get in first) on her way to becoming 'middle-aged coy' about her age.[37]

Another year was coming to an end. She was looking forward to seeing Hal Porter at a cocktail party in Sydney to launch Australian Book Week. When they met at the Australia Hotel it would be on pleasingly equal terms. *The Watcher on the Cast-Iron Balcony* had just been released and Astley and Porter could now enjoy each other's success. She would not forget Porter's support of her from the start. The Miles Franklin Award gave her a new confidence, but it also reinforced how important literary friendship and mentorship were and had always been to her.

The year's end brought an unexpected and sour parting from her most important mentor. Astley had been rattled when she heard that Geoffrey Dutton was not going to take *The Well Dressed Explorer* for Penguin paperbacks. She found it inexplicable as a commercial decision – always her complaint. Astley wasn't thinking about the quality of the novel; she was in the midst of her old argument with

Beatrice Davis about literary fiction and its commercial prospects. But when she called Patrick White to let off steam, she misread the dynamics. White was a longtime friend of Dutton's. His on-the-spot reaction was to condemn the book itself, making the kinds of blunt remarks she had first encountered in his 1961 letter.[38] It opened the old wound.

In twenty years Astley would have the satisfaction of Penguin republishing the novel, and Dutton himself would have long received his marching orders from White. However, White had been irritated by Astley for some time, 'lamenting the fact that she lived in a remote suburb and was forced to miss so much'. In 1964 he wrote to someone who would understand his disaffection with her – Laurie Collinson – the very person he had roundly criticised only a year before: 'I have always found she resented anybody's having a vacuum cleaner until she had one herself, when she had, she forgot about the vacuum cleaner and went on to something else. I found resentment building up over our move to Sydney, as though we might be doing better for ourselves ...'[39] White's reaction put an end to the Astley–White friendship for decades.

At 44a the routines of life enslaved and liberated. Only the previous year, after trying to write *The Slow Natives* in her holiday break, Astley had been like the prisoner who misses her chains. She had written to Forshaw that she couldn't wait for teaching to consume her energies.[40]

Just one year later, at the end of 1964, things were very different. Astley decided to take two weeks' leave from Cheltenham Girls' High – an exceptional act for her – to finish the final draft.

She had now been writing continuously for seven years, under pressure from herself, from Davis, and even from the public success she was starting to enjoy as a novelist. And now, as she was immersed in the last stages of *The Slow Natives*, Astley found herself beset by a series of irreducible anxieties. There was the state of her own marriage – 'hypothetically' marriage itself; the end of two significant literary friendships, one with White and the other with Forshaw; Phil's worrying predicament; her troubled relationship with her mother and Catholicism. How would that survive a book set in a convent full of priests and nuns behaving badly? She was also still agitated by what she saw as the slipshod treatment of writers by publishers, which had affected even that all-important relationship with Davis at A&R. By 1965, not only marriage, but Astley's whole existence was a state of 'armed neutrality'.

10

Writing as a neuter

I don't even know how women think. I've been neutered by society so I write as a neuter.

Thea Astley, interview with Candida Baker, 1986[1]

As Astley completed the draft of *The Slow Natives* she was increasingly aware of living a double life. Her domestic routines sustained the day-to-day process of writing but she found herself engrossed in writing about the duality of the married suburban existence, the very kind she herself was living.

Years before she had said to Beatrice Davis that she knew the territory she wanted to visit in her work; that had been the Dream Country of her early days in country towns up north. She was claiming new territory now. She was not intent on observing the 'prying eyes' of the local gossips; now her novelist's eye was turned inward, to a corruptible self behind the social mask of life. She discovered and enjoyed American writers who were expert in the form of urban social satire – such as John Updike and John Cheever (the 'Chekhov of the suburbs') – whose short stories she particularly admired; and so Astley knew what she was aiming at. While others in Australian letters were debating what was or wasn't 'The Great Australian Novel', it was an irony entirely to Astley's taste that her epic would be about the 'The Great Australian Suburbia'. The savagery and pathos Astley injected into this new novel reflected her increasingly disarmed psychic and emotional self.

Young Ed woke daily to the tapping sound of the Green Hermes 'Baby' typewriter. He was now in upper primary school but still needed to be dropped off at 7.30 in the morning so that Astley could arrive ready for a full day of teaching at nearby Cheltenham Girls'. Astley drove the popular German 'people's car', a Volkswagen Beetle. She hated driving but would end up driving more than most people, once Jack's eyesight became an issue. The sight of 'Thea in her VW', emerging with frustrated relief, became a familiar one to her colleagues. From third grade onwards Ed had been letting himself in after school with his own key about an hour before Thea returned home. Ed became aware that this was an unusual arrangement; in the early 1960s working mothers were still in a tiny minority. Jack's job at the Conservatorium in the city had even less flexibility. He took the 7.43 am train to Wynyard from Epping station, Thea and Jack's numeric talisman for the 'grind of life' they both enjoyed hating. Jack made Ed's lunches, a cleaner came once a week, and Jack and Thea, with little interest in gastronomy, shared the cooking of some very ordinary meals. Thea would retire for writing in the evening, Jack would go to his music.

Ed was now quite often playing at the homes of friends; with families who to him resembled the smoothly functional households he saw in such TV programs as *Leave It to Beaver* and *Father Knows Best*. His home, he knew, was very different. In these shows, not only were the roles of master-of-the-house husband and domestic-duties wife clearly spelled out, but family life seemed to be a model of politeness. The atmosphere at 44a was energised by his parents' repartee – he could see they enjoyed each other's sense of humour enormously – but there were spaces, silences and secrets. Slowly he became conscious of belonging to a one-sided family: there were regular visits up north to see Eileen but Jack's family visited rarely and seemed remote. Information was tightly held. Jack's former marriage and family were never mentioned; Ed would be nearly twenty before he discovered, by accident, that the story he had grown up with – that his grandmother had died after childbirth – was a lie; she had suffered severe post-natal depression and been institutionalised.

Jack had always visited her regularly, something Thea let slip one day, much to her husband's irritation. For at least three or four decades after Jack's birth in 1915, post-natal depression of such severity was barely understood and spoken of in hushed tones. Electroshock therapy was a common treatment for what was generally called a 'nervous condition', with little differentiation about the type of condition and the suffering of the individual. Jack had grown up keeping his own counsel about some very serious matters.[2]

All children hover at the edges of the adult world, watching, but Ed negotiated his own little family with an exaggerated sense of truths held just beyond his comprehension. He couldn't know that Thea and Jack had formed a bond early in their marriage against their respective families, largely because of the difficulties with Jack's earlier marriage and the Catholic Church.

As a couple they were naturally inclined to secrecy from the start. When he was much older, in his late teens, Ed worked out that their shared secrets were part of their bond, and that they often seemed at their best when teaming up against others. Only occasionally did he get to team up with his parents as the Astley family. This happened when Eileen telephoned, all neurotic fuss and concern, in the years immediately after Cecil's death. Eileen now represented to Thea and Jack a more extreme form of the conservatism of Epping, from which they had set themselves apart: the married couple out of step in a Barry Humphries-style suburbia.[3]

Since winning her Miles Franklin Award Astley's life had become more public and she was more inclined, and more confident, to speak out on various different subjects. If she was trapped by her particular writing style, as the critics said, she would still have her say. She enjoyed opportunities to undo what she saw as misrepresentation, trying to explain publicly what she was doing in her writing. In 1963 *The Bulletin* had proved the perfect place to express her need for distance from those 'Joe-meets-Mary, Joe-loves-Mary sort of Australian novels ... the old Vance Palmer sort of thing'.[4] The interview had been a particular success: she had declared herself 'intensely interested in style' (claiming White's influence). By differentiating 'story' from 'style' Astley was trying to stake a very personal claim to the aesthetics of composition, which was also partly a reply to her critics, but also the aspect of writing that still interested her intensely.

Personally, however, Astley was feeling stifled. Scribbled notes for the novel, to herself, on the back of postcards, lay all about: 'One of the exciting things about committing adultery ... was knowing it would not last, a knowledge that gave clutching the moment an acidic sharpness.'[5]

The idea of marriage with its repetition and tedium had proved great material but Astley obsessed over her avenues of possible escape. She could see none. Much as she was arguing a lot with Jack, he was not really the issue – it was beyond that. The tenor of their tiffs bordered on comedy, she knew: 'Even if you're in the midst of a domestic row you think, "God, this is awful, isn't it?" and you start laughing.'[6]

Astley was in fact thinking deeply about marriage, this 'primary magic' that didn't last, but it would take another thirty years – when she was well into writing books about old age – before she would ever publicly describe the extent of her disillusionment about love and marriage at this time in her life. Broadcaster and publisher Louise Adler, who published Astley's later novels, knew enough to enter the fray:

> Louise Adler: 'Only you could come up with "we bore each other rancid". Why are couples so endlessly entertaining for you?'

> Astley: 'Well, I think marriage is an unnatural relationship, don't you? It's gotta be – two young people get together – we gonna be together – not look sideways, forwards or backwards, we're gonna be together for ever – next 900 years – not gonna get bored, gonna find you totally fascinating …'[7]

In *The Slow Natives* Astley had disguised her frustrations, perhaps to protect Jack, by adopting a male narrative perspective. In her satire of the hypocrisies of suburban couple Bernard and Iris and their problematic adolescent, Astley allows Bernard to comment about their marriage: 'There she is, he thought, and we have known each other in romantic, disgusting and boring attitudes for twenty years.' He is aware of but unmoved by his wife's relationship with another man: 'They would discover that the relationship they had rejected and the one they now enjoyed and the one each might enjoy later on all went the same way.'[8]

It is this man who comes to reflect on love between men and women, between parents and children: 'Parental love, he told himself sourly, the only damn love affair that goes on and on. After all, loving only has to be active to exhilarate, and you accept that fact and they love you back sparingly because there is a natural wish to escape.'[9]

'To find love, not that you are loved' was the most crucial thing, according to Astley, 'the only fulfilment a person can have'.[10] The unconditional love of a child was the kind of love she had found, making her 'old slipper' version of marriage seem by contrast more stark and despairing.

Astley was obviously concerned about Ed, old enough now at ten to be affected by her relationship with Jack and the arguments in the house. What she suspected he saw appears in *The Slow Natives*, a world in which 'adults talked and corrupted each other, slandered, hated, betrayed, remained pathetically loyal and pretended self-containment, assurance'.[11]

Ed was leaving the hinterland of childhood but Astley was still at heart the ever-watchful and anxious mother. She was, as the poet Fay Zwicky recalls, a 'typical mother of an only son'.[12] Zwicky and Astley had talked as wives and mothers more than as writers, and it was hard for Fay not to notice how anxiety about Ed's welfare dominated Thea's conversation.

Germs were an issue. The local swimming pool was out of bounds. Bike riding was too dangerous (Ed was thirty-five before he got his first bike). Like many only children, he was often conscious of too many eyes upon him. Both Jack and Thea imagined the worst; other parents would be asked to watch out for him.[13] While they were undemonstrative as a couple and Jack was not an effusive parent, Thea was a very physically affectionate mother. As he wriggled free of her embrace, Ed would look to Jack, and sometimes catch him 'looking on, worried'.[14]

Jack's concerns were manifold. They came from a deep knowledge of the anxieties and neuroses his wife had always suffered. Nobody understood her compulsions better than he; early in their marriage he had worked hard on getting her to stop sucking her thumb. With Ed getting older, Jack was concerned about how Thea would cope once the tightly knit mother–child relationship changed. Jack also received disturbing news about his own daughter from his first marriage and the advance of her leukaemia. All these things exacerbated his natural tendency to withdraw into himself.

The previous year – 1964 – just before finishing *The Slow Natives*, Astley had become aware of her growing battle with nerves. She was not sleeping, and in the day was beset with phobias about small things, worrying, over-worrying, and returning to check on switches and the like. When she read Cheever's short story collection *The Brigadier and the Golf Widow*, she couldn't help admiring how he detailed such phobias, placed them at the centre of life.[15] Astley particularly liked the story 'The Seaside Houses' with its 'thrilling finality' of a long marriage. Reading it had worked in perfectly with *Natives*; she had luxuriated in the dialogue:

> The wife: 'Oh God, you bore me this morning.'
> The husband: 'I've been bored for the last six years.'[16]

It was almost as if Cheever knew her mind. She was not the only one fascinated by that double perspective of being and not being, of partners resenting but enjoying the safety of society's most prized bond. This fascination had once taken the form of a rather arch self-consciousness in her writing, as with Helen Striebel in *A Descant for Gossips*, who watches herself 'enjoying the externals, I had not given myself completely'.[17] Was Astley watching herself now? Was she concerned about giving *herself* completely?

Astley struggled with opposite needs, a psychic schism in which extremes of emotion are bound to flourish. The novelist Jessica Anderson once wrote about the way a human being can have twin needs 'for the shell, and the emergence from the shell', needs that are 'strangely one'.[18]

She could have been writing about Astley. Like so many of her fictional characters, Astley's needs and passions were out of balance with her opportunity to express them. Writing was a way of enacting her own boredom, an exercise in abjection.[19]

There was much boredom to draw upon. Astley had amused herself in *The Slow Natives* with the character of Father Lingard, describing his boredom with Mass and himself as 'the symbol of a yawn. A great yawn incarnate'.[20] For such moments, of course, Phil's life was always useful material. He was finding his second teaching role as a Jesuit very challenging. Increasingly, as he continued to struggle, Astley could see that the Church was taking its time with Phil, but also taking *his* time, his life. Writing a broad canvas of failing faith was a way to deprecate more subtly. She wrote it into the novel: 'This is death, Sister Matthew thought, to have confessed and feel no relief.'[21] It might not have been at all what Phil was experiencing, but it was something Astley herself was determined to put into words.

Astley had always had a preternatural sense of Time but now it was truly her enemy: she appeared to others worryingly anxious, rushing always to the next task – or just rushing – as she had along Dorset Street as a young mother pushing Ed. She was struggling a great deal with her own nervous energy; she needed a physical outlet. Something to do with her hands, perhaps? Some might take to needlework but Astley simply announced, 'I think I'll take up smoking.' Now she would be like Beatrice, with her own aid to conversation. Drawing on cigarettes made Astley's hands seem like extensions of her thoughts and smoking completed her conversion to one of those speakeasy dames of American popular culture she and Davis loved, deep-throated heroines with crackling wit.

It was the beginning of a breaking out that was also sexual. Astley was nearing forty. From this vantage point it was not difficult for her to see how marriage as a virginal convent girl to a man more than ten years her senior had retarded her sexual maturity. Astley was still conscious of her good looks, if not actually vain. Here she was writing about the corruptions and compromises of love and marriage, all the while experiencing a growing frustration about her own limited experience.

Hidden behind the talk of the boredom of long marriages was sexual frustration. Women friends were treated to declarations – the kind that had become Astley's conversational stock-in-trade and that were usually amusing, made for effect and not necessarily intimate revelations.

Margaret Smith, Astley's neighbour, remembers her friend Thea often holding court on the subjects of sex and marriage; she could spot within a few words or tone of voice that something very personal was bothering her, that a soliloquy was on its way. 'Thea would say, "Women have their needs. Men are just frightened of them. I've talked with Jack, you know, and he said, 'Go off and do something about it!'"

'Jack did seem aware. He'd say, "Thea's off with you-know-who somewhere ..."' Reflecting on the entire period decades later, Margaret realised she often did know 'who'. Astley's soliloquies revealed how anxious she was about her situation – 'perhaps there was some impact, too, of Jack having been divorced – not sure'. Yet the more forceful memory her friend has of the time is that at the centre of it all was Thea's 'absolute loyalty to Jack' and their union.[22]

Astley was saying nothing she couldn't say or hadn't said to Jack; it had always been that way with them and it was important to her that it stayed that way. Jack, usually absent from these candid chats, was nevertheless the most quoted 'giver of permission' for them to take place. Thea could 'look elsewhere'. Listeners were invited to draw some obvious conclusions. Discretion – though not secrecy – was appreciated. It was a strange pact. Paradoxically, Astley's outward consternations seemed 'highly moral'.[23]

In the end what really mattered to her was the moral code that she lived by, not social or religious dictates. She and Jack had been through all of that in their day, and they had a shared view of what it meant to be truly an individual. They had both wished to be free from institutions that seek to govern the self – particularly the sexual self.

This common ground probably prevented their antagonism becoming real. They were co-conspirators again, now openly sardonic about their union: 'till the last instalment do us part', as Jack was fond of saying. They both had significant and separate interests. Jack had his work and plans to travel; Thea had her writing. They both had music. Their own brand of humour broke the inevitable silences. In the larger matters of life, accommodations had already been made.

But outsiders found the atmosphere at 44a to be surprisingly convivial. Their place was a Saturday morning haunt for various friends and neighbours who sat around the bar counter planned in the early days as a central feature in the kitchen. Thea's limitless supply of tea was always at the ready. At these times, anything could and would be said and people loved Thea and Jack together. Jack's wit was drier but Thea was always ready with the 'the killer droll remark. It was fun'.[24] Jack was spending more time with Ed now that he was older, so on Saturday afternoons they listened to *The Goon Show* or jazz together, while Thea got on with some writing. If you didn't know she was writing a novel about the despondency of failed marriages, you could almost sense harmony.

When she wasn't writing, Astley read real estate ads. Shacks, shanties and boltholes of all kinds had always appealed to her, the more remote the better, somewhere to house a would-be runaway like herself. The dwellings that interested her were always modest and in north Queensland, a return to her Dream Country in all senses. Astley spent these years idly sketching floor plans, alterations, totting up building supplies and legal costs in her writing notebooks in pursuit of the lusted-after hideaway. Two incomes and the occasional advance from publishers, as well as Astley's prizes, brought the dream closer.

In her literary social excursions, Astley was attracted by the combination of 'intelligent buddies' and the prospect of sexual interest from men. She tended to think of herself as the kind of woman other women dismiss as offering no sexual competition, safe in the view that men were not attracted to her because she said too much, or said the wrong thing. This was not necessarily the case, but it meant that Astley could always deflect and self-deprecate. She was always ready to compliment the good looks of another woman. Later in life these seemed odd and arresting conversation-starters: 'God, you look about twelve today, really, you really do!' People could see she needed to say such things.[25] It was not really a way of putting herself down; it was an act of shyness first and foremost, a nervous way of diverting attention away from herself and onto others.

Any female contemporaries who dismissed Astley as being of no special interest to men had been talking to the wrong men. Astley was not conventionally good-looking, but many men did find her appealing. She had always had a strong physical presence, being slim with easy body movements. Even in her hand gestures, or the modulation in her voice when she delivered an unforgettable remark, there was a frank sensuality.

This was not the self she necessarily presented in her public appearances as a novelist, where she was careful with her diction, but she was toying with ideas and consequences in her books that were very relevant to her own life. She had after all created a husband in *Natives* who condones his wife's affair, accepting it as both cause and symptom of his own inertia.

The manuscript of *The Slow Natives* was now ready. Astley always put her work through several drafts, so that by the time it reached Beatrice Davis at A&R it had been reworked many times. The esteemed editor's faith in Astley was now well and truly paying off. The letter came back straightaway: Davis considered the new book a 'technical advance' and Astley's first 'properly constructed drama'. Astley's keen eye would have settled on the postscript: Davis was pleased with the 'more sympathetic tone'.[26] She read on and discovered a 'but': Davis found the 'happy ending' (the disaffected youth loses a leg but regains his parents' attention) too literal and over-explained. Astley bristled. She didn't agree and felt she had earned the right to have the words and story the way she intended. As she had before in a similar moment (with White and 'The Little Lie'), she decided to seek a second opinion – this time from Amy Witting.

Witting was strong enough to openly agree with Davis, not her friend, but Astley still backed herself, and stayed friends with Witting as well. In another seven years she would dedicate her favourite book, *The Acolyte*, to her: 'For Amy Witting, who also knows how the work goes naked to the weather'.[27] They both did. *The Slow Natives* went to print unaltered late in 1965. Astley watched the reviews with interest to see whether any of the critics said anything about the ending. Only one reviewer expressed concern about the novel concluding 'a shade too prettily'.[28]

She was now seen as a writer of the 'Australian suburban agony': serious, stylish and amusing. She was hailed as 'world class' and the novel as 'brazenly stylish' and 'limned with wit'. Only the prose style was still the sticking point – 'prone to pointless extravagance'.[29]

'Style' notwithstanding, *Natives* won both the 1966 Miles Franklin and Melbourne Moomba prize for fiction, a combined sum of $2,000.

This was about a third of an average yearly income, enough to buy any large household item, and a good windfall to buffer the cost of the in-ground pool that had been completed only the previous year. These were now serious sums of money for 'wage slaves' but Astley had lost none of her resentment about the financial exploitation of writers. Success meant that she had a chance to advertise these deficiencies: 'I make only $400 from the sales of my books – if I'm lucky,' she told one reporter. On the subject of her reputation, she commented, 'You never build a reputation here by winning prizes.'[30] The prizes were hardly hurting hers.

The prevailing view of her prose style, her tendency to 'sprinkle' novels with 'words that need dictionary interpretations' didn't go away.[31] Astley was now personally affronted by this reaction, claiming high standards of literacy in her defence, but her views on the virtues of 'style' were and would always be about the poetry of the word, the importance of making the best and most particular words dance together in new ways. Turning meaning around, to make a perspective swivel until it appears fresh – fundamentally what metaphor does – is what Astley regarded as all-important.

It was about this time, around 1966, that the young writer Tom Keneally first met Astley as a fellow guest at a literature conference at the University of New England. She had just won her second Miles Franklin Award. He was struck by this well-known writer who was absolutely 'obsessed with word play and imagery'. Minutes into their conversation, Thea leaned towards him and asked, 'Can I have that?'[32] *That* was a word, metaphor or odd phrase he had hardly remembered using but he could see that it was being stored up for the next book.

From Astley's point of view the meeting was well timed as Keneally understood completely her obsession with style – even if he thought she took criticism too personally. They both belonged to a group of writers within a generation for whom style was paramount. It was 'Patrick White territory but also Randolph Stow, Hal Porter' and, Keneally knew, himself.[33]

They were straining to conjure a mystical and visionary world with the use of evocative imagery but this way of writing was rapidly earning the dubious reputation as an Australian 'malaise of excess'.[34]

A long critical overview of Astley's novels by J. M. Couper appeared in *Meanjin* in 1967 and she eagerly bought a copy. It was the kind of serious attention she had been waiting for, but it was not what she had hoped to read:

> The writer is still succumbing to the temptations of writing, straining after terms and metaphors that are picked up like pretty shells, for they do not serve what she has to say ... It is possible that in Astley's style the distraction does serve her, not only in the pleasure of writing poetically. Heavy handed and hammering as her metaphors may be, they also serve as a mask to the nakedness of her pessimism ...
>
> It is unevenness that mars Thea Astley's novels, and it is caused by straining after effect to catch a suspected loss of attention, an application of zeugma, a bizarre metaphor, poetical fine writing, willful flashback, thought impressions by means of a mockery of cliché, the escape of any character in exigency into cultural parade, or of the plot into sensation.[35]

This was adding to a chorus of past censure: Beatrice's early warning about 'preciousness'; White's 1961 letter; any and all of her less flattering reviews over the years. Astley had grown up loving poets such as Hopkins and Baudelaire who believed in the auditory imagination as the most direct route to melodious writing and therefore to the heart. Astley saw words, poetry and music as a continuum and would have loved Ezra Pound's remark that 'music begins to atrophy when it gets too far from dance ... poetry begins to atrophy when it gets too far from music'.[36] Astley, like Hopkins, was trying to get at the essence of a thing. When she wrote she lived with the rhythms of the physical world, heard them pulsate in the heads of her characters. Character and landscape were inextricably linked in her Dream Country.

To Astley all of it was symphonic, as close to the 'essence' of human life as language can get, the reason she had always loved the sound-sense poetry of Gerard Manley Hopkins. Why did nobody seem to understand?

She was despondent. The people reading her scores were deaf to the music. Was it because she was a woman? Astley thought of other Australian writers – men – whose prose was not so different, but they were not criticised as she was. More than twenty years later she was still bitter: 'I used to get a lot of criticism ... when the most ornately rococo prose was coming out of people like Hal Porter. I don't know whether it was a sex thing or not – people just fell back with joy at Hal's prose, and I seemed to drive people into a frenzy of rage. Maybe I should have been called Theo or Jerry or something.'[37]

But despite this, Astley was receiving the kind of recognition that she wished for. A long personal letter arrived from noted Australian poet and critic Arthur Phillips praising *The Slow Natives* as 'a bloody good book which kept me out of bed too late'.[38] Other letters arrived from readers, the first she had received. Such careful commentary on her work by 'ordinary folk' – as she would call her admirers – was a pleasure Astley would come to appreciate more and more.

The most surprising letter, though, came from her past. Her old teacher Sister Mary Martin asked Astley whether she would like to write the preface of a book for teachers about how they might inculcate the principles of Christianity in their teaching. This was bizarre: perhaps Sister Mary hadn't read *The Slow Natives*, set as it was in a convent of deranged nuns and priests. Pious folk had already criticised it, though she hadn't heard a word from her mother.

If Astley really believed she had been neutered by society, she soon discovered there was much interest in her 'female' point of view. These were to become rather excruciating showdowns for her, struggling as she was with contradictory thoughts about her own life.

No, she said, she didn't hate men. She just thought they were 'illogical and devious, and emotional exploiters of women'. At the same time she would hate to see Australia become a matriarchy. Under the pressure to justify her words, Astley would often pick up speed, running with her argument to bag an entire collection of often unrelated ills. She railed against the new permissiveness of 'arty' parents; about 'women's new approach to sex morality sponsored by the Pill'. She didn't believe 'sex equality' could really exist because she thought 'most women still want their men dominant and virile'. Men, for their part, had to accept that women 'had ideas' – were not just 'wives or mistresses'.[39] It was a farrago of ambiguity and defensiveness.

Astley looked like a most reluctant feminist, despite a lifetime of bemoaning the lot of women. Her ambivalence was complicated by an inbuilt distaste for dogma, which made it hard for Astley to say 'yes' to anything that looked like an '-ism'. The effect was to make her seem more conservative than she actually was, for behind these postures of grievance were softness and vulnerability. However, these shadows of self-doubt were hidden, at least for the moment.

In 1966 Robert Drewe was a twenty-one-year-old journalist on his first job at the Melbourne *Age* when he met the prize-winning novelist for a newspaper story. The woman he met was very self-conscious, obsessed with her age and looks; there had been several phone calls about the best photograph to be used in the profile.[40]

He tempted Astley into what he suspected was a self-commentary: 'Women are very sad things when you think about it. When they reach forty-five or so their marriages are usually pretty arid and they command no respect in any sphere at all.' (Astley was forty-one.) 'They aren't sex objects, as Western society demands, any more and they usually have no intellectual pursuits. If they are intelligent they're regarded as screwballs.'[41]

This was not the mood Thea was in when Tom Keneally met her at the University of New England. Thea Astley, he thought, was a 'very good-looking woman'. She was accompanied by the well-known political journalist and author Don Whitington, who was not himself a guest at the event.[42]

Thea found it necessary to explain to him that she was not really 'with' her husband, leaving the young Keneally to decipher exactly what that might mean.[43] For most of the next five years afterwards, whenever Keneally saw Thea socially, she was nearly always with Don. As chance would have it, not long after the conference meeting the whole Keneally family moved near the Astley home in Epping, so they would be close neighbours as well as friends.

Don Whitington was fifteen years older than Thea, and had divorced some years before, in 1961, leaving the marriage for another woman – but that had not lasted. At this time he was a well-known public figure, widely considered courteous and highly principled. Don had published novels, written plays, and his lively group biography of Australian prime ministers, titled *The Rulers*, had been published in 1964. He revered Astley professionally and respected her achievements. As a writer himself, he certainly knew her worth. They could also share the experience of the 'settled suburban existence'. Don had spent the last few years of his marriage rushing between hard drinking after work with other journalists to quiet domestic weekends with family. Thea understood why he wanted a life more about ideas, the arts.

Don was shy, awkward even, and had a stutter. It was an appealing combination: worldliness and vulnerability. He was slightly built, not particularly tall at less than six feet and not good-looking, but Thea could see why women were attracted to this attentive, patient listener. There was nothing predatory in their encounter; here was a man who appreciated and listened to women, was not afraid if they had ideas. Don liked attractive women, but it was clear to Thea that he did not require them to be silent.

Knowing what she did about the 'silence of long marriage' Thea listened sympathetically to the story of his divorce. Don was very involved with his third child, Richard, nine years younger than his other children. While Richard's siblings were past school years, he

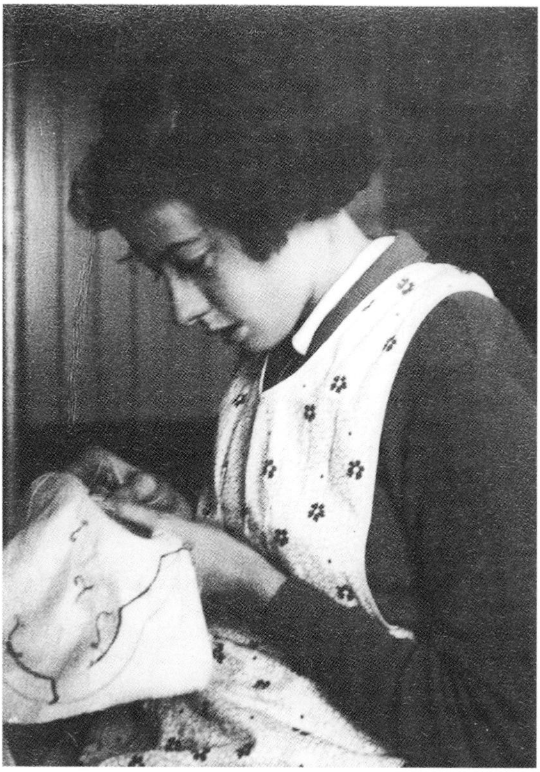

Thea Astley aged eight or nine years old. She would grow up to have much to say about all matters domestic.

Thea dressed for her First Communion, c. 1933. Her troubled experience with Catholicism influenced much of her writing.

Thea at Kirra Beach on the southern Gold Coast with her mother, Eileen, and older brother, Phil, in the early 1930s. Thea's fondest childhood memories were of her family's beach holidays.

The Queensland 'beach shack' of Thea's youth, c. early 1930s.

Thea's father, Cecil, in the 1940s. A senior newspaper sub-editor, he prided himself on the correct use of language – a quality Thea would inherit.

Eileen and Cecil Astley in the 1930s. Their unhappy marriage created tension in the family home throughout Thea's childhood.

Thea (far right) and friends on a day out, c. 1940s.

The Barjai writers' group, at the University of Queensland, provided Thea (back row, second from right) with the opportunity to socialise with other young writers and to develop her literary voice.

Thea Astley graduated with a Bachelor of Arts from the University of Queensland in 1947.

A devout Catholic, Phil Astley began training with the Society of Jesus (Jesuits) in the early 1940s.

Cecil and Eileen Astley and guest at Phil's ordination gathering. They were very proud to have a priest in the family, but Phil faced many personal struggles throughout his life in the Church.

The newly married Mr and Mrs Gregson on a night out in 1948.

Thea sitting in the foundations of 44a Dorset Street, Epping. She was the creative energy behind the uniquely modern design of the house.

Construction of 44a Dorset Street was completed in 1956.
Thea would write eight books over twenty years in this house.

Thea with a young Ed in the front garden of Dorset Street.

Jack and Thea with Ed in the kitchen of the Dorset Street house.

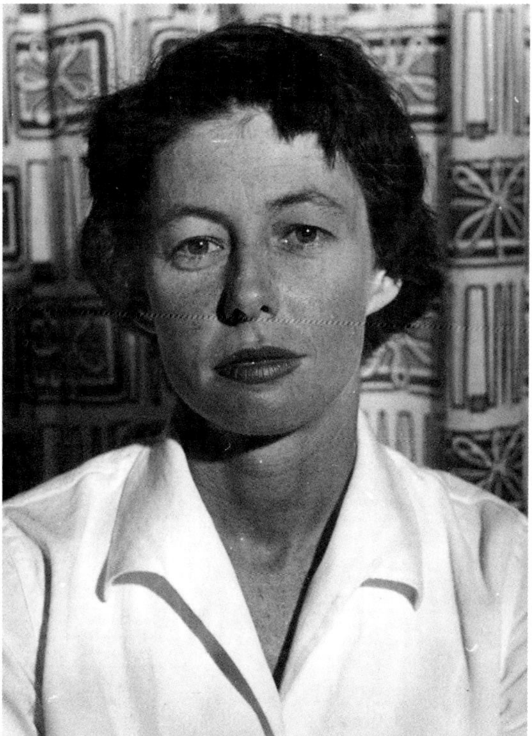

Thea in 1958, the year her first book, *Girl with a Monkey*, was published by A&R.

The first publicity photograph Thea had taken for A&R, c. 1962. She sent the photograph to her editor, Beatrice Davis, with the note: 'Glorious photos of me with my wrinkles smoothed out and my ego trimmed en brosse ...'

Thea reading *The Well Dressed Explorer*, for which she won her first Miles Franklin Award in 1962.

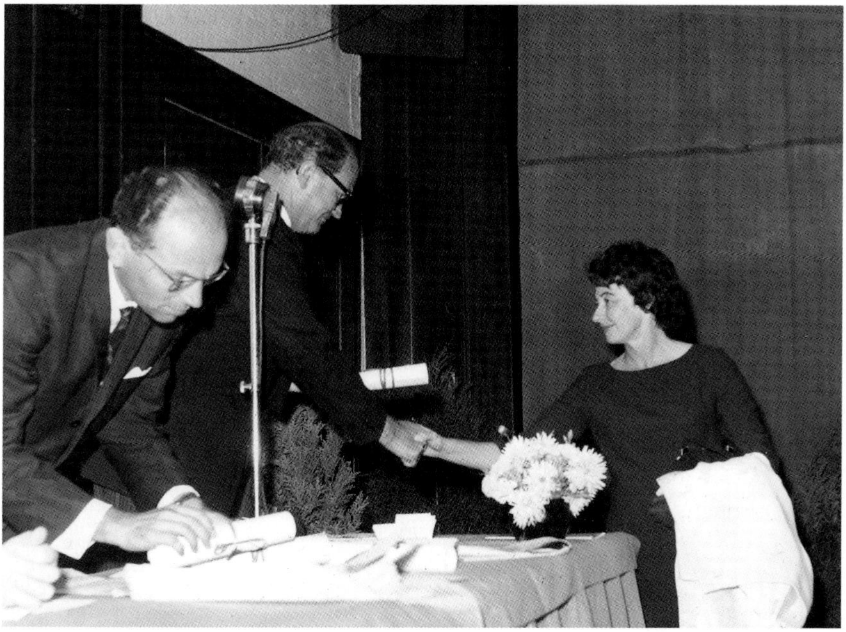

Thea collecting the Melbourne Moomba prize for fiction for *The Slow Natives*, which also earned Astley her second Miles Franklin Award in 1965.

Thea at the Adelaide Writers' Festival in 1979 with her friend and fellow poet Fay Zwicky (second from left), as well as poet Andrew Taylor (far left) and writer Barry Oakley (second from right).

Thea befriended some of her students at Macquarie University. Here she is with Jeff McMullen in the mid-1970s.

Thea with US academic Robert Ross in Memphis, where she was the writer-in-residence at Memphis State University in 1988.

Thea at the Adelaide Writers' Festival in the late 1980s, with Robert Brown and Laurie Muller from UQP.

Thea at Macquarie University. Photograph by Graeme Kinross-Smith.

Thea relaxing at her Kuranda home, relishing that 'do-it-tomorrow feeling' she so loved about Tropical North Queensland.

Thea and Jack in the lounge at their Kuranda house, 1979.

Jack, Thea and June at Michelle and Ed's wedding on 15 July 1988.

Thea and Jack in the late 1980s.

Thea remained very close to her brother, Phil, over the years. Here they are outside the Carmelite Monastery, Melbourne, in 1990.

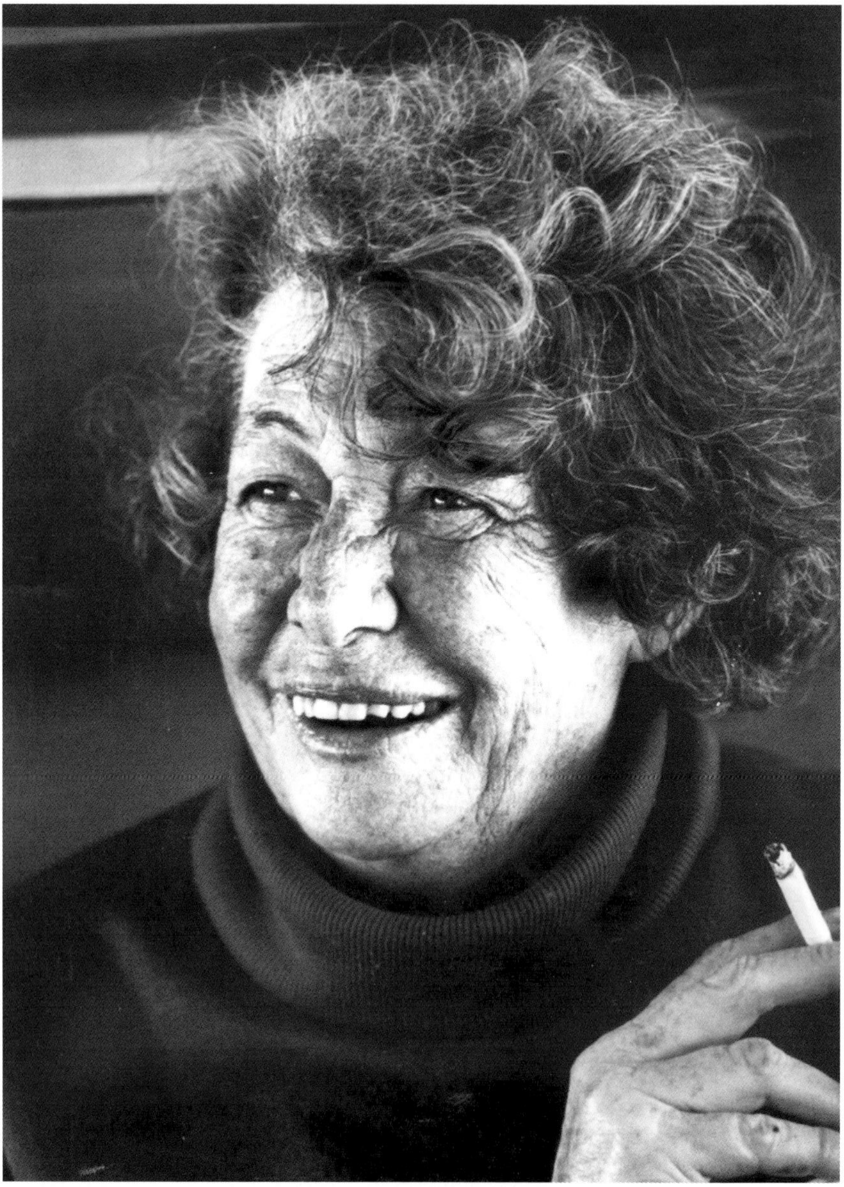

Thea, with her signature cigarette in hand, on the 1990 Writers' Train that travelled throughout rural Queensland. Photograph by Ray Cash.

was still a teenager. He and Don were living in their small recently purchased terrace in the eastern Sydney suburb of Woollahra. Don and Thea swapped stories about teenage boys, though Ed had barely entered his teens.

Don was in his mid-fifties, while Astley was just over forty, and he had seen much more of life than she had. He had had many jobs, including whatever work he could find throughout the Depression. He was heavily involved in the Australian Journalists' Association with a fierce regard for journalists' working conditions, issues about which Cecil Astley had been passionate throughout his daughter's childhood.

Astley admired her new friend's determination to write books, not being, as her own father had been, a slave to the daily grind of news deadlines. He and Astley shared a sense of the world being composed of 'feet, boots and mats', a larrikin sense of humour and deep empathy for the less well off. Don Whitington, in short, had the potential to enlarge and fulfil Thea's life in new ways. Their relationship would not be easy, given Astley's other loyalties, but they had a strong and mutual sense that it might be worth the effort.

By early 1966, on Friday nights, Don and his son Richard would drive from Woollahra to Epping, a long trip across Sydney. Richard recalls that his father never explained why this was happening. It just became the accepted way: have an evening meal, listen to music, sometimes greet Jack and sometimes not – he was usually out at a music concert. Ed, much younger than Richard, had dinner with them but was in bed soon afterwards.

When Richard first walked into 44a he forgot for the moment to be bored by the grown-up company; the Gregsons had the most sophisticated sound system he had ever seen. He soon realised that this visit to this house was different in other ways, though at fifteen he could not quite articulate what they were.[44]

People who met Don at this time could see not only why Thea liked him, but how Jack might too. Tom Keneally remembers thinking that if he and Whitington had met at a cricket match or a concert, they would have got on like a house on fire.[45] Astley's neighbourhood friend Yvonne Wyndham also recalls how this new frequent visitor to the Astleys' in Dorset Street had quickly became accepted.[46] Astley had no intention of being alone – she could not bear it – and Jack would never leave her. She had worked her way towards being comfortable with a very public secret.

Soon, partly to share the driving, Thea began visiting Woollahra. There was a reason, or perhaps an excuse: she was coaching Richard, a student at Sydney Grammar, in English (finally improving his results). On a Friday or a Saturday Richard could expect to see Thea's familiar Volkswagen. Richard said, 'Dad and she would go out in his car to various functions – I was out a lot too at that age – I'd come home, both cars were out front. Thea was never there in the morning.' On one occasion Richard took Thea's VW Beetle, started it without keys and crashed the car. Richard commented, 'The strange thing is I don't recall any consequences from either of them – insurance claim or anything.'[47]

Only later in life did Richard contemplate how awkward this must have been for Thea. She needed a car badly, for driving Ed and to get to her teaching job at Cheltenham Girls'. At home, too, there must have been the awkward sense of something overt that was usually unseen.

As time passed, there were trips out of Sydney. In the years after his divorce Don had bought a sailing boat. The vessel appealed to Thea for its 'knocked-up-from-nothing' quality. It was the converted lifeboat from a large ship, very plain with a mast and with weight in the keel which made it less sailable. For Thea, it was the sailing equivalent of her beloved out-of-the-way shack. Friday nights could now extend to some weekends, and Ed, too, could enjoy the novelty of boating and picnics. Literary friends became used to seeing Thea and Don together, although their private time was limited.

One day Astley's former neighbour Betty Judd, who had moved

up north some years before, received an unexpected phone call from her suggesting they all – that is Astley, Ed, Betty and her children – go for a holiday at Red Rock, about forty kilometres north of Coffs Harbour, a relatively unspoiled part of the coastline offering tranquil bush and beach. Settled into the rented holiday house and catching up with Thea about old Epping friends, Betty was surprised when Don arrived; he had not been mentioned in the original arrangements. She didn't feel like challenging Thea over it. Betty had known Thea for many years: apart from the fact that she didn't think that whatever was going on was her business, she knew how important Jack was to Thea.[48] It was hard to imagine that changing.

Richard found the public Thea Astley, considered to be a woman of forcefully voiced opinions, at odds with the woman he was coming to know. To him she seemed shy, respectful, mostly reserved. He noticed how she was not as comfortable with Don's set of friends as they all were with each other. He also noticed a nervy, apologetic tendency in her, a sense that she was at fault, often over small things. 'Thea would walk over to turn off a light, absent-mindedly, then say "sorry, sorry", as though she'd done something terrible.'[49]

However, when they were alone together and away from the city Don and Thea could relax. They bought a small ramshackle house together at Killcare on Broken Bay, north of Sydney. It was tranquil and rural, decades before the area became suburban and dotted with expensive houses. What it offered in 1966 was privacy and isolation. Weekends shifted to accommodate these new arrangements.

It is not possible to know exactly what led to the final parting between Don and Thea after about five years but Richard had noticed a worrying acceleration in Thea's nervous compulsions, including her constant apologising and paranoia she had done something wrong. When Astley visited her Dorset Street friends the Smiths, she said 'hurriedly Thea-style': 'I didn't run over one of the boys, did I?' Margaret Smith was concerned for her friend:

> [At her worst] she couldn't walk twenty metres without saying something about what she'd done. It was bizarre. I was worried but I thought it best to laugh it off if I could. I knew things had to be worse at home.[50]

They were. Thea was now constantly agitated, worried about switching things on, and off, then on again. Thea kept asking, genuinely fraught, 'Have I put glass in the dinner?' Ed, who was already used to his mother's volatility and the hostility between his parents, now saw his mother weeping and talking of suicide. 'It was scary at the time. Jack stayed as calm as he could but it was hard for him.'[51]

Astley's circumstances were deeply distressing. Guilt had become her entire world; she even felt guilty for being miserable. But apart from that, she was confused by her success as a writer. It didn't feel real; it didn't feel right. She did not know whether she deserved it. For the first time in her life she was unable to laugh off tedium and routine. Suddenly the source of her creativity – the place where she had found expression of herself – was terrifyingly out of reach. And after more than twenty years of effortless classroom management, she was now finding teaching near impossible.

Jack and others knew that some accommodation had to be made urgently. It was decided that Astley should take on some correspondence teaching – a holding pattern of sorts – with the hope that other possibilities might gradually emerge.

Thea's troubles virtually paralleled those of her brother. Only a year before, he had been sent to Loyola College in Watsonia, Victoria, allegedly for a fresh start, but Astley knew his Order had arranged for him to be hospitalised for depression. His was proving a long and difficult journey out of the darkness, but the entire body of Jesuits stood by him, visiting so often that he was rarely alone. Astley heard that he was recovering confidence slowly with the help of his brothers in faith. Phil then made a very important decision: he would return to music as the central expression of his faith; he had always loved church music, especially Bach. Phil discovered a new life within the Order, playing for church services and ceremonies, and here he found his niche. He became known as a fine musician with a special talent for the organ.[52] It was an important reminder to Astley of the music she and her brother had loved as children. Perhaps her own suffering might also find its salve in music.

Her neighbour Margaret Smith was studying piano and offered to put Thea in touch with a good local teacher. Astley grasped the opportunity as if her life depended on it, which for the moment it did. The piano was moved into her study so she could practise all night if necessary and she started playing once again, starting with calming Beethoven sonatas.[53] For years after this she was candid in radio interviews about this 'therapy': 'I'm trying to learn thirty-two Beethoven sonatas – I'll be around 120 when I get there.'[54] In this particular interview she can be heard lighting up cigarettes, and her voice is shaky.

There was another saving grace. Towards the end of 1966 Astley saw an advertisement for a tutor in the English Department at the brand new Macquarie University, so new that it had not even been built. The site was fairly close to where she lived. Astley acted quickly, asking Beatrice Davis for a reference. As Astley was the author of four published novels, two of them Miles Franklin winners, it was no exaggeration for Davis to describe her as one of 'the most talented of contemporary Australian writers'.[55] Any reference hardly seemed necessary but Astley was diffident: this was 'university', not a writing award, and certainly not high school. However, she instinctively felt that the change could save her. Those closest to her witnessed conflicting reactions as a result of this: a renewed sense of self-belief, diffidence, a sense of insecurity, defensiveness. This was not an equation that lent itself to being solved.

PART 3

NORTH OF NOSTALGIA

11

The oldest senior tutor in the Commonwealth

It is now abundantly clear to me, the oldest senior tutor in the Commonwealth if not in living memory, that the school has neither the wish to make me a lecturer nor the slightest intention of doing so.

Thea Astley to the Head of School,
Macquarie University, 1976[1]

Astley's time as a senior tutor at Macquarie University would prove to be one of the most personally satisfying and productive periods in her life. Under its benevolent influence she produced five books and won a third Miles Franklin Award. Sydney's third metropolitan university had ambitions for a new, more democratic age in education. Even the name was telling, after Governor Lachlan Macquarie, a Scot known for his humanitarianism and keen interest in education. A university proud of its Australian heritage would have impressed Astley; the university motto 'And gladly teche', from the General Prologue to *The Canterbury Tales* by Geoffrey Chaucer, even more so.

In 1967 Macquarie University consisted of a set of ideals, sketches and building works. Astley negotiated a trip to the MLC building in North Sydney – Macquarie's temporary campus – where the situation was refreshingly ad hoc. There couldn't have been a better way for Astley to start this new phase of teaching, for this was what it was to her. No personal challenge had changed her deep instinct for the profession. The staffroom was cosy, with only five or six in the fledgling Department of Literature and Linguistics, most of whom were Oxbridge-educated academics. Despite this, the inaugural professor Herbert Piper was utterly committed to Australian literature – a focus still reasonably foreign to Australian universities in the late 1960s. Piper, a graduate of Adelaide and Oxford, was a specialist in the Romantic period – and originally had the kind of British-imported vision of university life one might expect from such a background and interest. Yet as head of the English department at the University of New England, he had invited Australian writers such as novelist Frank Hardy and the poet Kenneth Slessor to visit. By the time of his 1966 appointment to Macquarie, he was more than ready to embrace new areas of interest in English studies such as American and Australian literature.

The department that Astley joined differed significantly from those of other Australian universities, both in terms of its members' intellectual and creative interests and their attitudes to students. From the start, management planned for students to have mentoring support from staff. In time attempts to formalise this within the teaching structure broke down, but the effect of the original intention remained in the teaching culture.[2]

The new Macquarie students were often women with family responsibilities, free to study for the first time. Astley at forty-two could identify with them. She might invite a busy young mother to meet her for a coffee if that was more convenient than a university office interview. In this setting, and mindful of the problems many women faced in returning to study while still carrying out domestic duties, she might unveil her 'three washing basket' philosophy. There should be one basket for the mother, one for the father, and one for the kids, and Astley instructed: 'You must only wash clothes in your basket.'[3] This was a special kind of mentoring, kindness, too, since Astley had scarcely enjoyed this privilege in her own young adult life; no older women had been there to guide or support her.

Astley's American-born colleague Joan Kirkby had not been long in Australia, and remembered the excitement of these early days when teaching students seemed like 'having a lot of friends'. However, Astley was never completely comfortable with her position at Macquarie; she never quite resolved the tension between literary scholarship and her position as a writer.[4] She felt accomplished but undermined from the start because she was ambivalent about her status as an academic. As an American, Kirkby had also felt she was being put down and that she and Thea were both outsiders. The two women formed a bond as friends rather than colleagues. During their lunches in the city Astley enjoyed sending up the imagined superiority of academe.[5] Kirkby was surprised to see Australian anti-authoritarianism displayed in a woman who was also reserved, even polite. In the staff common room, she watched Astley enjoy the frisson she created with what colleagues saw as her 'penetrating assessment' of various pomposities.[6]

Not everyone appreciated this; some were irked by what seemed like defensiveness. The duality in Astley's role – a creative writer teaching alongside academics – was awkward for others to negotiate. In its way this served Astley's interests well: her creative self, as always, depended on being both inside and outside the group. Astley's relationship with literature was emotional, which made her inherently suspicious of literary criticism 'the starmakers, not the stars' as she called critics. She was still smarting from the recent *Meanjin* overview-article of her work by the well-known Scottish-born critic and poet J. M. Couper, who was to become a senior lecturer at Macquarie, right in her area.[7]

When the journal's editor, Clem Christesen, asked her to write an article on a planned issue discussing the 'temperament of generations', Astley declined due to work commitments and the novel she was trying to finish, but used the opportunity to vent: 'After reading Dr Couper maybe I'll chuck the novel away. He was kind to devote space to me but he made me feel I'm wasting my time. I couldn't understand all [*sic*] his article ... But then I'm not academic, so it was probably over my head.'[8]

This kind of capricious response made Astley's university position more than problematic, since she also appeared to desire scholarly critical appraisal. Nobody felt inclined to engage with her over this point, but few academics would have joined in with her irreverence for the holy grail of academic publication. To her friend Joan Kirkby, however, it was all part of 'Thea's way of being in the world', which seemed to her not only legitimate but also embodied the very best of Australian character.[9]

Astley was fun, and fun to be with. Her nerves had recovered a little and she was ready for engagement; she was also one of those people who become energised by an audience without necessarily being an extrovert. Macquarie offered relief to Astley from the difficulties of her own life, which often seemed such plain hard work. Some of it still was: getting around Sydney could be exhausting. She had always hated driving but Ed needed to get to music lessons and elsewhere. He was also now reaching an age where he needed some separation from her. He escaped from the house when trouble broke out at home, which still happened, though less frequently than before, and he would go on long walks to neighbouring suburbs.

Neighbours Tom and Judy Keneally were close to Astley. In Tom, Astley had someone who could understand her upbringing from the inside, a fellow Catholic and a Queenslander too. Together they talked frankly about the compulsions that had lately become so acute for her: 'One thing we had in common and talked about explicitly and implicitly was the obsessive-compulsive thing,' recalled Tom.[10] They swapped theories about it, not always seriously: was this kind of obsessive compulsion caused by the ritual and repetition of the Church? Did the Church instil it, or just make it worse? Ex-Jesuit Keneally believed that the Church actually encouraged obsessive-compulsive behaviour: 'Not only is there concern about hygiene, but concern about sin, about being morally culpable for everything that goes wrong.'[11]

Very few people could have provided this kind of bracing criticism, allied with laughter. Their relationship meant a lot to Astley. Keneally, too, was indebted: he loved Astley's writing, had felt 'succoured by it'. As a relative novice in the writing life, he had felt encouraged that 'she had been doing it for some time. It could be done'.[12] It is hard to think of Keneally as ever having been a novice in the writing life; at this time he had already published two novels and was on the brink of winning his own first Miles Franklin Award for *Bring Larks and Heroes* in 1967.

The stimulation of Astley's new job brought calm at home, and more congenial work commitments meant more time to write. Astley had kept up her weekly tutoring of Don Whitington's son Richard and had organised a writing-research trip to the New Hebrides (Vanuatu) with Don, which ended up being their last close time together. In the last couple of years she had been working on another novel, *A Boat Load of Home Folk*. She signed the publishing contract at A&R in January of 1968 – as Thea Gregson with Jack as a witness – as was usual.

If there is a book by Astley that ought not to have been published it is *Boat Load.* It extended the life of her *Slow Natives* couple, making a doomed marriage and other dismal partnerships once again centre stage. It is, to quote a publisher's reader, 'a study in unhappiness and frustration' and a 'depressing, unlikeable book'.[13] Yet the book passed through the hands of a significant number of people in-house – odd in itself given the author was by now certainly well known at A&R. Possibly Davis didn't like the book either but felt too compromised by her past support for the author to say so, and she might also have been aware of Astley's fragility in the face of criticism.

The setting of an isolated island (Port Lena) and a bit of cyclonic weather do not in themselves seem plausible bases for despair. The despair, of course, was the writer's. In this Astley was like the Australian historian Manning Clark, who tended to project his own dark moods onto his versions of Australian history.[14] Whether truly forbidding or not, everything came under the same dark spell. It was Astley who felt that 'everybody was living on a cyclonic edge'.[15] This was how she experienced life.

Like many of us, Astley found no difficulty in accepting her state of mind as reality. In this mood, Time really did cast its shadow. She was creating characters who suffer from life erosion, a state she would later refine in the phrase 'putrefaction of the spirit'.[16] These would become acidly detailed portraits, often in just a few words: 'Trembling sexagenarians, hearts pausing – but not for joy: eyes cataracted, prostates swollen or excised, livers cirrhosed, hearing dimmed.'[17]

The Slow Natives had featured a 'dried-out version of a society hostess who lived it up with bulk liquors, brass costume jewellery and lots of hair rinse'; in this new novel there were 'Boutiques. Girls in boutique wear. Old girls in better boutique wear'.[18] Misses Trumper and Paradise are 'two maiden ladies in the sad years'; one has hair that 'hung like old grass' and 'raggedly applied lipstick whose end result was sad'. There are 'seedy men with their limp manhood between varicose thighs' who know they are 'still grandiose because of being male'. Stevenson, a ship's captain, feels 'enormously sad for that time of morning'. When his phone doesn't ring it is 'silent as old marriage'; Father Lake is 'a quietly exhausted forty-three'.[19]

Astley, not so quietly exhausted these days, was nevertheless also forty-three and seemingly hell-bent on representing abjection of the kind unleashed in *Boat Load*. This bleakness had been apparent in her other work. It is there in *Girl with a Monkey* when clumsy Harry calls out to Elsie, 'I brung ya some fruit', only to be met with her frozen self-centredness; it is present in *Descant* when the excruciatingly lonely Vinny Lalor is destroyed by sneering peers; in *Explorer* George Brewster uses his wife to model a sweater he has bought for his mistress.

When in *Boat Load* the unmarried Miss Paradise announces to her companion Miss Trumper that the latter has bored everyone for years, there is also the echo of John Cheever's dialogue between a bored husband and wife that Astley loved so much. She resisted the accusation that such portraits were cruel, saying she had made her observations in sympathy, that 'those two elderly women – Paradise and Trumper I felt sorry for – they were not married – and before World War II you just had to marry'.[20]

By 1968 Astley had built something of a written dossier of treachery, betrayal and self-loathing. Why? If it was based on self-knowledge, it was certainly not kind – and in her late teens she had written in a school prize book that 'kindness was more important than cleverness'. She was thinking of kindness to others, not to herself. The belief that 'self' was not important had become a spiritual rock around her neck; Astley's concern for others was genuine enough but it was also a nervous playing out of imaginary or real guilt she associated with herself and her own behaviour. In the end her writing suffered.

A Boat Load, according to the A&R reader, was not enough like White or Keneally to be attractive to the educated reader and too disjointed in construction for a popular market.[21] But it did have one of Astley's signature characteristics: she knew how to send herself up and she often did. Even in this bleak book there is a wonderful spoof based on her own poor culinary efforts: short on ingredients, a character simply tears up cardboard to make a sauce. This lighter comic strain would yet be redeeming; almost from the start Beatrice Davis had seen Astley's ability to express anguish through self-mockery.

While Astley waited for the reviews, a well-timed letter came from Hal Porter suggesting they meet up at the Phoenix Bar in Flinders Street, Melbourne. It was an opportunity before the university teaching year began to celebrate at least getting the book off her hands. Always the tongue-in-cheek flatterer, Porter urged, 'Keep in mind, young woman, the fact that I am coming 142 miles to keep this appointment.'[22]

The reviews concentrated on the two aspects of her work that had been most unpopular with critics: Astley's Catholicism and her rather ornate prose style. As the book was full of priests and Catholic rituals it was perverse for Astley to think this criticism was unfair, but she had become adept at attracting this kind of criticism and then crying foul. All four of her novels were in print, and she could even play overseas comment against negative local comment. The year 1967 had been a good one, with a letter from the actor Anne Baxter reminding her that the film of *Descant for Gossips* remained a possibility – though Astley knew that the world of film was full of well-meant gestures that did not come to fruition – and *The Slow Natives* had been published in the United States.[23] This was particularly satisfying for Astley, who hungered for attention in the US; she was very pleased when it gained a favourable review in *Time* magazine. Beatrice Davis wasted no time in telling the A&R London marketing people that her author had been named as the best woman novelist to appear in Australia since Christina Stead.[24]

It was no doubt on the strength of that comment that late in 1968 Alec Bolton, A&R's manager in London, sent *A Boat Load of Home Folk* to Stead for comment. What came back was a disconcerting mixture of flattery and criticism.

> Dear Mr Bolton,
> … I have now read the book and would say that, without presuming to give a serious opinion, Thea Astley is a vigorous emphatic writer, very much steeped in the idioms of modern success writers, Maugham (background and interpretation), Graham Greene (persons and themes), and even James and Woolf: she imitates them and quite powerfully, though at times with pretentious clutter. She has real originality in description of sight and sound, vigorous and striking; her hurricane is good; and it is delightful to have original poems in a novel. These white shadows in the southern seas (to quote) are more Maugham (himself a fading shadow) and Greene, now theme-weary, than 'native' – it seems to me. Everyone has a right to ply tunes on

the old harp of course and sometimes the old airs please more than unheard tunes. Perhaps that is what she wants. But does she? She is a gifted writer and could see with her own eyes.

The frenzied cruel pursuit, for example, of old maids 'angular' and 'withered', the contempt for middle-aged married men (I won't quote the descriptions), the sympathy, sole sympathy for the erring cleric, a homosexual, is really too Maughamesque; it is a parody. (He deserves it.) I believe she is gifted. Probably this is just a sketch, an experiment, such as everyone does.

Kind regards,
Yours truly, CHRISTINA STEAD[25]

Nothing in Stead's letter could be used by Angus & Robertson for publicity. Astley did not see the letter until the mid-1990s, when this author gave her a copy; obviously nobody at A&R had felt inclined to risk her reaction. Bolton wrote to Davis about 'C. S.'s incisive comments', obviously in agreement with the thrust of them.[26] He didn't much care for the work, and even wrote to his senior editor John Abernethy at the Sydney office.

Dear John,
I've been meaning to say to you how aghast I was at the awfulness of the new Thea Astley. It's not just that her view of personality is so anarchistic, it's the mannered, arid style that she affects all the time. I dragged myself right through it and hated every word. If there are going to be any more of her novels, perhaps we should come right out and promote her as an utter bitch? We've got an ad in the *Bookseller* tomorrow which I believe will sell this book to the libraries, but it's misrepresentation.
Yours,
Alec[27]

Astley would have been devastated by Stead's criticism, for she felt an affinity with her. In 1981, without having seen this letter and fifteen years after it was written, Astley expressed this herself:

> Perhaps it is because I am a woman – and no reviewer, especially a male one, can believe for one split infinitive of a second that irony or a sense of comedy or the grotesque in a woman is activated by anything but the nutrients derived from 'backyard malice'. Assuming these particular qualities – sense of irony, the eye for the comic or the grotesque – are indications of intelligence and believing a priori that no woman is intelligent, critics assign the evidence of humour, irony or comedy to darker forces at work; the Salem judgement comes into play and the lady writer is most certainly for burning. It is hard to understand why else a writer of Stead's calibre could for so long be ignored in her own country.[28]

Boat Load was clearly not to be one of Astley's great books but there is something in its savagery that was to remain important in her work. Classically educated, Astley would have understood this as an Orphic descent. But even as she wanted her words to be 'vernacularly right', as she often said, her aesthetics belonged to ancient traditions in mythology and literature, particularly the myth of Orpheus, which is founded on the seduction of sound.

Enjoyment of despair was now the core of Astley's aesthetic energy. There was pleasure to be had in indulging the irony of even the worst of things, and her own peculiar mixture of bombast and anxiety could leave her real pain hidden. Colleagues were diverted by her wisecracks but Joan Kirkby, closer to her than most people, realised that this style of relating to other people made her seem fiercer than she really was. Kirkby wondered whether this kind of deflection prevented Astley from taking her own pain seriously.[29]

To Astley compassion was a gift of the imagination. And to her, whether a person possessed a soul depended on their sensitivity –

sometimes, it must be said, on their sensitivity towards Astley. Early one morning a fellow staff member walked past Astley's open door and saw her sitting weeping at her table. He went away, made a coffee, handed it to her and closed the door quietly. Later, she remarked to her colleague John Ryan, whom she considered a fellow outsider, 'I know one person on staff who has a soul. I know nothing about him but I know that.'[30]

To be so vulnerable while being accused of cruelty must have been very taxing for Astley, but the psychological nakedness of *Boat Load* had left her nowhere to hide: inevitably there would be inferences about the writer behind the work. She became more self-conscious in interviews, endlessly wrangled over the perfect photo, asking journalists what was wrong with the expensive publicity shot she had already paid for herself.

It was harder to hide from Eileen, who had made plain her concern about the world's view of her daughter. In early November 1968 she wrote to Thea:

> I found it [*Boat Load*] quite interesting but sad and unhappy. I seemed to be reading episodes from your life in some of the disguised characters. But Thea why spoil such good writing with such awful sexual details? Love means <u>self-sacrifice</u>, not <u>sexuality</u>, which is <u>lust</u>. And I feel quite ashamed about how you wrote about Fr Lake, whom I remember was in one of your other books. You certainly do hate everything Catholic. What a pity. There are lots of beautiful and lovely good people to write about. And things. After all what gifts and talents you have are given to you by God.[31]

Eileen didn't like her daughter using the word 'lousy' in a *Women's Weekly* interview. 'People will say you must be like the way you write,' she said, adding for good measure, 'I have read Charles Dickens' works … 800 pages in small print and not one foul suggestion and every page full of interest. Perhaps you have not heard of him. However I wish you every success and happiness as you truly are a hard worker.'[32]

Eileen's was a pinched version of well wishing, her letter a curious mixture of scornful pride and open disdain. It had been nearly ten years since the return of the marked-up copy of *Descant* and this response made the wounds raw again. Some questions were silent and unanswered still. If Eileen assumed from the tone of Thea's novels that their author was a tough customer, then did she know nothing of her daughter's true nature?

Possibly feeling guilty, Eileen wrote a week later about being on the lookout for mentions of Thea or reviews of her books. Astley maintained her apparent resolve not to quarrel with her mother. In their still very regular correspondence (almost weekly), she was careful to talk lightly of life, of how she liked the new 'university work', filling the required pages with news of Jack and Ed. She would work on *The Acolyte* over the next three years, all too aware that Eileen would probably find fault with that novel too.

There were lighter moments, weekend trips to Killcare on the NSW central coast or to the beach with Don's friends, but some of the strain of the last couple of years was breaking through with an intensity that affected that relationship. Don had bronchial problems (like Thea, he was a committed smoker). A warmer climate might help, but less than a year later he moved permanently to Canberra, where Richard attended the Australian National University. By mid-1969 Richard had left university and returned to Sydney. The Woollahra house had been sold. Everyone's life seemed to be taking a different path; that year was the last time Richard recalls seeing Thea.

The years of contact with Don's son had given Astley a glimpse of the late teen years that lay ahead with Ed. How would she handle his emerging sexuality? The university world meant she was in close contact with young adults who were already exerting pressure on the sexual mores of their parents' generation.

None of the students Astley taught knew more than the barest details of how she lived her life. The younger students seemed to her selfish in their freedom and what she saw as their escape from any responsibility. Her hearty endorsement of individual will was pitted against resentful censure. Students of the time talked about 'dropping out' in the great quest of self-discovery but Astley couldn't relate to it – 'an entirely immoral philosophy ... a very selfish philosophy'.[33] She couldn't see how her own version ('I've always thought myself to be a bit of a misfit') was in some ways quite similar.[34]

Astley became known as a crusader for language and in public would deplore what she saw as a collapse in literacy standards: 'Half of Macquarie were going into teaching and I used to wonder what would happen.'[35] Her idiosyncratic views emerged from her own experiences. Her misfits were outsiders excluded by the group because their individuality affronted the status quo, mirroring her own predicament as a young woman. This was all in her mind; outwardly Astley was socially conservative in her conduct, very much so. All of it was tied to Church and society, to the 'congregatory aspects of abrading'.[36] If she wrote about self-involvement it was only to prove, as she would later say, that 'looking inwards ... is the death of the personality'.[37]

Astley was witnessing big social changes but they only led her to concentrating on the aspects of human beings that stayed the same, which was the theme of her story 'The Scenery Never Changes', her contribution to *It Could Be You*, the anthology of Australian stories Hal Porter was editing.[38]

Astley was preoccupied by a 'geometry of living', some kind of 'single theorem' that could explain what human beings did to each other and why.[39] She could summon mathematical metaphors with surprising ease. Paul Vespers's description of his relationship with the musical genius Holberg and his ménage in *The Acolyte* is an early example: 'Take four points, A, B, C, and D, and join them with lines that connect but never never never intersect. You have us, a trapezoid of needs that pass from point A to point B to point C to point D and that is all.'[40]

Henceforth, ideas for Astley would always need to be logically connected. In fact, this went back to her early poetry, a bringing together in words of 'The wanting and the will at variance'.[41] It became a special kind of mathematics for her; in later books her 'vanishing points' would draw on Euclidean geometry, parallel lines that could never meet. These were *her* emotional and intellectual *sorites*, that is, forms of argument with each premise leading to a conclusion, which then forms the premise of the next argument. For Astley, it offered a set of endless alternatives with which to map the genealogy of character.[42]

All this careful plotting in her writing was at variance with Astley's public face. When she rushed to take up a position on something she often became a victim of her own angry persona. A colleague at Macquarie remembers her response to a young male student wearing a fashionable chest-revealing shirt. 'You'd walk into the staffroom and Thea would be complaining about the flaunting of flesh … There was something contrived in that anger, I always thought.' It was as if her response had been designed to attract attention rather than to express any real disgust.[43] Astley's response to openly discussing sexuality was complex and ambivalent.

But Astley was learning to harness anger creatively. A picaresque sweep of revenge pranks can be found throughout her novels (slingshots, models of 'The Big Developer', after the real-life Big Pineapple in Queensland), characters firing 'cannons of classical music' in protest. Not that Astley was really angry – the Macquarie years were proving vital for her wellbeing. Three years of university teaching had alleviated her nervous energy but there were signs that life was still taxing. Eileen wrote, glad that Astley had a 'day bed' in her office to help her relax 'mentally as well as physically' but she had 'no confidence in psychiatrists'. Eileen was referring to Phil, whose whole personality in her view had changed since he had 'electrical treatment in Melbourne'.[44]

Astley had been in regular contact with Phil, had recently sent him a clipping of a newspaper profile on her. Phil's position in the Order and the closeness to Eileen must have made it difficult for him to openly support his sister, at least to his mother. His sister's critique of Catholicism had been an embarrassment: there was gossip about him having asked for her books to be removed from the Campion House library.[45]

As the years passed, however, Eileen had become more capable of praise. In 1969 she confessed in a letter that she read Thea's books 'often' and thought the 'satire brilliant'.[46] Perhaps this praise was too little too late, but it is one the few letters Astley kept, a rare tangible sign of maternal support long withheld.

With both of her children experiencing such acute mental suffering in middle age, Eileen's letter is a remarkable tribute to the powers of parental denial; she had always thought the cure for everything was good food, lots of rest and fresh air and exercise. She was now just on seventy years of age and various irritabilities crept into her letters. The smallest thing could attract attention, such as Ed adding his name as a P.S. (an afterthought not appreciated), or a letter arriving days later than expected. Any cash money sent by Thea and Jack was accounted for in detail in a follow-up letter, all purchases itemised according to their practical use (cloth for dress lengths and cash for a holiday). Astley was like her mother in this way: never tardy in taking great pains to write thankyou notes for kindnesses, no matter how slight.

12

North of nostalgia

North: Some Compass Readings: Eden
Title of first story in *Hunting the Wild Pineapple*
by Thea Astley, 1979[1]

In 1976 Astley gave an ABC radio interviewer a copy of her most recent author biography, asking for it to be read aloud at the start of the program. It is an updated version of the style of biography Astley had given A&R in 1958, almost twenty years before. 'Astley, Thea, aged 50, mother of one son, Ed, Queenslander who is having a late maturing love affair with the place though she's been in exile in New South Wales for the last 17 years, teacher, at it for 30 years though being a tutor at Macquarie University hasn't eased the pain of marking essays and last of all, writer.'[2]

The deliberate order of the items in this checklist seems especially pointed. Apparently little had changed in the way Astley thought of herself and her writing, at least publicly. Fifteen years later, in a 1990 interview, she said she had been 'at it' so long that she was tired. ('Yes, I'm dispirited. It doesn't seem worth it really.') And besides, essay marking was like 'digging ditches – writing too – from one ditch to another'.[3]

But she had returned to her Dream Country, literally this time. In 1973 she and Jack purchased a north Queensland 'shack' near Kuranda, a 'wild dream of achieving a Somerset Maugham existence – keeping a low profile', Astley had said. The university semesters afforded the opportunity for extended stays up north. They could live there for a few months of the year.[4] By the early 1970s Ed was out of school and independent.

Astley's rather bleak self-portrait on radio was rescued, even overturned, by a spliced-in segment from her former student Mark Macleod, who was teaching at Macquarie and who knew her well. His words gave listeners a glimpse of an 'alternative Astley' – the way she often appeared to others – as a person of extraordinary energy 'kung-fu-ing the lift button'. Here was Thea Astley as a person of simple tastes, whose favourite food was poached eggs on toast, who admired the then PM's wife, Margaret Whitlam, not just for her politics but 'for appearing in public having only run a comb through her hair'. Astley described the university cafeteria as a 'Clark's Rubber Store because of its cannelloni and pizza with a wallpaper print on top' – but went there anyway to buy chips, though she enjoyed complaining about the lack of salt.[5]

Astley didn't set out to assert herself in the English Department and in time she formed strong friendships within the broader university. Instead, she concentrated on this new kind of teaching, with small groups, treating her students to a *tête-à-tête* with Ms Thea Astley, the writer who was their tutor. Astley influenced a generation of young people, a surprising number of whom became writers, broadcasters, editors or publishers.[6] Broadcaster Jennie Brockie remembers Astley's verbal directness, her seemingly 'huge authority' within the department.[7]

University teaching continued to be the tonic Astley had badly needed. Neighbours were seeing the 'old Thea' again, enthusing wildly over any of these new students she thought brilliant. She often mentioned Mark Macleod. As a young student he had not expected to be bowled over by the attractive woman in her forties who 'walked into the room, lit up a cigarette and started talking about D. H. Lawrence and sex'.[8] Astley made sure she never presented the face that her students were expecting. As in her previous teaching positions, it was that quality of frankness that thrilled her pupils. Many were young people who were forming their first sexual relationships, and here was an older adult prepared to talk openly and honestly about sex in the literature they were studying. Astley could challenge students to think beyond their own sexual freedom, to the 'corroding effect that sexual relationships have'.[9]

It was rare for her to speak about her own writing – her presence spoke for it – but her personal contact was encouraging for any aspiring writers. Many of the mature-aged women students saw her as a role model: an academic taken seriously as an author, who was also a wife and mother. One of Astley's female students majoring in English observed that Astley did not discriminate about disciplines; she concentrated on each individual, on his or her capacity. Astley became a key person who encouraged this student to go as far as she could with Earth Sciences. This former student remembered Astley teaching Australian literature with passion, and with a strong historical and social inflection. In this, she resembled Leonie Kramer, whose lectures on Australian literature also included history and sociology.[10] Kramer and Astley were of the same generation, almost exactly the same age, in fact. By this time Kramer was a highly influential person in Australian literary circles, especially because she had taken up an appointment at the University of Sydney in 1968 as the first female professor of Australian literature.

Astley loved her student audience and was quizzical during lectures in a way that appealed to them.[11] In their eyes she was a refreshing addition to scholarly life. Astley and the poet Alex Craig were some of the first writers to encourage what would become a national push to involve creative writers in study at university.

Astley formed very close relationships with her students. The young men, she thought, were not unlike Ed, who by 1973 was about their age. The mother of a son is perhaps bound to identify particularly with young men, and Astley was part mother, part teacher and part chum. When Mark Macleod took his first steps towards postgraduate work in the same department, Astley was firmly behind him. They became close friends. He came to understand Astley's contradictions fully but unlike others he accepted them more readily. He was softly spoken, accommodating and alert to the sensitivities in a woman he had already known and liked as his tutor. It was to Mark that Astley ventured her candid views on the academy as well as staff attitudes towards her.

Astley had sensed a lack of approval from other women on staff and often felt slighted. Rightly or wrongly she felt they regarded her as privileged, somehow exempt from the ordinary issues of domestic life. This irritated her: 'I cook dinner and I write books,' she insisted; she felt her workload to be very unfair and sexist.[12] She saw in the academic hierarchy the same order of jobs she had seen in the Catholic Church: the men taking the honours and the women doing the lion's share of the work. As a tutor she worked longer teaching hours than other academics, and her thorough marking habits, carried over from schoolteaching, almost doubled the time it took her to comment on student work.

The role Astley loved most was that of self-appointed counsellor, and she was good at it. Advice beyond academic matters was her specialty. Married woman who were falling out with their husbands, or were just confronted by life, made their way to her office. The tears flowed. One story often told is of how Astley suggested that an appointment at the hairdresser was what her student really needed. Above all, these new interactions were great material for her novels.

However, this could lead to a perception that she wasn't really listening, but observing for her own purposes. Mark Macleod once confronted her by saying that as a young student he had always felt she was not listening to him as much as watching his hands and face. The remark was met with a silence that he knew was her way of acknowledging a truth. He also saw that she had a way of backing out of an unwelcome conversation, usually by lighting up a cigarette, though she rarely retracted what she had said.[13] This was unfortunate since what might have begun in humour could easily turn to anger – for instance, a conversation that allowed her to say anything about women as second-class citizens. It could be too much for people. Astley 'acted out' much as she had as a schoolgirl, and would think nothing of leaving a staff meeting suddenly, announcing a dubious attack of diarrhoea. Her anger over time seemed to attach itself to all manner of subjects: the university, students who shouldn't pass, academics, anything in the political order she didn't like. She was often quick to judge others but confident in her own judgement. If she got it wrong, she would move on without feeling guilty. Her targets, mostly those in power, hardly needed protection.

Not all students loved Astley's style – her sarcasm in person could be as scathing as in her novels. Anyone who was noticeably late for a lecture or tutorial suffered nothing short of public humiliation. Astley did encourage young writers, but not indiscriminately.

Jeff McMullen, who later became a respected senior journalist with the ABC, was one of the chosen. When they met just after Astley had joined Macquarie, he was studying part-time as well as working for the ABC. It was a very difficult time in his own life. His mother, who had had fallen into a coma and suffered partial paralysis from a car accident a year earlier, had died from her injuries, at barely fifty years of age. It was not difficult for Astley to enter imaginatively into the sheer magnitude and terror of that loss to such a young man. She was clearly affected, and all she could say, McMullen remembers, looking at him as if he were a child just home from school, was, 'You have to write about it.' He did.

His drafts were highly personal and a bit strange – 'schizo', Astley said – but she listened, and listened. It was this listening that McMullen took into his own journalism, understanding the space that silence gives to story. Their friendship became a place of remembrance for his mother. She had been a woman of a type Astley would have liked, wide-trouser-wearing, practical, country-born; Astley warmed to her idea that a white tablecloth and a single rose on the dinner table were all that were required for a civilising influence. To those in pain Astley could give the kind of advice that could have been expected only from a family member.[14] Both Macleod and McMullen, in their different ways, became for Astley the sons who would never leave.

McMullen went on to travel the world covering major news events and Astley would pump him for all the human detail, mentally writing it down. This was not prurient curiosity: she wanted to understand and to pit external events against her own prevailing fatalism. Her interest, McMullen noticed, was almost obsessively in the small things, joy and struggle, family as the centre of aspiration, tolerance and endurance. Behind this she had a strong sense of 'the feminine struggle constantly in motion' as Astley endlessly visited and revisited questions of relationships, fairness and balance.

McMullen was fascinated to see that the long partnership between Thea and Jack was in a state of constant evolution. He knew nothing of Astley's private life at this time and was instead struck by the way Thea – obviously so individual and spreading her wings at Macquarie – had not 'signed off' on Jack nor the marriage, amid what were often plainly scenes of exasperation with each other.

Jack's world-weariness – usually about politics – seemed to infect Thea with a kind of benign resignation. Jack more than anyone wanted her to be herself, so much so that McMullen came to see that 'the two of them knew what they had'. Jack at this time was glad of the stability that the Macquarie position had given to Thea. He never gave in to Thea's manufacture of drama, but always tried to make sure they worked out whatever the problem was. However, increasingly and willingly Jack went his own way and Thea hers, by mutual arrangement. In the next few years Jack would travel alone to the US.[15]

Students probably sensed some drama behind the politics of the department when Astley spoke cuttingly of her colleagues and other writers, as she sometimes did. She continued to feel undervalued and out of place, an unresolvable issue since promotion would always be tied to scholarly publication and Thea did not publish in scholarly journals. It was also fertile territory for stored resentments ('what would I know about it, I'm just a writer'). In fact, the creative writing program was a niche for Astley in a way that a scholarly position could never be.

Astley knew that academic rigour had little to do with the originality she wanted to encourage, but she would turn people inside out, exposing vanity or conceit. With only four or so students in a tutorial, this method naturally created nervous tension. It was difficult for students to feel entirely safe; one former student recalled the personal dynamics of the discussion taking over from concerns about the literary quality of the work. Astley came across as accomplished, razor-sharp and disarmingly sure of her own originality, but she also gave her students a chance to shine. She usually praised the student's voice, and inflated talent with compliments, saying, 'I wish I could have done that at eighteen.' She also managed to pull the more talented writers away from mimicry and towards a critical sense of their own work and its value.[16]

In her teaching Astley indulged her passion for contemporary American writers – especially Cheever and Updike – not always in the traditional syllabus; she had no interest in drawing up boundaries of value and form. Macquarie was still making itself up as it went along. Students walked through the grass paddocks to class and the main library was still under construction; the first groups to study creative writing were abuzz with the sense of being part of an important experiment. The atmosphere was almost intimate, apart from the monolith of the W6 building, where you could find Astley's door always open.

The writer Wendy Blaxland came to think of Astley as everybody's favourite.[17] This was true for those she favoured: she made sure only the most able students were allowed to take her classes in creative writing. Among the chosen ones, at student parties, she would join in (having a little to drink but never too much); always the informal staff member sans title. The students heard all about Ed, of course, and indulged her unabashed devotion and candour. Astley made her priorities abundantly clear: immediate family then writing. When she was writing a novel, the practicalities of teaching became as they had always been, a conflict between duty and what she knew she was meant to do.

Astley was ferocious in defence of standards of literacy – she was prepared to fail students who wrote illiterate essays – and there were heated arguments on campus about the place of Australian history or literature in the new curriculum. The move from temporary accommodation to the new North Ryde buildings had spotlighted claims for a new 'Australian university'. In this climate Astley – as serious as anyone about this – was nevertheless determined not to take the situation seriously. She moved into her new office: bare walls, empty bookshelves. Staff shuffled about quietly arranging stationery and chairs when a voice rang out in the corridor: 'But there aren't any books!' The next thing they heard was Astley's very recognisable 'posh voice' on the phone: 'Is that the bookshop? Could you send a yard of Penguins, please.'

There was a chumminess that hid some unpleasant staff relations of the kind sometimes peculiar to university English departments. Macquarie's combination of literature and linguistics was somehow uncomfortable for those involved in pure literary studies, with the belief that literature was 'the key to understanding the universe' as many, including Astley, felt.[18] It was with lecturers in the History department, only one floor below – not necessarily her colleagues in English – with whom Astley found camaraderie. What these friends had in common was that they were all – like American Joan Kirkby – outsiders in some way. John Ryan, in History, was like Astley, having arrived at university teaching via schoolteaching. Even her

English department colleague John Bernard had an unusual previous life as a chemistry buff.

John Bernard's office was directly opposite Astley's and, like her, he started the day early in the morning. Astley was dashing – always in a hurry, it seemed – and anxiously muttering that she had knocked someone over, or run into a car or something. John was a calm person and his demeanour worked a charm with Astley at such times. He knew she liked to be contrary; had heard she took a book and ostentatiously read it while at a Test cricket match. On one occasion the odd drop of slivovitz Astley happened to have in her office (the presence of plum brandy there was a long story) added to the mix. John Bernard knew Astley was not any kind of a drinker but somehow this crazy out-of-character act matched the moment. Exhausted after late lectures Astley the non-drinker now took to ordering exotic high-powered tipples – the more elaborate the name or colour the better.[19]

It was Bernard who witnessed at close hand the steady rise of Astley's resentment about her academic status, and he noticed that this would break out and become attached to literary matters. He said that 'when Colleen McCullough's *The Thorn Birds* was so successful Thea became paralytic with rage', claiming that she was much better and got no recognition.[20] When Macquarie wanted to give Astley an honorary doctorate years later, she flatly refused. She would never forgive the university for what she considered its lack of regard for her.

In John Ryan and John Bernard, Astley found two men she could be frank with about her life, including her marriage, and she often spoke graphically about sex. 'Ya gotta read *Lolita*,' she'd urge John Ryan. 'Just imagine all those men driving in cars, sitting there with testicles and balls, squashed to nothing,' she'd say to Bernard.

In the end John Bernard found it hard to know exactly what Astley thought of men, or whether to take any of what she said seriously. John Ryan, too, wondered the same but in relation to the Astley marriage. Jack was somehow central to her views but he seemed a remote figure, watching. 'He had a stand-back assessment of things and people – as if his work at the Conservatorium meant he was used to dealing with erratic people,' said Ryan.[21] Dinner parties with Macquarie colleagues were odd, with Thea's male friends privy to a side of Thea that Jack seemed to understand, yet nobody knew to what extent. Thea appeared to be breaking the rules of married life and Jack didn't seem to mind. Her colleagues liked Thea as a woman and saw a soft underside to her brashness. For all the talk they had as friends, much of it gossip about colleagues, Astley gave off the sense that her world was larger than that. The world of university pettiness, however irritating, really didn't impinge. 'If you went over there, there was just the typewriter on a table. That was it,' said John Bernard. It certainly was. For three years before publication of *The Acolyte* in 1973 Astley had been working long hours, writing, teaching and lecturing. She was also the watchful mother of a teenage boy and maintained a range of literary friendships, while sometimes attending to the development of her own literary profile.

This attention to her reputation was not always to her liking; she was becoming alert to being manipulated, and her position about this could be contradictory. She was sensitive to any suggestion of her success 'as a woman', though she was herself an advocate for women's opportunities; she was pro-women and anti-feminist. She did everything she could to help married women previously unable to study at university to enter the system now that the Whitlam no-fees era had arrived. She said, 'If they do not get jobs then they will go mad. They cannot be satisfied with the traditional routine of family charring and social outings. They want something more.'[22]

Yet, in conversation she reverted to her 1960s comment that 'women are sad things really'. Unable to resist one-liners – her father's failing – she would describe the university as 'menopause manor'. Like many women of her generation, she had internalised a male negative view of women, and it was bound to tie her up in knots. It showed in her work: one critic commented that the women in her novels were 'mostly nervy if not neurotic ... unsure of themselves ... building or shoring up defences ... often at the mercy of men and abased by them'.[23] It would be a long time before her 'vein of bitchy black comedy' (as *The Acolyte* was dubbed) could be understood as a legitimate critique of male–female relations, and in the early 1970s the author was hardly obliging.[24]

Even twenty years later, she was equivocal about the 'F' word, saying in 1990: 'Even now I'm not entirely comfortable with feminism. I think it has become a perverted term rather than a description of natural justice.'[25] She added, 'I'm a normal heterosexual I think, I hope – but I grew up in an era when women weren't supposed to have any thoughts at all, and if they did express thoughts then either no attention was paid to them or they were considered brash and aggressive ... I sound aggressively feminist, don't I?'[26]

If feminists wanted her in their camp, they had picked the ultimate non-follower, for Astley still rejected any '-isms'.

She thought nothing of declaring that 'all women are whores' and, like the writer Katharine Susannah Prichard before her, she tended to look at women in terms of 'an idealised self', or a 'despised alternative'.[27] The masculine women in Astley's novels are like those evoked by Henrietta Drake-Brockman's phrase 'always the better men'.[28] She hated the 'approved whores' – married women – and the 'tea-makers for God' women of her Catholic upbringing. Women still had few alternatives that she could see; little chance to 'invent their own weather'.

This tension between apparent feminism and her innate conservatism was impossible for Astley to resolve. She did not believe one generation learned from the next. Hers, she said, was a 'feeble hand flapping in protest' in the face of what would always be an inequality between men and women.[29] Fatalism was a stronger force in her than feminism could ever be.

If she was a divisive figure at Macquarie – she could 'cut through people' – Astley didn't have a lot of time to dwell on it.[30] Her twin roles as teacher and writer did not coexist comfortably unless Astley was editing a book of stories (as she did with the Angus & Robertson anthology *Coast to Coast*) or when she set for her students books by writers she admired who were also friends, such as Hal Porter (she set his *Handful of Pennies* at the earliest opportunity). Porter, she knew, was writing *Mr Butterfly*, and a collection of his stories was being put together by Leonie Kramer. Much as she was pleased for Porter, and disdainful of academic work, Astley knew she had not yet received that kind of attention from such a noted literary academic.

Sometimes she ran to the limelight. Astley was adamantly anti-censorship even though she found quite a lot of the emerging fiction of her contemporaries in bad taste. She had just given a lecture, 'The Author as a Critic of Society', in which she referred to 'the excremental vision of *The Vivisector*' and to the 'trend towards sickness' in the work of Patrick White, Hal Porter and Tom Keneally.[31] Having heard that A&R were fighting a censorship case against the banning of Philip Roth's *Portnoy's Complaint*, she went public in her support of her publisher, unhesitatingly writing herself into the public drama. Patrick White gossiped that she had been 'trying to work everything to appear as a witness'.[32]

Porter was keeping her up to date on A&R's dealings with him (he was cross, privately, at least to Astley, about the appalling number of spelling and other mistakes in the Kramer collection). He still did a good line in flattery ('dazzling Thea'). It was not all innocent goodwill: Porter was conscious of Astley's favour to him – setting his texts in her courses – and knew how to ask for a favour as well. As the 1971 academic year drew to a close, he wondered whether she might use her student groups to conduct a 'Gallup Poll' of their favourite Porter stories. 'Sorry to bother you, honey, with my whimsical notions,' he said, but he asked anyway.[33] Astley would have noticed how little in these letters was about *her* work. She had had a completed novel at A&R for weeks, and had heard nothing.

Like many other Australian writers, Astley was genuinely anxious about developments at A&R. The appointment of Richard Walsh as publishing manager in 1972 had brought various long-standing in-house hostilities to a head there, and these were to affect the next period of Astley's writing career. It would be the end of the only style of Australian publishing she knew, but she also remembered their failings: their sale of *The Slow Natives* as a paperback to Sun Books, without much apparent success in sales, which had made her want to recover her rights to that title. However, Beatrice Davis eventually wrote that *The Acolyte* was 'very stylish' and 'the best thing Thea has done' with only a quibble about the 'comic ending'.[34]

But the two male readers had not recommended the manuscript for publication. They said the male narrator was not always convincing, that the tone was 'negative, sardonic and self-destructive'. The conclusion was that it was 'not an important work of literature'; and one reader in particular could see no reason why it would sell.[35]

Astley knew nothing of this but would have guessed that London, as of old, had been invoked as the arbiter of decision-making about Australian titles. It is possible Davis had told Astley about her own battle to remain at A&R, for Astley wrote a rather cryptic letter to her with the overtly droll comment that she had written the book 'with an eye to an Aussie market rather, as I've never been what one might call a big seller in UK'.[36] Astley's sixth novel, 'Thurlow's Answer', had been rejected, with no Davis to save it. 'Death should be distinguished from dying, with which it is often confused,' Astley had written on the manuscript.[37]

In Australian publishing there was an increasing emphasis on commercially viable decisions; it seemed to Astley a concocted and expedient form of reasoning – a version of 'literary books can't make money' thinking – but there were harsh realities overtaking Angus & Robertson. A&R was short on resources and the publishing side of the business was in substantial debt. In-house tensions over editorial control were mounting. Davis was at the centre of this, but by August of 1972 the publication of *The Acolyte* was already secure and Astley could rest and wait.

There would never be a time when Astley was happy with the attention, or type of attention, paid to her work. If this mattered more now, it was because – as she said to anyone who asked – *The Acolyte* was her personal favourite. The satire allowed Astley to disguise reality with fiction; in her *roman à clef* she had vented her rage at 'followers' of all kinds, which could be read as a critique of 'followers' of the literary critical establishment. She had left cryptic codes within the novel – about sight/blindness, genius/follower – a running analogy for the whole literary critical exercise: 'Ultimately of course their names are wrapped round meat.'[38]

Versions of this were repeated in interviews Astley would give later in life – 'I suppose the critics are the flies on the meat, aren't they?'[39] Or later still, with a touch of mordant fatalism, 'Books die within six months, don't they? Unless you've written *War and Peace*.'[40] In *The Acolyte*, for the first time, the narrator's verbal mannerisms resembled their creator's. Passive, cynical, self-aggrandising and melodramatic in his role, Paul Vespers is difficult to like, no better than the blind monster-musical genius Holberg. Perhaps this was one answer to Eileen's complaint about Astley's 'unlikeable' characters: make them all equally unlikeable.

Astley's relationship with a number of people, especially her publishers, was now 'locked in irons'. She knew she had to a take a more assertive approach to the publication of her novels. However, the reputation as a novelist she would one day enjoy among Australia's publishers owes a great deal to the dying days of her relationship with Angus & Robertson. When publishing manager John Abernethy died suddenly, Richard Walsh took over the position. He recalled inheriting 'a nest of vipers', an atmosphere of resentment between Abernethy and the editors who answered to him (Beatrice Davis and Douglas Stewart). Walsh agreed with Abernethy's unpopular view that A&R's comparative failure to encourage new writers was largely due to the conservatism of Davis and Stewart. He felt that younger writers couldn't relate easily to Davis, that a style of 'literary peerage' had developed.[41] Needless to say this reflected on favoured writers, Astley among them. Ironically, it had been Davis who, back in the 1940s and 1950s, had modernised the company's list.

There was some truth in Walsh's criticism. Davis had an editorial manner that suggested hauteur and her assumption of authority could make her intimidating, especially to younger writers. According to Walsh, new in-house literary opinion sent Douglas Stewart into a rage, which caused him to leave. Davis chose to follow him: she was not sacked, as was commonly believed at the time. Observers asked why Davis, who had been at A&R for over thirty-five years, would have left in an apparent fit of pique. Davis also told people, including Astley, that she had been fired. Walsh was at pains to point out, when asked, that he had offered Davis a consultancy role that she had refused, using in subsequent discussions, the rueful phrase 'we had to let her go'. [42]

For Beatrice to be suddenly gone from A&R (Beatrice to Astley *was* A&R) seemed utterly implausible. There was certainly widespread indignation among the old loyal A&R authors at the way the publisher seemed prepared to lose its two long-serving and esteemed editors. Several of Davis's favourite writers, including Astley and Hal Porter, left A&R in protest and loyalty.

Astley still depended on Davis for editorial support, even though she could be discouraging. Astley had been researching the Kanakas, and Davis had warned that 'the South Seas is, for some unknown reason, repulsive to the G[eneral]. P[ublic]'.[43] But Davis continued to support her favourite author. She was the chairman of the Miles Franklin judging panel in 1972, and gave the $1,250 award to Astley for *The Acolyte*. It was Astley's third Miles Franklin Award. By 1974 Davis had moved to Thomas Nelson publishers.

Astley was angry with A&R for other reasons. Her award-winning novel *The Acolyte* had been poorly distributed; Astley was appalled to find that a large number of copies were still stacked in the warehouse. Here was her most recent book, the winner of her third Miles Franklin Award, and she still had no confidence in being published with commercial respect. This mattered – would always matter – to her. Her attitude was still a little more forthright than that of other Australian writers of literary fiction. Early in 1973 she had initiated an exchange of letters, some legal:

> Dear Richard [Walsh] and Michael Johnston,
> I'm unsure how to address this as my last letter addressed to Mr Johnston was answered by Mr Walsh … I have decided to solve it by writing to you both.
>
> Actually I had given up hope of an answer when, with mind-boggling anachronism, the publicity section sent me with their compliments a copy of the *Sun Herald* review of *The Acolyte* which was published (the review) last August or early September. Tell them they can stop sending that particular review now. I have five copies. It would be funny, wouldn't it – it IS funny! – but it's sad …[44]

Astley was now intent on selling overseas rights, particularly in the US, and several American publishers expressed some interest, including Viking. However, they did not act on this for more than a decade (with *Beachmasters* in 1985). Astley was faced with a situation where all her previous titles were in the care of a publisher whom she had left and with a publishing manager who was not personally committed to her writing. Walsh seemed to like her company but she knew he felt that she over-wrote.[45] As editor of the magazine *Nation Review*, he had attempted already to edit one of her stories – a far more rigorous edit than Davis would have given her.

It was easy for Astley to make Walsh a focus of the resentment about A&R's treatment of her writing that had been building for years. She requested a reversion of rights on various earlier titles, particularly anxious – somewhat unfairly, considering how recently it had been published – to regain control of *The Acolyte*. A&R refused, giving Astley the rights to the previous *A Boat Load of Home Folk* instead. There was some suggestion that *The Slow Natives* might go into the new Paperback Classics series. Astley commented that this would be acceptable only if the paperback binding glue, so weak that the 'books don't stick together', could be stronger – an unusually understated criticism of what was by common consent slipshod binding.[46]

Tension continued to develop between Astley and her former publishers. She was now convinced that A&R were deliberately acting against her interests, and stayed on the lookout for misdemeanours. She suspected that other publishers (Penguin, for instance) had been or would be interested in *The Acolyte* but were being put off by Walsh. Astley asked Anne Godden, the publisher at Thomas Nelson, to enquire about Penguin's supposed approaches, leading Godden's colleague Bob Sessions to comment to her that he had 'the distinct feeling that we are being played off against one another!'[47] He was right.

Astley was determined to look out for her own interests and by 1980 she had finally reclaimed the rights to *The Acolyte*. From here on she would remain vigilant about the performance of her publishers, dealing with three in the next ten years alone. In 1980 it came to light that only a few years after their falling out, back in 1977, Walsh had sold a large quantity of authors' manuscripts to the Mitchell Library for a lump sum. Astley had not been told about this, had received no financial recompense and, outraged all over again, spoke out against A&R and its director. Walsh could not be as certain of the legal situation as he appeared because he had requested some confirmation of such undertakings from Davis about the storage of Astley's manuscripts, which Astley probably knew about.[48] It therefore came as no surprise that Walsh didn't want paperback rights to the 1979 story collection *Hunting the Wild Pineapple* due to 'our present strained relations with Thea'. And so the relationship between an award-winning Australian novelist and Australia's oldest literary publisher came to an end after more than twenty years.[49]

13

Living is serial

Birth, marriage, death, re-birth. They're the only endings, traditional culminations for living – for books, even – and what bogus back-watering punctuation they are! Living is serial, an unending accretion of alternatives.

Hunting the Wild Pineapple by Thea Astley, 1979[1]

Astley was embarking on another stage of life. Jack was now only about half-a-dozen years from retirement and Ed was a young man. Nevertheless, she continued to fuss over her only son. When she burst into the department corridor at Macquarie talking about cars that might 'warm a young man's testicles', colleagues were straining to discern the poetic reference.

Astley's particular form of motherly worship had taken the form of searching obsessively for Ed's all-important first car. The plan was to buy it herself, but Ed would be the main driver. It had to be large, in case he had an accident, and she searched all over Sydney for something suitable. She settled upon a Swedish car, a Saab with heated seats that the ad said offered 'protection for the urogenital system'.[2] Previous Astley vehicles had been the humble VW Beetle and a Toyota Corolla, both a far cry from the very expensive $5,000 she paid for this new European car. The choice was pure Astley: if Ed was to have the best it might as well be amusing and exotic.

However taut – even strangling – the strings of motherhood seemed to others, possibly including Jack, this apparent over-protectiveness was not the whole picture. Astley was utterly committed to making sure Ed did not have to live with the social censure about sexuality that she had endured as a young woman, forgetting that as a young man from a later generation this would not be his lot. In this respect, despite appearances, she gave him unusual licence. Astley delighted in removing life obstacles for Ed and she tried very hard not to overwhelm him with her own expectations. To those who knew Thea well this 'free zone' seemed more an extension of her own anxieties. One friend commented: 'She was determined to make his life as uncomplicated as she could – perhaps to make her own life smooth? – but she didn't let him develop.'[3]

While other parents fretted about their children undertaking university degrees that would lead to prosperous professional lives, Thea and Jack were happy with Ed's decision to study guitar at the Conservatorium. Ed had taken up piano at ten with his mother's encouragement, learning from a teacher Jack knew from the Conservatorium, but Ed switched to guitar two years later. His parents both felt that study for a more stable career might be necessary one day but music, life, mattered more now. Ed, whom everyone suspected wasn't especially interested in what his mother might want anyway, nor at this stage the books she wrote, seemed more like Jack than his mother: even-tempered and savvy about the world. He did not seem to need extreme measures of protection.

Local parents speculated about possible 'Thea–Ed' scenarios. They said they couldn't see Ed staying at home much beyond school (he didn't) and wondered how Thea would cope with his absence. Others tut-tutted about the teenage sexual antics they suspected took place at home when Thea and Jack were not there. Not Astley. She made a point of leaving the house, 'so that [the kids] can have their time,' she said as 'eyes widened'.[4] If this was parental neurosis, it was an unusual expression of it. But then Astley had once been that young woman in small towns that 'lay idle under the hot sun waiting to devour reputations' and so now seemed like as good a time as any to turn brazen.[5]

In allowing Ed such freedom Astley might also have been trying – albeit in an odd and even desperate way – to lengthen Ed's time at the family home. If this was her intention it failed; Ed embarked on a spirited series of relationships in the well-off eastern suburbs on the other side of Sydney, often with older partners. His activities provided Astley with a whole new set of tales about him; the Smiths next door grew used to multiple versions of 'he's seeing this girl and I don't like her'. Ed was coming home with expensive gifts; Thea worried about why. Jack, with typical bluntness, answered her: 'Because he's good at it, Thea!'[6] Not so funny was that Ed preferred calling on the phone to visiting. He was gone.

'Time' really was 'the great heel', as Astley had once scribbled in her writing notebook. Lives were brief: 'you live, you work, you die', as she was fond of saying. In this mood she received a letter of thanks from her old All Hallows' teacher Sister Mary Claver. Along with other past pupils, Astley had written a retirement tribute to the sister for *The Sydney Morning Herald*. It was long and congratulatory, written from the perspective of a colleague rather than a former student, and full of news about the old days at the school. It took Astley back to the days of the Warwick evacuation during her final school year – almost the same age as Ed was now – and their 'open-air' classrooms 'under the pepperinas'.[7] Life had a way of accreting in layers.

When Ed was in his senior years at school and could be left on his own, Jack and Thea travelled regularly to the first holiday house they had bought at Ball Bay, thirty-five kilometres north of Mackay. It was a simple beach house – it cost less than $1,000 – and its simplicity made it look a little like the Epping home. It was not remote or north enough for Astley. They decided to keep an eye out for another property near Cairns, something more than a beach shack, with a view to living there permanently later. Astley was now thirty years away from her direct experience of teaching in small towns in Queensland. Yet everything about her writing was subject to a force of exaggeration, a subconscious antagonism, which found its locus in the tropical far north of her home state.

Astley purchased the next house (Jum Rum) in the little village of Kuranda, twenty-five kilometres northwest of Cairns, just off the road to the Barron Falls. This house was an interesting mix of stained glass and timber, all covered in vines and tropical vegetation – almost looking home-made, or even trendy. Balmain in the jungle it might have been, but it was not a lifestyle choice as much as an act of the imagination.

It had been a while coming. In 1971, when Astley toured Queensland on behalf of the Commonwealth Literary Fund, she had surprised herself in her encounters with isolated rural audiences in such towns as Mount Isa – bringing 'the miners to heel', as Porter had expressed it.[8] These were the same people she pilloried in her novels, though not apparently those who attended her readings. Engaging with such audiences was Astley's idea of sensibility in a hot climate. Not since the days of Barjai had she experienced this sense of culture besieged, undone by mediocrity and crass materialism. Astley even thought of dedicating her next novel to the avowedly anti-intellectual 'screwball' Joh Bjelke-Petersen, then premier of Queensland.[9] The fight was on: literature to the rescue.

Astley would soon be steeped in nostalgia, comparing the gallant efforts of the early settlers struggling to offer Shakespeare to miners with the 'middle-class pretensions of first-nighters in Sydney', forgetting for the moment that by education, disposition and cultural tastes she herself was one of those first-nighters.[10] The CLF experiences and those Queensland towns had melded in Astley's mind and were ideal settings for novels, especially the one she was now writing (*A Kindness Cup*).

She was also extending her imaginative range, looking at the colonial devastation of the South Pacific rim. Despite Davis's opinion that the public did not read novels set in the South Pacific, Astley continued researching the history of 'blackbirding' – native populations of Pacific islands forced or tricked into working in the canefields of the north – but that book (*Beachmasters*) was some years away. For the moment she was preoccupied with the absurdities of life in Queensland. She was attracted to perversity, and her home state delivered that.

Eileen, on the other hand, was dubious about Astley's possible move to the far north. She had urged her daughter to give up smoking so that she could enjoy this new home 'amongst the trees' – despite the 'mosquitoes' – and concluded with, 'the heat is dreadful'. Eileen would never understand why Astley rushed towards it.[11]

It was both incredible and somehow predictable that as an ex-but-always-to-be Queenslander, Astley would run into her own past, even in the far north. After almost forty years she wrote to Moira Knudson, her rebellious pal from All Hallows', asking whether Moira knew somewhere Astley and Jack could sit on top of a mountain in the rainforest and look over the sea and play loud lieder and chamber music. There must be total privacy and room for one very large piano.

After telling Astley that her books reminded her of the work of Carson McCullers – 'You couldn't have said a nicer thing,' Astley replied – Moira told her that a property right on the nearby creek had come onto the market. In no time at all Thea and Jack were looking at the Kuranda house they would buy, while Thea and Moira observed each other with the curiosity of girls who suddenly realised they were fifty years old.[12]

Meanwhile, Thea continued 'rushing about in Sydney', as Eileen saw it, and there was plenty of evidence that life back in town was indeed very, very busy. It was not just that Astley's life was full and her reputation developing rapidly; change was in the air, much of it brought on by the election of the Whitlam Labor government the previous year, in 1972. With that came the much-talked-of changes to cultural funding, with the Australia Council replacing the old Commonwealth Literary Fund. The cultural powerbrokers of the time, later to be called the 'first eleven', were to make up the first Literature Board. Astley was invited to join.

She was finding the work at Macquarie more than enough, with rising student numbers, and she was now being called upon for advice as an experienced member of staff. Without the title or the salary to match, she was less than flattered. She pushed on, quietly furious, unable to find people who would understand and care about her feelings. Several of Astley's award-winning books had been displayed at a university open day, and she took to pointing out how much more creative work she had produced than other staff members, many of whom were likely to be paid more than she. So the invitation to be a member of the Literature Board, a part-time commitment, was a welcome acknowledgement of her worth. This would not be about the academy: it was about books, *writers*, *her world*.

Many on the original Literature Board were people she knew: Richard Walsh, A. D. Hope, Elizabeth Riddell, Thomas Shapcott and Judah Waten, for example. Rodney Hall, an English-born writer from Brisbane whose path (surprisingly) had not crossed with hers at any point, had helped set up the new board. Astley worried about meeting him. Years back she had written a negative review of one of his books, saying that an Englishman couldn't write about Australia, a comment she now regretted.

From Hall's point of view, Astley had published a story about unpleasant characters that he was convinced were modelled on two of his closest friends. Without having met her, he decided he didn't like her. Astley could have guessed he would feel like this. Australia's literary community was a tight-knit one; Hall had not been in the group favoured by Beatrice Davis or Douglas Stewart. And Astley had her own bone to pick with newly appointed chair Nancy Keesing, who had written a negative review of *Boat Load*. There would always be this kind of tension in such circles with occasional genuine feuds, offset by what Astley called 'flummery gossip', which she enjoyed.

With the 1974 Adelaide Writers' Festival coming up, she decided the best thing was to be direct with Rodney Hall. She spotted him talking in a doorway, went straight to him and said, 'Oh, we haven't met and I've got a bone to unpick with you.' It was not friendship – yet – but Hall recalls it because 'it was such a ringing sort of thing. Very Thea, to start off with, "We've got a problem, let's see what it is."' She carried this approach into board meetings. Hall said that when Astley came out with 'incredibly definite ideas' at board meetings, often expressed humorously, they would lead to 'wonderful conversations because she wasn't locked in – she'd fire a whole lot of shots across the bow and see what came out of it'.[13]

Literature Board meetings were efficient and members got through a great deal of work, but with Astley the meetings were also fun. She could spark off others in the group who were also lively and outspoken characters. Members had dinner together after meetings and visited each other's homes. Partners, including Jack, added to the throng once the work was done.

The room was unapologetically smoke-filled. Between them, Astley and Fay Zwicky created an oxygen-free zone that would be impossible for today's non-smokers to survive. Michael Costigan, then director, thought the two women were very similar in personal style – throaty, confident and outspoken. While they 'talked kids' he appreciated that they seemed sympathetic to him as the father of a family of young children.

It was a friendly board during these years, and there was little open hostility about decisions. Astley was polite enough but others sensed ambivalence in her attitude towards government funding for writers. Her often generous attitudes always had an underside like this: she affected a 'nobody helped me and I did it, why can't they' attitude, which broke out now and then in off-the-cuff remarks.[14]

Astley had a similarly ambivalent response to the growth in university creative writing degrees, which she sent up even though she had been one of the first teachers of creative writing.

Like so many of her positions on issues, this condemnation of government support for writers didn't ring true in practice. Whenever Astley met beginner writers, she couldn't wait to share the hopes and woes of the 'craft'. She did this, while trying not to question government help for writers per se; indeed, she was well aware that she could never have written at least two of her books (*The Well Dressed Explorer* and *The Slow Natives*) without help from the Commonwealth Literary Fund.[15]

The hard work involved in being a board member must have weighed on Astley at this time: before external assessors were a part of the assessment process, the board members did all the work. This meant reading hundreds of applications from writers about proposed books, and dozens from publishers about subsidies for books they hoped to publish. Back in the early 1970s, Costigan recalls, Thea did not generally oppose many of the decisions, including a contentious publishing subsidy for the multinational William Collins, who were bringing out the monumental *Poor Fellow My Country* by Xavier Herbert. She was no fan of big money going to publishers (at the expense of writers, in her view) but she knew that an Australian novel that took on the dispossession of the land from its original inhabitants had to be published.

Aboriginal history was now in any case foremost in her mind. She had been appalled by the living conditions of Aboriginal families in the north, near her Kuranda house. She had just spent over two years, between 1972 and 1974, writing a novel based on an old true story from the area about an Aboriginal woman who was terrorised, chased and forced to suicide, child-in-arms, over a nearby cliff edge (known as 'The Leap').

Astley knew that this newest novel, *A Kindness Cup*, published in 1974, would bring nerve-wrecking public exposure because she was examining the politics of race. The central character is bitter teacher Tom Dorahy, who returns to the town where he had brought classical education to the unwilling outback inhabitants with a 'zealot's earnestness'.[16] The book is particularly violent – something Astley had objected to in a novel by the American author Robert Coover some years before.[17]

In a radio interview she had said that Australian writers were 'jumping on the US bandwagon' and that such issues were overriding the importance of character.[18] However, in writing a novel about the cruelty of white settlement and its effect on the Aboriginal people, she needed to describe physically gruesome episodes. It was the only outlet for her anger, apart from activism.

Jeff McMullen, now a friend of some years, had initially been surprised by Astley's empathy with the Aboriginal population near Kuranda. He knew that socially and politically he and Astley cared about the same things; their discussions were always animated. For Astley, the answer to 'what was to be done' always came back as 'she'd write the story of how it came to be'.[19]

When the heat wasn't overwhelming, Kuranda in the long university breaks breathed freedom into Astley's writing. She would always be drawn towards 'that do-it-tomorrow feeling ... the plants, the rainforest, the water cobalt off the shore, the tropicana'.[20] When Tom Dorahy announces, 'I'm single and thirty-seven and in love with landscape', it is a fair expression of Astley's sentiments at this later time in her life. Astley became defensive – 'I'm not really trying to be Jane Austen of the rainforest. The setting is as much an emotional one as a physical one' – and had to reclaim her work from the trivialising effects of the exotica of the north that she herself had nevertheless stamped on every page.[21]

It was hard for readers to decode this odd combination of 'stern high-mindedness' and 'a whole-hearted delight in the sensual qualities of the physical world'.[22] *A Kindness Cup* won the Melbourne *Age* Book of the Year Award in 1975 (worth $3,000 and therefore twice as much as the last Miles Franklin), only the second year of the award. The advance against royalties she had signed with Nelson publishers had been $600 on signature – prizes were becoming more generous than advances. Astley's change of direction and subject in an 'incipient tragedy' that 'degenerates into uneasy comedy' did worry some reviewers.[23] Some saw a writer running out of teachers, small towns and islands.

Astley felt hesitant about being seen as part of the established literary culture. New, younger writers had been the subject of discussion – not only at the Literature Board meetings but in publishing circles and in the press generally. The culture of publishing had changed as these emerging writers such as Peter Carey and Murray Bail were 'chatted up', encouraged and offered deals by publishers in competition.[24] Nobody was going to chat her up because, as she took to saying, she wasn't part of the 'ghetto de Balmain'.[25]

As a member of the board Astley saw some of this new writing, and was less than impressed with it. She was sensitive to what she saw as a lack of writing craft in these new works, all present-tense sludge piling up, with little authorial shaping. An in-house memo at Nelson paraphrases her: 'If only they could see the crap I've been reading accepted by other publishers.'[26] However, as she watched these new writers become increasingly prominent, she feared ending up left behind or overlooked as a writer. Her multifarious resentments now included lack of critical attention; publishers and their trickery; disrespect for the 'craft' of writing; disdain for the academy and its view of writing; poor treatment of her by Macquarie University; and declining literacy standards.

She had championed the cause of writing but was also convinced that these 'new writers' were getting serious critical attention that had been denied her. Frank Moorhouse and others were writing short fiction – Moorhouse's were 'discontinuous narratives' with a group of characters, known to each other, floating in and out of each other's story – but she had always written stories too. Astley chose not to acknowledge her very public awards, not to mention the growing list of her titles now coming out in paperback. Instead, she brooded over the worst examples of her treatment by journalists, such as the time *New Idea* magazine had run an article on her handwriting, describing it as 'slightly emotional but realistic' and asserting, 'I have to repeat that Ms Astley's writing shows a wonderful brain.'[27] No, she wasn't associated with the 'ghetto de Balmain', Astley's phrase for a local inner-city-based arts culture of younger writers she didn't in fact want to be part of, but she also didn't want to lose readers. Astley's need for approbation would always be too strong to moderate this mood. Mark Macleod wondered whether she was becoming a 'victim of her own diffidence'.[28]

Doubts fed other doubts. Years before, in *The Slow Natives*, she had written of the 'brain in splints limping home to its last haven'; now she felt as if hers were in the same situation, without the haven. On the surface everything was fine but there was always an underside. Ed was making great progress with his music – but what about a secure job? Her brother, Phil, was settled at Campion House in Melbourne but his fragility could not be denied; Eileen was less scornful than she had been but repeated herself in letters, her health declining. Evidently it was Thea's health that bothered her mother.

Thea and her family had survived Eileen's most recent visit well enough, with Jack doing the cooking and Ed offering a trip into the Conservatorium, but Astley sometimes found difficulty in enjoying even the pleasant things.[29] This was Eileen's last visit before Jack departed for his 1975 trip to the United States as a sixtieth birthday present to himself. Thea, who was to be a writer-in-residence at Rollins College, Florida, and Ed would join him later. It would be a welcome break for Jack and Thea. 'Thanks for putting up with me,' she had written in his birthday card.[30]

In the meantime, Astley got through at Macquarie as best she could. Little things niggled; her responses flooded even simple conversations with what seemed to others disproportionate angst. Astley took perverse amusement in her own rages.

She was enjoying a new-found public reputation as a curmudgeon. What did she have to lose? Her chief target was the 'numbers game' of education, the need to pass a certain proportion of students, who knew already that she could be more likely to fail them than other staff members might. This echoed her own irritation with the university's treatment of her. And besides, she always insisted on the primacy of correct as well as beautiful language. Speaking on radio in 1977 Astley was blunt: 'I do think the new systems that are less demanding of performing the basics have given an enormous tail to the unis.'[31] What she saw was like a beast, growing beyond its habitat; the politics of education driving it towards the commerce of numbers, with drastic results.

She had burst into print in the national newspaper *The Australian* on the same subject in 1975: 'Grammar' was 'now the dirtiest seven-letter word in the language,' she declared. Referring to Judith Wright's 'Bullocky', she quoted a student: 'In the poem "Bullocky" she describes the bollocks and their tracks that are gone and made what for a different type of life.'[32]

Frank Devine, who would later become a columnist and editor at *The Australian*, had sent the draft of Astley's article to the poet A. D. Hope, now nearing retirement from the Australian National University. His reply to Astley made writing the article – and the frosty looks in the staffroom – worth it for her. Hope reminded her of better days, 'that splendid lunch' at Macquarie with Alex Craig and Professor Piper, and her 'even more splendid irreverent asides – not always so *sotto voce* that their victims could miss them'.[33]

He had spotted a despairing recklessness that had crept into Astley's sense of persecution.

Jack's letters from the US, arriving almost weekly, had been a real comfort – pages and pages of news and concern for her. Astley did not express her bitterness about Macquarie. She was looking forward to her trip to the US the following year, a punishing backwards and forwards plan from Florida, to Orlando, Seattle, San Diego, and back to Florida, visiting university campuses. Ed would go his own way but fly in from Las Vegas to meet her in San Diego. Then there were four more years to her retirement in 1979, when she and Jack would move to Kuranda.

The first few months of 1976 passed without major event. Astley's university position was discussed without mention of retirement, and she agreed that she would like a lectureship. There were quite a few issues of concern closer to home. Eileen had developed the irritating habit of commenting on the works of Australian writers Astley was teaching; Patrick White's *The Vivisector*, she decided, should be banned.[34]

This might be ignored, but Phil was again not well, and that was much sadder. He never missed a family birthday and always visited when he passed through Sydney, preferring to stay at the Stella Maris Club for Catholic Seafarers than with his sister; some of his hideouts were exotic enough for Astley's novels. She enjoyed the warmth of their shared bond. He kept in touch – not just politely – but in letters fondly reminiscing about their favourite poems and music. She still had the poems he had written in 1943 as a novice priest for *The Canisian* – all Gerard Manley Hopkins-type imagism – and his musings on music in the form of poetry.

Astley had been a schoolgirl when she knew that she wanted to be in the world in a way that Phil wanted to be out of it. Music and poetry were pathways to another world, one they could both be in. Yet here was Phil all these years later, unable to hear confessions because of his poor hearing and unable to preach because of a nervous stutter. Eileen was depressed by Phil's fate, blaming it on the treatment for his previous breakdown.[35] Astley now recognised in letters the nervous mannerisms that seemed to belong to the whole family, each of them taking turns to worry out loud about someone tampering with the mail or trying to steal it.

Eileen was still living alone at the Ashgrove house but her future was becoming increasingly problematic. She was growing older and her memory was failing. Thea and Phil were in constant contact about her, though Phil did most of the writing. Astley promised him she would write to their mother every few weeks from overseas; Phil planned to be in Brisbane the following year. Neither of them expected Eileen to deteriorate quickly; they did not know what to expect from an elderly parent of increasing frailty.

This experience with the parent–child bond led Astley to look at her relationship with her own son. Perhaps because she had accomplished so much already with her writing, she could always see what motherhood had brought to her that nothing else could have or would do. She declared, 'I'd give all my books away for the privilege of having a child ... Ed was the best thing that ever happened to me in my life.'[36] Theirs had been a strong bond from the start and as Ed entered adulthood their witty rapport only got stronger. There were no jokes better than those they shared; Ed came to understand her not just as his mother but as the individual she was. He was exasperated by his mother's behaviour and their relationship was often tempestuous, but they could always overcome such times. Humour and music guaranteed a deep affection.

Astley's novels, and the stories she was now assembling for a collection to be called *Hunting the Wild Pineapple*, were full of portraits of sensitive young males, such as the narrator Keith Leverson (the young boy from the 1965 novel *The Slow Natives*). Beatrice Davis at Nelson was uncomfortable with Astley's shift in literary style from novel to short story, but also her change in tone, to harsher satire about 'youth'; she was writing about 'the modern young seeking escape and the good earth and the dole queue'.[37] Davis wrote to publishing director Robert Sessions: 'I wish it were one novel rather than a series of stories. But there seem to be few rules these days (Wilding, Moorhouse etc) and the writing is outstanding.'[38]

Hunting the Wild Pineapple would be launched (reluctantly) as a discontinuous narrative, interlinked stories much like Frank Moorhouse's work. Two in-house editors had to be mollified by Davis's promise that Astley would follow her editorial advice and all would be well. Davis's attitude to Astley's writing was typically blunt, and it would have infuriated Thea had she ever seen it, repeated often as it was: Astley was 'no best-seller' but 'a writer who adds distinction to our list and we can't afford to lose her'.[39]

Astley still had one last salvo to fire at the university. She noticed on return from her overseas study leave that all talk of a lectureship had evaporated under the familiar excuses about policy and promotions. She wrote to the Head of School, Professor A. Gibbs:

> It is now abundantly clear to me, the oldest senior tutor in the Commonwealth if not in living memory, that the school has neither the wish to make me a lecturer nor the slightest intention of doing so. I find the attitude grossly expedient and cynical towards me as well as the students in this matter; it becomes a case of Leacock's boarding-house geometry: 'All Double rooms being taken, a single room may be said to be a double room.' … I have been teaching for ten years at Macquarie now. During those ten years I have produced three books of my own (two of which won three major national awards) and edited a fourth. Four books more, I would suggest, than ninety per cent of the staff has produced. Admittedly they were fiction; but listening to critical theories of some who are hierarchic seniors while being twenty years my junior I must confess to curiosity in another branch of fiction whose inane currents I have never ridden.[40]

In fact, Astley had been thinking of adding critical writing to her credentials. She and Mark Macleod had been sharing lectures, with Astley speaking on Barbara Baynton and Patrick White, but she wanted to write about the poet Bruce Dawe and her friend Tom Keneally. The *Pineapple* stories must take precedence, however, and she would see what (if anything) came of the other academic work in due course. Towards the end of 1977 she was appointed a fellow in Literature and Creative Writing. It was a placatory gesture on the part of the university and it came too late to please Astley, though she accepted it. Why should she be grateful?

Her mother was of the opinion, as usual, that God had been good to Astley and that she should thank him by going to Mass. God was nearer than even Eileen thought. Cecil had now been dead sixteen years and she had managed a life alone extremely well, keeping close to neighbours and family, but also managing a house and garden with a degree of physical stamina that alarmed Phil ('I hope you don't mow the grass. It is really too much for your years.').[41] Thea and Phil's letters about Eileen were never about her physical frailty: aged eighty she was old, of course, but her mind was the issue. In recent months Astley had noticed a plaintive tone creeping into Eileen's letters, hints that perhaps she should be in an old people's home.[42] In the New Year, in tremulous handwriting, she confessed she had forgotten her daughter's address. 'Time, the great heel', was getting ready to stomp.

By May of 1978 Eileen was miserable and every small task was a huge effort. She told her children that she intended to go into a nursing home, an unusually self-possessed decision given the circumstances. Phil used his networks in the Church to find the right one, and eventually discovered Villa Maria in Fortitude Valley, about ten minutes by car from the Astley family home in Ashgrove. The home was dedicated to the so-called Black Josephite order, not the Brown Josephs, as Phil told his sister, a distinction Phil made in deference to his mother's devoutness as much as from his meticulous knowledge of ecumenical history.[43] According to one of Eileen's neighbours, Eileen was crying for joy because the nuns would be close.

A protection order that let the state trustees deal with the estate would help see to the sale of the family home and distribution of the assets; neither Phil nor Thea had any wish to be involved with those details. From Villa Maria they received weekly reports on Eileen's wellbeing – much of it heartening (she was gaining weight). However, on 26 August 1979, the day after Astley's own birthday, the 'war against clocks', as Astley liked to call it, was lost for Eileen when her death came suddenly. She was buried next to Cecil, whose gravestone carried the traditional 'may his soul rest in peace'. The wish for Eileen was that she would also rest in peace, though there was no mention of her soul.

14

Jane Austen of the rainforest

I'm not really trying to be the Jane Austen of the rainforest. The setting is as much an emotional as a physical one and a gesture towards the long-standing love affair I have had with the geography of this state.

Thea Astley, 'Writing in North Queensland', 1981[1]

Her mother's death was a reminder to Astley that all human life is the victim of time. She hardly needed to be reminded: this was something she'd expressed in her earliest poetry – 'Enter – harshness/ The facing of the world'.[2] The 1979 move up north in the December heat had been taxing, the weather turning thoughts into electronic circuits with tiny filaments charging each other. Weather had its way of making all wounds fresh wounds. Living seemed a paltry business; so too the business of writing.

In the months following Eileen's death Astley was facing publicity for the *Pineapple* stories in a grim mood, as usual talking down any possible success: winning the Miles Franklin Award, she announced, was the 'kiss of death'. Writing was 'private'. 'Mixing with other writers is wasting your time.'[3] In reality, Astley was now mixing with many writers, and was engaged in a more social network of literary activity than she had ever been. The move north would not change any of that. Her life had become steadily more gregarious since her Literature Board involvement, which had brought some close friendships with other women writers on the board such as Fay Zwicky. Fay shared Astley's view that bringing the arts to regional Australia was important; she was an advocate for Western Australia, knowing how much more was needed for a region just as geographically remote as Astley's Queensland.

With increasing invitations to writers' festivals and residences and with Kuranda as a refuge, Astley moved back and forth as needed, just as she had been doing during university breaks. Ed remained at 44a Dorset Street. He was happy there with his 'little pals', quite the grown-up and even giving dinner parties. Irritable as Astley could be with life, Ed could do no wrong.[4]

Back in Sydney, Astley took a bath to remove an engorged tick ('Jack, watch out for them in the jungle'), which had safely transported itself from Queensland, and contemplated her split existence. Kuranda was next to rainforest. Astley was awed by the place, which was already indivisible from the characters forming in her mind. She was now moving away from the urban satire for which she had become so well known; she was discovering a different voice for herself in this fresh situation, drenched in the tropics she loved. She thought about the Djabugay people's ownership of the land. She knew that for them it had been a place where young people were taught stories, culture and language, a far cry from the hippie culture that had supplanted it.

Or was it? The bohemian young people who sought an alternative life in the wilderness had their stories too, like the character 'Wait-a-while' in the *Pineapple* collection. Astley had named him after the plants (*Calamus* spp.) that were all over the forest, boasting little hooks that allowed them to climb tree palms and stick to visitors' clothing. New tracks over several swampy low-lying areas had been built so that visitors could 'walk one track', as the elders said. It was a sentiment that appealed to her.

The place, the stories, and the stories to come were always on her mind whenever she returned to the city, which she did for remaining commitments at Macquarie and with the Literature Board. Leaving Jack behind, she wrote, 'The south is so dull after the north', 'Uni is the same', and, 'There's more social life where you are, love. It ain't here.'[5] It was half of the truth: their comfortably divided lives were blossoming in Kuranda among the conviviality of the Knudsons and near neighbours, a community in which a new 'Thea and Jack' seemed to be forming. This was now a partnership without the rancour of the earlier years of their marriage and with all the good things – wit, history (theirs alone), Ed, tenderness – still intact. It was like love as a form of benign fatalism, perfect for Astley.

She and Jack always exchanged letters when apart (though to others Astley would claim 'letter-writing quite an effort' and that she actually wrote few), and among the domestic trivia of car bills, power bills, banking and tools for hacking away at tropical undergrowth, all tallied in columns of figures by Thea, there was real warmth of feeling. 'When are you are coming up, Thea?' Jack wrote at the end of one letter and, more intriguingly, 'You are in for an absolutely delightful surprise when you enter the second bedroom.'[6] He had bought her what she most desired: a piano. He was missing her.

Because Jack was ten years older and had been such a strong emotional support, it was hard for Astley to think of him as frail. Back in the late 1960s he had had 'giddy spells', as Eileen had called them; now he was complaining about his eyesight. He had macular degeneration and needed to have an eye operation in Cairns.

Eileen's estate was worth \$17,530, shared equally between Phil and Thea. Cecil and Eileen and Ashgrove and Brisbane and all that life added up to \$17,530.[7] There it was, thought Astley. No matter what the amount, the sum was the same: you live, you work, you die. We 'walk one track'.

Jack and Thea shared this fatalism, laughing in the face of it all. Here they were, two 'superanuands', as Astley took to calling them, with sixty years of the 'daily grind' between them. Now in retirement the habits of frugality persisted, even though Jack and Thea were not short of money. Being careful with finances was a state of mind rather than a necessity. Bare simplicity in matters of house and furnishings might have been aesthetic, but Jack and Thea's meticulous care with expenditure was psychological and emotional.

Good things came Astley's way but always, from her point of view, too late. Her one venture into literary criticism, *Three Australian Writers* (on Bruce Dawe, Barbara Baynton and Patrick White), seemed amusingly post-the-point, published in 1979, just as she had left academe. Kuranda had its dangers: living there gave Astley time to think, worry, imagine, visit and revisit wrongs. The litany often started with Macquarie's treatment of her but embraced her publishers' treatment too, ranging over her critics' misunderstanding of her and the underestimation of her work. She used acceptance speeches for her awards to air frustrations about writing and her jaundiced views of readers, a perverse thing to do in the circumstances: 'I think they think that having exposed our pips of souls, our mini-talents, we're fair game. I mean they don't have to pay to hate us. They can borrow us from libraries. Maybe that's why they have this marvellous contempt for writing activities.'[8] She concluded that writers were resented.

'It's lonely at the bottom,' Astley wrote in pencil on her typescript of this particular speech. Perhaps, but was she at the bottom? Was Australian writing even at the bottom? Hardly. She could be difficult to follow for audiences: celebration and deflation in one act.

Astley could persist in this state of mind despite all manner of good omens. In the early 1980s there were plenty of these: she had been invited to visit Canada; the *Pineapple* collection had won an award from the James Cook Foundation for Australian Literary Studies; her friend Hal Porter had written to say he loved the collection; she had just been named as a Member of the Order of Australia (AM); and that grand dame of literary academe Professor Leonie Kramer had written congratulating her – something Astley would have valued enormously.[9]

Fay Zwicky was keen for her to come to a residency at the University of Western Australia the following year.

Astley could choose to receive her Order of Australia in either Canberra or Cairns, but she chose to go nowhere. She was brooding about her battle with Richard Walsh earlier in the year, about his selling of her original manuscripts to the Mitchell Library without her knowledge or consent. That situation had epitomised for Astley the powerlessness of the writer in the publisher–author dynamic.

In Astley's view publishers were tyrants and cowards, 'entrepreneurs of the book', no more deserving of credit than the mobs of sweltering businessmen carving up the tropical north. (To add insult to injury, Richard Walsh had been near Kuranda and hadn't called in to see her – his apologetic Christmas Eve letter did nothing to mitigate this.[10]) At the same time she was none too happy with Nelson's handling of the story collection, writing fiercely to Davis about the review list and the poor distribution of *Pineapple*:

> … why oh why would the PR girl send copies to *Woman's Day* and *Women's Weekly* and OMIT the *Bulletin* and the *National Times*, reviews in both of which would please me far more than any amount of notice in those other ghastly mags – Knit Your Own Royal Family …[11]

Astley was seriously beginning to think she needed a new publisher. She had kept secret from Davis and Nelson the approach of the American Frank Thompson, publisher with the University of Queensland Press. He had impressed her the previous year with his offer to reissue her personal favourite, *The Acolyte*, in paperback, and the fifteen per cent royalty he was offering was double her last royalty percentage. It was the kind of literary commerce Astley had been dreaming of for thirty years: she, a serious writer, was at last being taken seriously. Even she was beginning to feel that the battle lines were slowly shifting: literary writers were becoming valued, and this time she would be a front-runner. She decided to accept Frank Thompson's offer, which had firmed up very quickly after their initial contact. It was satisfyingly appropriate to sign the contract in her own name, not her married one, as she had done before. But her distrust of publishers generally was not quite dead: she decided to hold off on signing her next work of fiction over to UQP. There might even be a chance to up the ante.

Astley had just written about the literary scene in north Queensland for a literary magazine, published in 1981.[12] Non-fiction writer Patsy Adam-Smith had been in west and central Queensland for work on her book *The Shearers*, and sent Astley a postcard describing the area as 'an open-air asylum'.[13] The two women had a lot in common, being of the same age. Adam-Smith was passionately interested in railways, having been adopted by railway workers, and this would have appealed to Astley's love-hate relationship with 'rail motors'.

Astley certainly knew about open-air asylums. She saw landscape as Tom Keneally did, as a 'pressure on character, as a foil, as a parallel big world to the little world of man's soul'.[14] Astley was writing about the Australian tropics within a European, almost Conradian tradition. Instead of the observer in *Heart of Darkness*, she has the most ordinary of folk, 'oddballs', somehow not-so-innocently implicated in the dark events she describes. When *Hunting the Wild Pineapple* was published in America by Putnam's in 1990 – ten years later – reviewers noted her 'dark assessment of the world' and wondered why 'women in general … [didn't] fare very well'.[15]

One woman in these stories does fare well but critics could have been forgiven for not noticing the self-portrait in the character Mrs Waterman in 'Petals from Blown Roses'. Fifteen years later Astley had certainly not forgotten her. When she stepped onto the stage for a small reading at Jimmy Watson's Wine Bar in Carlton, Melbourne, in 1993 she gave the impression of re-enacting an old friendship: 'We need to catch up with Mrs Waterman. I've always had a sneaking fondness for her. She is a straight talker. And …' (Astley was whispering) '… she has tits.' The audience laughed, seeing that Astley was similarly endowed.

She continued, 'Tits are important. No, I *mean* it! Look, I'll tell you ... how I came to write Mrs Waterman ... it was up north, terribly modern with loud music and lots to drink and everyone got their gear off and swam in the pool – well, it WAS hot, I suppose ... and look I was amazed ... Aw God, how can I put this without sounding ... at women who were, well, lacking in any mammary development. Well, this one woman – who hadn't been joining in – decided to have a go. All eyes were riveted as she undressed slowly (I think she was sober) and someone yells out, a man of course, "Look, she's got real ones!" It was one of those moments.'[16]

Mrs Waterman is a 'yummy forty-five', ten years younger than Astley when she wrote the story. When talking about herself growing older, Astley often said, 'Look, for a long time I was arrested at forty-two.'[17] This was the age she had been when she still enjoyed teaching at Macquarie and Don Whitington was on the scene. Mrs Waterman exudes sense, sensuality and, above all, control. For once Astley was describing sex in terms of sensuality, not a power struggle.

It had been over three years since Don's death in 1977, but closer to ten since they had finally parted back in 1970. Just a few years after Don's permanent move to Canberra, news filtered through of Don's remarriage to a woman nearly thirty years his junior, which could only have fed Astley's fatalism about romance: men did that, didn't they? She didn't attend his funeral. Astley was well on the way to developing her theory of the four ages of women: 'bimbo, breeder, baby-sitter, burden'.[18]

Astley still tended to interpret heterosexual relationships as intrinsically degrading to women, while accepting them as the norm. But as she grew older she began to adjust her own memory. Whereas in the mid-1960s she had pronounced women to be 'sad things' as they age, she was now thinking about herself ageing, about those strong women who were eccentric in their independence (cowboy-attired Aunt Sadie in *The Acolyte*, for instance) but who were still very much female. Her story 'Ladies Need Only Apply' in the 1979 *Pineapple* story collection attracted a lot of comment from colleagues who had read it because of what was seen as its excruciating portrait of a woman at the mercy of her own sexual needs. Fay Zwicky's view was: 'It was Thea questioning herself, I think – was she a lady?'[19]

She was interested in women who still desired men. 'What do you do for sex?' is a very Thea Astley kind of question. Marie, in *Boat Load*, downed sex like gin and tonic; opera-singing Gracie Tilburn in *A Kindness Cup* was highly sexual, but Astley was not comfortable with granting her characters sexual licence without humiliation. It was vulnerability that mattered and that was asexual; she had explored this in her first published story, 'Cubby', about a young boy's sexual awakening.

Astley chose to write in a female first-person perspective for her next novel, *An Item from the Late News*. It had been over twenty years since she had done so. She rearranged her characters in notes, carefully numbering incidents in a tight logical track – she knew exactly how tragically the scenes would play out. If Mrs Waterman was an idealised self-portrait, then Gabby Jerrold, the protagonist in *Item*, was an antithetically dark self-portrait.

While UQP wrestled with editing and managing the forthcoming *An Item from the Late News*, Astley was strongly connected to Penguin about the future of paperback editions of earlier titles, including *Hunting the Wild Pineapple*, with others to follow. Astley had been a 'gloom bug', she knew, when she had met her Penguin publisher Brian Johns in Brisbane, even though it was great that he wanted to republish her earlier books.[20]

There had been the usual request for a photo, too, which Astley considered a punishment, as it was forcing her to watch herself ageing. With classic deflection she described the enlargements that had just arrived from Townsville: 'They are nicely vague. And I prefer the one with my eyes cast down. I wasn't asleep. I was just lying on the grass at a beach home at Yorkey's Knob, examining a Barringtonia nut.'[21]

Astley's 'gloom bug' effect shows how sensitive she was in this immediate post-Macquarie period. Her demeanour could be a bit wearing, even for good friends like her colleague John Bernard. He and his wife, Judith, were among those whom Astley invited to join her at the little settlement at Mantaka, near Kuranda, with its set of half-a-dozen European houses and Aboriginal shanties. Astley had already regaled them with stories of the Aboriginal children who swam among the freshwater crocodiles.

When there had been 'unkind reaction' to Astley's representation of Aboriginal people in the *Pineapple* collection, it was Bernard who best understood Astley's hurt. He had seen himself the genuineness of her response to those Aboriginal children, though he knew that was not necessarily the same as writing about them with sympathy and compassion. He suggested Astley's particular style for that subject made for unstable sympathies. He was tiptoeing around her vulnerabilities about her wordy 'style' that went back decades, but he did not succeed. 'Well, I suppose we don't *have* to be friends,' snapped Astley. There were no further visits to the Bernards in Sydney.[22]

Astley had felt wounded leaving Macquarie, let down by Nelson, and was now miserable in Aarhus, Denmark, where she was a writer-in-residence. Astley had agreed to visit the Commonwealth Literature Centre at Aarhus University in the early months of 1981. She was one of many Australian authors that the centre's director, Australian-born Anna Rutherford, had encouraged to visit. The conditions here for writing – forced if pleasant company by day and behind closed doors at night – mirrored exactly her early years as a teacher in small Queensland towns. She seemed to have come such a long way, as a renowned international guest-writer, yet in a way she had come nowhere at all. She was still imagining her characters' worst psychic distress in the tropics 'writing out the things that bothered her': in this novel, Gabby, a visual artist ('I've been painting the heart of boredom'), is recovering from a serious depression. She is a woman hiding from herself; one whose birth-given secondary role of 'female' breeds a gap between who she is and who she feels she has to be. All the while she practises the 'protective veneers of womanhood'.[23]

Gabby is covert in her relationships with others, surviving by keeping her feelings in that 'inner country', her 'screwed-up rag of a self'. 'There is no talent in me, but I do have a flair,' says Gabby.[24] She expresses herself in the nervy self-talk so familiar in Astley's earlier protagonists, a 'chronicle of self-appraisal and self-doubt'.[25] Gabby is the ultimate extension of Astley's original portraits of self-regarding young women caught up in small town hostilities, a character to showcase the author's unassuageable discontent. Astley wrote to her editor at UQP, D'Arcy Randall, obviously closely identifying with her character: '[Gabby's] just this poor old failure of a dame writing it and writing it and writing …'[26] The female first-person narrator Gabby is a bridging character to the women of Astley's later fiction. She couldn't know it, but she was already influencing women writers of the day, including Kate Grenville. As Randall later commented, women writers were joining UQP's list on the strength of Astley's work.[27]

The year 1982 began well. Astley received her $2,000 advance for *An Item from the Late News*. This, in addition to the twenty per cent royalty rate, meant that her contract with UQP was the most generous she had signed. A residency at the University of Queensland could only bolster the relationship. The ABC was developing a telemovie based on *A Descant for Gossips*, the 1960s film prospect having vanished long before. Best of all, Penguin were likely to put more of her books into paperback; she had been thrilled with their cover for *Hunting the Wild Pineapple*. She had sent Penguin publisher Brian Johns a copy of *A Boat Load of Home Folk*.

The contracting of *Item* to the rival UQP meant she could expect his final decision to be influenced by that – and perhaps slow in coming. However, 1982 proved to be a year of small but satisfying machinations of a commercial literary kind. Astley now had the time, the energy and the inclination to chase down all her publishers and ask for the royalties due to her.[28] Nelson did not reply quickly to her letters requesting information on payment of royalties – perhaps there was nothing sinister in that – but Astley thought that managing editor Bob Sessions was being less than co-operative because she had sold her most recent novel to the University of Queensland Press.[29]

Kuranda was a fortress from which to sling all manner of arrows and make decisions about allegiances without necessarily being able to see the consequences for those on the receiving end. There were many visitors – from the Macquarie years, other writers, Ed and his friends – and the combination of the silence necessary for writing with well-planned episodes of conviviality afforded Astley the perfect double life of the writer.

Beatrice Davis had been one of the first to take the trip up north and arrived to hear Astley complaining about badly edited and mistake-ridden proofs. Which proofs? Davis knew of none. She realised for the first time that her favourite author had changed publishers. Thus it was that Bob Sessions at Nelson heard of Astley's defection, and he wrote to her expressing regret at losing her from their list. Astley rallied to her own defence by citing UQP's enticing substantial advance before seeing the manuscript; with characteristic understatement Davis wrote to Sessions, 'I take it she missed me as consultant in writing and editing.'[30] Typically playing both sides, Astley was complaining about UQP and the proofs while telling Davis how much she missed her. Knowing that she had introduced UQP's Frank Thompson to Astley's work with *Girl with a Monkey* back in 1958 must have been even more galling for Davis.[31] It was a sad end to their long creative association, but the two women remained friendly. Within a year, Davis retired from Nelson.

Emboldened by the interest of several publishers in her work, Astley became mischievous in some of her dealings. She pretended mystification when it came to the payment of royalties, sometimes suggesting easier and more direct methods that would get the money to her – fiddly and unorthodox practices from a trade perspective.[32] Astley's particular combination of assertiveness, financial savvy and professed naivety persisted in other financial dealings too. She hoped that using her married name of Gregson might confuse the tax office; she paid and then reclaimed lump sum deposits on blocks of land, beach shacks, taken on and abandoned sometimes within the space of a week. Subject to multiple changes of heart, Astley astonished real estate agents. Sometimes she simply forfeited the deposit. Ed was frequently called in for a second opinion.

> Thea: 'Whadya think?'
> Ed: 'Nice location, great little house.'
> Thea: 'Do you really think so?'
> Ed: 'Yes. You do realise what that is?'
> Thea: 'What?'
> Ed: 'The boat ramp.'
> Thea: 'So?'
> Ed: 'A *speedboat* ramp.'
> Thea: 'Oh, Gawd!'
> Back to the agent.

Astley might have known to the last cent what her publishers owed her but in these matters she was almost completely reactive. She was already starting to think that her first Penguin edition was her best publishing moment but while she corresponded with Penguin regularly about *Boat Load* – 'I think I would prefer the date of my birth to be omitted from the jacket'[33] – it was the reception of *An Item from the Late News* that was preoccupying her and, as always, the writing of her next novel.

Astley made sure to send a copy of *Item* to Beatrice, the person whose opinion had guided her writing for more than forty years. Beatrice replied:

> I shall treasure it of course, but what a terrible story – so powerfully told that the devastating tragedy made me feel truly sick. Greed plus brutality, with Gabby the informed onlooker. I couldn't believe in her, though unhappy and frustrated in her love, behaving with such bitter spirit. Yet this is the basis of your sad tale. Can't say more at the moment, being too close to this horrible small town world you've conjured up, too close even to snipe at you for being at times too clever by half. Congratulations and love, Beatrice.[34]

Did Davis really think that this was a nasty book written by an unhappy writer? Perhaps Astley had offended the doyenne of literary publishing by her defection.

Ed, now twenty-five, had met someone two years before and the relationship looked serious. He and Michelle Barbour did everything together, or so it seemed. It was hard to know what to make of her, a beautician – 'for heaven's sake, *a beautician*,' Astley took to telling people loudly, as if the word attracted its own damnation.[35] Under the cheap jokes was something deeper: anxiety about the inevitable changes Astley foresaw in her own relationship with her son. Michelle was a serious and tough-minded young woman who did not melt meekly in the face of Astley's histrionic one-liners nor the quieter tactics of irony. Michelle had laughed knowingly when a previous girlfriend of Ed's had leaned towards her and whispered emphatically, '*What* about that *mother*!'[36]

When Jack and Thea met Michelle's recently divorced mother, June, many things fell into place. June was living the kind of independent life Astley admired in women who had managed to extricate themselves from marriage. Thea, Jack and June got on well. June, like Jack, was happy with a scotch and somehow able to survive Thea's chain-smoking – and June loved to read. She knew, appreciated and respected Astley as a writer. The family get-togethers became easy, open and relaxed in ways that Astley had never enjoyed in her own family life.

June quickly became a firm friend to Thea and Jack and a support to Ed and Michelle. She enjoyed a very close relationship with her own children, which Thea looked upon almost in awe. June was amused one day to hear Thea coming down the stairs, announcing to all, 'Michelle. I can hear you and you're talking to your mother as if she's the *Queen*.' In private with June she would sometimes ask, 'Why don't Ed and Michelle treat me the way they treat you? Why don't they love me like that?' June could see why: Thea was Thea. She was different, that was all. And all children, as well as parents, had their particular ways of showing love.[37]

If anyone understood this it was Ed himself. After leaving school he had spent some years trying to sort out the mixed messages from his parents about his life. There seemed on the one hand to be a total and passionate commitment to his choice of a career in music performance, but then there were the regular little worried speeches about the importance of having 'something to fall back on'. His confidence was being undermined and by the time he met Michelle he had begun to distance himself from his parents' advice. Michelle helped him to understand their views while continuing to maintain a close relationship with them.

It was an important development, since Ed was their closest relative. Jack saw little of his own wider family. His father and brothers were all still alive and living in New South Wales. Thea had visits from Phil when they both happened to be in Sydney several times a year. The merging of family groups through Ed and Michelle, now living in the Epping house, unexpectedly created a new family for all.

Time was bringing all sorts of natural life changes but many of the things that seriously bothered Astley in the past still clung to her. Vanuatu in July had been hard work. Astley had been researching the background for her novel *Beachmasters* in which the original inhabitants of the island colony of Kristi stage a brief rebellion. She was writing the new novel, thanks partly to a residency at her old university in Brisbane. It was now 1983 and she had been writing for forty years.

She was unable to shake her animosity towards the entire commercial machinery of the book trade, despite Penguin's publishing the paperback of *An Item from the Late News* and UQP's acceptance of *A Descant for Gossips* for their own paperback list. Mixing with other writers led to odious comparisons, with Astley finding out what publishers were doing for them and by implication what they weren't doing for her. David Malouf had talked of the 'dozens of interviews' Penguin had organised for him. It rankled Astley. She wrote to Julie Watts, her editor at Penguin:

> I was rather hurt when Penguin gave no publicity at all for *Pineapple*. For *Boatload* [*sic*] I rated *one* radio interview with the ABC in Tasmania at a breakfast talks session. When I suggested to the Penguin girl ringing me – can't remember her name – that *at least* an interview with Brisbane or Cairns might be more apposite, she replied that the ABC were very choosy. Now, frankly, I found that pretty hurtful. Really, I'm not writing Mills and Boon. I think I have a fair track record.[38]

She was 'sad and bitter'. To others her wounds always came across as emotional and complicated by resentment and ambition.Her strongest complaint about the Australian response to her books was its failure to look at her oeuvre as a whole. As she later commented to Rodney Hall, 'Why don't they just take a look? Why don't they just say, let's look at her – she's written all these books, some good, some not so good – but what do they add up to?'[39]

In reality, Astley was faring reasonably well in terms of academic recognition, and she knew it. Journal articles had been appearing for some years – in *Meanjin*, *The Southern Review* and *Kunapipi* – and five years earlier, Astley had asked Beatrice Davis if the author of one such article could review the *Pineapple* collection.[40] But the Australian literary world was small and Astley craved the broad engagement with books that she saw in the American mainstream press. She had always felt that 'the standard of competence in writing since the war' lay in America and 'not in England at all'.[41] Some on the Literature Board had misgivings about the expense involved in promoting Australian writers overseas, but Astley was not one of them.

Astley told Penguin's Brian Johns that she was getting tired of living in north Queensland, which she said was 'full of Real Estate Agents and hookers'. She had tentatively offered her next novel to UQP on the proviso that they would sell and promote her work into the US. 'I hate breaking my word,' wrote Astley to Johns, 'but I think their chances of getting me US pizzazz are remote.' Since her father had bought ninepenny Penguins when Astley was a child, she had been a fan, and the thought of having her work published as Penguin originals, not paperback reprints, was immensely attractive. She was delighted when Penguin decided to publish *Beachmasters* in Australia and sold the American rights to Viking.[42] In fact, a new era of Australian–American publishing was just beginning. With more Australian authors employing literary agents to represent them, many soon found themselves splitting and selling the rights to their work in separate territories.[43]

The Penguin publishing coup accelerated Astley's growing dissatisfaction with Queensland, the conservative politics of which she hated with a passion. She wrote to Ed, 'This is a banana republic and if Joh doesn't go I feel myself like shifting to northern NSW. Didn't know I was such a political cat!?'[44] Large areas around Kuranda were being developed. A few years later Astley explained to an audience at a literary event: 'I was having a love affair with the scenery in that area. Every departure from the place hurt … [but] the developer rot had set in and the hi-rise had started and the bulldozers were out along the Cape Trib track and real estate agents were selling two-acre lots at Cow Bay.'[45]

This despoliation seemed to Astley peculiarly Queenslandish. Life at Kuranda was also becoming much more difficult. The heat made doing the everyday tasks – especially keeping the grass under control – exhausting. Jack's eyesight was seriously deteriorating and he would soon need to be near specialists. They were a long way from Ed. The remoteness, once so attractive, was turning into a liability. 'It's hell at this distance,' she wrote to her Penguin editor, Jackie Yowell, as she struggled with editing and proofs.[46] 'Typists in Cairns are rare on the ground and from reports I've had, the spelling errors they include are amazing.' She asked Penguin to copy her manuscript for her, not believing there was a Xerox machine 'in cooee up here'.[47]

In 1984 computers and printers existed, not that Astley owned them. The Green Hermes typewriter had given up the ghost and in Cairns she had purchased its modern cousin, the Cream Hermes Baby typewriter. She was 'bashing out' drafts – except for *The Acolyte*, she always put manuscripts through at least three. Somehow feeling geographically removed from the place of publication increased the emotional isolation of writing books. This was particularly true of *Beachmasters*, caught up as she was with the complexities of dialogue in English as well as French-influenced pidgin.

Astley was still capable of taking offence, nearly always about finances, offers and contracts. If there was a price to be paid for being a Penguin author, she wasn't having any of it. Anticipating her 'American moment' for *Beachmasters* later in1984, she was making suggestions for covers.[48] Within ten years Astley would secure contracts with a right of refusal for the cover.

Astley could give off contradictory impressions about her life at this time. When a US interviewer asked her during her *Beachmasters* tour whether she talked and visited with writers much, she said that she didn't. 'I don't feel it's important for writers to mix with other writers. It's a very lonely occupation. I don't think you need other writers. Jane Austen proved she didn't need anyone except her own community. God, how well she did that!'[49] But despite this self-consciousness about reputation, most people discovered that to meet in person Astley was vivacious, warm, vital, and interested.

Her life was a contradiction because her needs were contradictory: insider-outsider-solitude. If she didn't 'need' other writers, she certainly enjoyed the camaraderie she felt in their presence. By now Astley was a regular guest at nearly all major writers' festivals around Australia and was frequently asked to launch the books of other writers.

Astley's very active literary life provided further incentives for her to move south. It was time for another escape. The previous three years had been busy ones: Astley had been in Santo, Vanuatu's largest island, for research for *Beachmasters*; at the University of Queensland in 1983; in Darwin in May 1984; at the Harbourfront Writers' Festival readings in Toronto, Canada, in October 1984; and at Biloxi, Mississippi, USA, for a residency and readings as part of a special session on Australian writers, a promotion supported by the Literature Board. Travel would be easier from virtually anywhere in New South Wales, though neither she nor Jack considered a return to Sydney. Anticipating the restlessness that was so much part of her character, Phil's Christmas card for 1984 hoped her life would remain 'calm and tranquil'.[50] It was a hope against hope that only proved how well he knew his sister, for her life was not standing still. She had sustained an important loss with the death of Hal Porter in September 1984; he had been in a coma for months after being knocked down by a car.

Thea and Jack decided to move to New South Wales by the end of 1984. They had found nearly six acres of sloping bushland on a hilltop property in Cambewarra, two and a half hours' drive south of Sydney. Within a few months of settling into their new home, Astley would see their decision vindicated by a small incident she felt justified her antipathy to Queensland. She had been asked by the Queensland Arts Council to conduct a writers' weekend workshop, but her name was given as 'Thea Ashley'. The name had been queried by the Arts Council, who said that a writer by that name didn't exist.[51] It was a simple misspelling but it was enough to recharge Astley's anger towards what she saw as the wretched, shoddy attitudes of Queensland, the disrespect for writers or for achievement in anything that didn't involve sport or money. She tossed off a furious letter of refusal. Damn Queensland!

Astley hoped to see her American star rise with the US publication of *Beachmasters*, her ninth novel. However, just as she faced the move to Cambewarra she read a review of her Toronto public reading in *The Strand* magazine: 'Thea Astley, narrating passages from her latest book *Beachmasters*, was engaging, but her lengthy reading became self-indulgent. The romantic form of the novel was tiresome and strained.'[52]

A furious Astley wrote immediately to Penguin, 'I do think that this published review is damaging to future sales and reviews of *Beachmasters* and I would like Penguin to take appropriate action.'[53] A year of positives was turned around in a moment: it seemed that she would begin her new life in New South Wales once more feeling that she had been misunderstood. The Australian launch of *Beachmasters* was a few months away. Would they get it right?

PART 4

PERSONAL WEATHER

15

Pictures from a family album

But no one seems to hear her and she isn't altogether sure if she has said what she intended saying. All her life has glittered with moments when the words uttered were not those meant, the phrase angled for caught up and wriggling on the hook of her tongue as something quite other.

She goes back to the start of things.

It's Raining in Mango by Thea Astley, 1987[1]

Newly arrived in Cambewarra, Astley got busy with a rush of tree planting, perhaps trying to turn southern New South Wales into Queensland rainforest. The effect was to virtually obscure the very view that she and Jack had purchased. People who knew their ways decided not to comment. The move had been the subject of years of hints and exclamations but, like many Thea-driven property purchases, was beguilingly rash. After a Canberra Wordfest in 1984 Astley had caught a long-distance train north, got a taxi from nearby Berry and looked at some properties in the Cambewarra area. She chose the third one 'because she couldn't be bothered looking anymore'. Astley's near neighbour at Cambewarra, Marin Martinelli, could easily relate to this story. This was the Thea he would meet in cafés, umming and ahhing over menus. 'Her eyes would close, a finger would go up, then slam – it could drop on just about anything in the menu. "I'll have that!" she'd say to puzzled waiters.'[2]

Lot 9 Emerys Road, Cambewarra, was not as isolated as Kuranda had been, and that was the main thing. It was Thea who was more concerned about the need to be near amenities and health services, especially for Jack. His deteriorating eyesight due to macular degeneration would take its course and they needed to be ready. Thea was writing more or less constantly and Jack, as always, knowing how important this was to her, also agreed that being near other people might be good for both of them. Public commitments were now taking Thea away often and she knew that Jack found his solitude a little oppressive. The partnership had been – still was – generous to her.

The new property, more than six acres, brought with it a level of upkeep that they hadn't anticipated. The land boasted not just a view but a spread of Paterson's curse and blackberry brambles. There were also large areas of grass. They would have to purchase a ride-on mower. Thea mentioned in letters that this was intended for Jack, 'saving his seventy-year-old bod', but shortly after they moved south, his eyes became so bad that he was no longer able to drive at all.[3] Thea as master-mower was something to behold if you happened to arrive at the right moment. Her small frame would be perched atop what was really an open-air tractor, giving the impression of control that was not necessarily evident in the expression of intense concentration on the driver's face. The whole business was described as an adventure; Astley enjoyed the fact that it would shock people who thought a woman nearing sixty years of age was 'past it'. But her bravado hid some bitter realities: Astley knew her role as a carer for Jack was beginning in earnest.

These pressures, and awareness of her own ageing, were taking their toll. Astley had been agitated about women as second-class citizens for decades, on the record, off the record, in her novels, but was now seeing for herself the double discrimination that came with ageing and being female. If you were older, female *and a writer*, you could make that three. In 1985 a review of *Beachmasters* entitled 'Writers Contrast in Age and Style' by well-known Sydney academic and writer Don Anderson appeared in *The National Times*. The novel, Anderson remarked rather pithily, was like a 'sort of *Absalom, Absalom!* in the South Pacific, without Faulkner's intellectual complexity'.[4] This touched a hot wire of fury, so Astley wrote to him:

> Dear Don Anderson,
> Well, that *was* a nasty little review – but I'm glad to have broken the cycle. Mark Macleod once indicated to me that most of my unpleasant notices come from women ... (Incidentally, I'm old enough to be your grandmother, too. Time out here for horrified denials of such genetic antecedents being possible on either side.) I don't mind a bit being fifty-nine, nearly sixty ... But I do get the impression from your review that you resent my age. Do you feel I should have hung up my typer the moment I hit fifty? Is there to be nothing left for the tottering senior citizen?[5]

Thoughts of the 'sick state' of Queensland politics were already giving way to nostalgia for the tropics Astley had just left. The story she had on her mind now was based on her own family history, but she wanted to write about a matriarchal family in the early days of such remote places. It would be about the pioneers of the tropic north, slogging it out through floods in crazy outback towns full of rotting mangoes. How many novels had mango in the title? It had to happen.

Since her US trip in 1984 Astley had been more alert to her publishing future: the last thing she wanted was premature memorialising. She was looking forward to reminiscing with Robert Ross, an academic who was researching and writing about her work, from Dallas, Texas, who was coming to Australia mid-year.

The smallness and intimacy of the University of Queensland Press seemed all the more obvious to Astley after her overseas experiences.

It was a poorly resourced operation that had purchased its first office computers less than three years before; typed carbon copies of letters and handwritten production cards were the norm.[6] Astley was looking carefully at the state of the copyright of her works and had convinced herself that *The Acolyte* was out of print, which it wasn't, but she was keen to know what she could offer new publishers. She had also been seriously put offside by the UQP-attached university bookshop's alleged 'neglect of her presence' two years ago when she had been a writer-in-residence. After being told *The Acolyte* was not out of print, she followed up with another letter complaining about the absence of any display of her works, which she described as 'offensive'.[7] At the same time, Astley was now actively looking for a US literary agent and probably already knew that a small publisher such as UQP would not be her future, despite its reputation for originating and promoting Australian fiction.

'Bluster and bully[ing]', wrote the UQP publishing editor Craig Munro, was part of 'Thea's usual style/charm!'[8] In fact, the press had worked hard to appease Astley. They had tried not to mind having lost publication of *Beachmasters* to Penguin while they themselves were dealing with reprints of *Item* and versions of the paperbacks of *Descant* and *The Acolyte*. Publishing director Laurie Muller wrote a long letter answering a list of Astley's complaints – the lack of a launch for *Item*, no books at the Guggenheim and Toronto readings the previous year, and so forth – concluding with his plan to pulp and reissue the paperback of *The Acolyte*, replacing what he regarded as 'one of the most appalling jackets of all time'.[9]

The publication of *Beachmasters* kept Astley firmly planted in the moment. It was a novel she had worked particularly hard on, but so had Penguin. The use of dialogue in pidgin languages had been problematic and taken many extra hours of specialised editing by Penguin's Carla Taines. After the launch in early 1985, even Astley was feeling a bit sheepish about her frequent despairing letters to Penguin. There had been, she wrote while still packing up Kuranda, 'a wonderful launching party' in Melbourne but it was the 'decent review in *The Australian*' that really restored her spirits, a way to repay Penguin for 'taking a punt' on her, she said, deflecting in her usual way.[10] This time, Astley had to admit, they had got it right.

With the nasty *National Times* review behind her, Astley was agitating for extra copies of *Beachmasters* to submit for national awards, having given them out 'like lollies' at the recent Canberra Wordfest, and she asked Penguin to organise this.[11] Astley was meticulous in these matters, more like her own mother than she might have been prepared to admit; Eileen had never wanted to take liberties, nor to feel obliged. Thea did not want to appear profligate or presumptuous in having 'wasted' copies. Would they deduct the cost of copies from her own royalties? asked Astley. She also enclosed unused Cabcharge vouchers – just in case someone 'got hold of them and decided to travel by cab to Broome'.[12]

With the US publication of *Beachmasters* Astley had achieved an ambition dear to her heart, seeing her work emerge as part of the global book market. Five years earlier, in 1981, she and Fay Zwicky had had their doubts about the Australia Council's new era of sponsorship.[13] However, as recipients of financial assistance from the board, they both knew personally the value of the help.

Astley had been a board-sponsored writer-in-residence at the University of Queensland for 1982–83 and *An Item from the Late News* published by UQP had also attracted a publishing subsidy.[14] The push to promote Australian literature overseas was a huge affirmation of her standing in the literary community and her 1984 trip to America had been generously sponsored by the Literature Board.[15] It was not only about Australian literature either: the planned readings at the Guggenheim Museum (where Astley was joined by David Malouf) coincided with a major Australian art exhibition. For Astley, the trip was a moment in her writing life that would prove crucial.

In the US, she had been mixing with writers from a very different publishing context. Astley heard their talk of agents, the necessity, even, of having an agent; how you had to push your own commercial interests and publicity. Only a year before, Astley knew, the Literature Board had engaged New York book publicist Selma Shapiro to assist in the promotion of books through more extensive reviewing in the US press.[16] The amounts of money being paid to writers were much greater too – not something Astley would ever miss.

It was during and after this trip that many thoughts long buried began to surface and influence her sense of the novels she would yet write. For interviews, Astley had probably intended to run off the old lines – 'I was always led to believe that books by women had no credibility' – but hearing them in this new context – the fact that she was now a US-published author – changed everything. Astley's sense of herself as an author permanently shifted; simultaneously, so did her perspective on that past self she was describing.

It seems likely that this was the moment when Astley realised she could do it – no, that she *would* do it: she would write the stories of women. The new novel with 'mango' in its title would be a beginning. For most of her life she had identified with her journalist father. It was noticeable to many how she never mentioned her mother. Now she thought: what about that other journalist, the runaway Con (Cornelius), her mother's father? What about the life of the women he left behind? For a novelist who was one of those women, it was an irresistible line of descent for her new work.

Astley had already lived through a great deal of change in the world of Australian writing, but now it was changing again before her eyes. Her work was a bridge between generations of writers. Her new novel, which she titled *It's Raining in Mango*, was a way of celebrating her own family's past while looking to a new writing future.

Many younger Australian women writers admired, even hero-worshipped Astley. She was now meeting many of these but also female publishers, editors and academics who understood her work. She was hearing their personal stories too. Astley, the self-described 'people freak', was always a talker – she would engage people in conversation at bus stops, cafés, anywhere – but more often now she spoke to women about themselves. In her early days of marriage, she had been close to some of the women of Dorset Street and Cheltenham Girls'. In literary circles of the 1950s and 1960s, Beatrice Davis had been her chief woman literary confidant and there had been women friends from the Barjai days. However, she had tended to form closer bonds with male writers such as Hal Porter and Tom Keneally.

Now there were many women who were not in the world of married couples, both independent and unmarried, such as Michelle's mother, June, divorced and living a busy and productive life. Astley had always been fascinated by the romantic myth of love and marriage, but was newly intrigued by the 'alternatives to the burden of marriage' that these women had apparently found.[17] Friendships with other women writers were becoming a key aspect of her life, and with her attendance at writers' festivals, the list was growing: Fay Zwicky, Judith Rodriguez, Carmel Bird, Helen Garner, Patsy Adam-Smith, Glenda Adams, Janette Turner Hospital, Elizabeth Jolley, Kate Grenville, Gabrielle Carey. Suddenly, the world seemed full of Great Dames.

Astley's way of writing about women was also changing. There were no more Gabby Jerrolds (the character from *An Item from the Late News* who had so dispirited Beatrice); no more nervy, inward-looking portraits of the artist-as-a-young girl. Astley's novels featured women such as the suave and sexy Mrs Waterman (from the *Hunting the Wild Pineapple* story collection) who would be comfortable speaking their minds, a new version of femininity that appealed to the mature writer. The women in Astley's novels were strong, with the kind of strength she had admired all her life, starting with the more forthright nuns in the Church.

Astley's career could have ended here, with an estimable body of work resting respectfully on library shelves. But she had time to write and much to write about, and nothing to lose. But even she could not have predicted that her changes in subject and attitude would lead to half-a-dozen highly successful late-career novels, beginning with her 'pictures from the family album' (*It's Raining in Mango*). Others followed from the mid-1990s onwards, including *Reaching Tin River*, *Coda*, *The Multiple Effects of Rainshadow*, and her last novel, *Drylands: A Book for the World's Last Reader*. From the writer who thought she might have 'missed the bus' in writing about women now came a second body of work to attract a new generation of readers.

Astley's ideas about romance, love, sex, family, duty and self-sacrifice were all still in flux. She had not yet articulated male–female relationships in Euclidean theorems (parallel lines that never meet) as she would in *Reaching Tin River.* Astley was delving deeply into her maternal past, looking for that 'female strength' that would give new vitality to her work.[18] This became her way of negotiating between the attitudes about women she had grown up with and those that now surrounded her.

Many of the Astley women in these late novels are in the process of a similar weighing up. Taken together Astley's character types shaped the possibilities of womanhood as she saw them: strong and independent women, married women (resigned or disaffected) and whores (actual prostitutes or simply slaves to sexual desire). Positive examples of female sexuality would still be rare. Writing about sex itself remained a difficulty for Astley. She preferred to write about expert managers of Life such as the eccentric cowboy-attired Aunt Sadie in *The Acolyte* or Doss in *An Item from the Late News*, who is accused of being 'unwomanly' for shunning marriage and who succumbs to it 'more from exhaustion than desire'.[19] Jessica Olive in *It's Raining in Mango* runs a pub. Astley was seeing women she now met compromise and negotiate (as she had in her own marriage), but continued to write of how 'men can shrivel a woman in a marriage'.[20] But leaving a marriage was not often an option for Astley's characters, as she had felt it was not for herself.

No one should underestimate the energy that reciprocation brings to all relationships. Astley was now ideally placed to benefit from her new associations with younger women writers. She was the female mentor with the sage wit, the elder stateswoman who was ageless in her camaraderie and off-the-cuff encounters; she could even blow her own cool smoke-ring. Her early tendency to 'burst in' or demand friendship – as she had with Patrick White – was now in reverse; she waited for people to come to her.

Astley did at times resent the success of other writers, including the media response to them, but she could also be extremely solicitous of those still making a name for themselves. Carmel Bird remembers her phone ringing one morning during a writers' festival, with the unmistakeable gravelly voice declaring: 'This is Thea Astley,' and confessing, 'I've been awake for hours hanging on for a respectable hour to call.' It was 7 am. Astley said she admired Bird's writing and wanted to meet and support her.[21]

Other kindnesses followed (encouraging comments scribbled on book covers and suggesting Bird as the editor for an anthology), but Bird most clearly recalls the way Astley related to her as an equal; it was this that Bird felt was her real generosity.[22] It was a quality Astley brought to group settings as well. When Helen Garner met Astley during a writers' lunch, she couldn't get over 'how relaxed she was, in just hanging out with people she probably didn't know all that well'. It was as though 'she'd spent years practising in pubs' – something Garner knew wasn't the case. Garner noticed something else: 'a bright face, looking from face to face as people spoke'. She realised that Astley had 'the ability to sit in a group of people and see things'. She was moved by that; it was a quality she'd long noticed tended to disappear as people aged, with only the historian Manning Clark being the exception.[23]

This kind of writerly intimacy suited Astley, involving as it did lots of confidences and anecdotes for the keen listener but little else expected. It could be a powerful one-way connection for certain individuals who met Astley; a repertoire of 'friends' was building – at least people who felt they were friends – but without anyone actually getting close. Helen Garner wondered about this aspect of Astley. When she visited her in Cambewarra their shared love of music had been a welcome diversion from Jack still being 'stroppy' about a critical review Garner had written of *An Item from the Late News* years before. She and Astley danced to jazz. It was a sweet memory until ten years afterwards, when Garner read a feature about Astley. In the magazine article, the scene appeared almost exactly as it had happened to Garner, but the dancer was now Astley's interviewer, the writer Mandy Sayer. 'Maybe that's the act Thea puts on,' thought Garner.[24] What was one to make of it?

Astley was not being insincere, but she was a performer. She was one of the first Australian writers who seemed to know instinctively that in this new public world of writing there could be no dissembling, except for the staged dramatic kind at which she was already expert. Where some writers bemoaned having to entertain, it suited Astley's personality. She had never wanted to be seen to take herself too seriously and she developed a persona as a knockabout lady writer, full of stories. What her audiences saw was an entertainer; they were being primed for laughter. Whatever future nerves might take over, Astley had proved something to her own satisfaction: it was safest if you stuck with the laughs.

Perhaps her performances did look rather slick to others, as though Astley was just a savvy soul who had learned fast, but to her it must have seemed as if it were the world that was catching up. The fact that Astley could be extremely funny did not mean that she wasn't deadly serious about life, especially about writing. Her performance, her projection of self, could harden at times; her one-liners could seemed forced and not particularly amusing. It was often social ineptness disguised as the desire to shock with humour. Ed was not unlikely to find himself wincing in restaurants as his mother all but shouted, 'He's my son, not my toy boy' to patiently smiling waiters.[25] It is possible that with time we all become caricatures of ourselves but it was as if, once her public persona was perfected, Astley clung to it as emotional protection.

People thought Jack must be long-suffering but their relationship was not so simple, nor had it ever been. Many, like David Malouf, didn't 'get' Jack, but Jack got Thea in a way that nobody else did.[26] The confusion about Jack and Thea as a couple came out of the way Astley wrote about marriage in her fiction. Assumptions about Astley's own marriage were not borne out of the reality. Her descriptions of marriage ('they bore each other rancid', 'the silence of old marriage') seemed so natural coming from Astley, yet they scarcely matched the real-life partnership that greeted neighbours or visitors to Lot 9 Emerys Road, Cambewarra.

The move to New South Wales had paid off in the way Astley had hoped. Not only was it closer to Sydney (and Ed) but it was near a largish town. Nowra was really a tatterdemalion clutch of centralised amenities in an otherwise pleasant coastal region, but it suited Astley's needs. Within a couple of years Astley was nevertheless using her relative isolation to escape various offers to speak publicly – '14km from the nearest railway', 'I *never* drive to Sydney' – evasion that was relatively new.[27] More than ever, being available for Jack and his needs was priority. All sorts of people made efforts to visit – Ed and Michelle and her mother, June, of course – but also writers, editors, publishers and people from the Literature Board past and present. Young Jesuits, including Michael McGirr, who knew Phil from Campion House in Melbourne, would come up from their holiday house at nearby Gerroa for a 'grand afternoon tea' – and a fair dollop of Astley's views on Catholicism.

To them her opinions were entertainingly familiar but also perverse: the nuns worked hard, the priests were lazy, why did they get rid of the Latin Mass? Guilt ghosted every conversation. But in their way these young Jesuits were paying court to Astley, and she loved it. She was flirting with exposing the absurdities of the Church as she had known it – or the Church as Astley's parents had known it and had made it known to her. In this company she was protective and defensive about Phil: she knew he wasn't an achiever in an order that 'boasted a climate of achievement'.[28]

Close neighbours quickly became friends. Nowra was a place where one might find the kind of coffee shop Astley loved: all white plastic doilies and equally plastic bread, milk and sugar bowls. It was somewhere a writer could smoke and idle away time. Nothing in the fresh air of the new hilltop home had put Astley off smoking; she seemed immune to this anti-nature habit amid nature. This was how she appeared when she first met her neighbour Marin Martinelli. As he sat at the end of a pathway under a tree he saw Astley track her way down to him. 'Ah, how terrific to find someone to share a cigarette with!' she said. He sat there for their long first conversation, with Thea convinced he was smoking. He did not smoke, but he became a genuine confidant in a way that few did.

Marin's life offered a rich set of circumstances and experiences that fascinated Astley. A gay man, he had been raised in an orphanage, travelled around the world for most of his life and most importantly was happy to talk about sex, any kind of sex. Even to him Astley never spoke about her brother as being gay, saying, 'Phil was a nice quiet person' – but Marin sensed her curiosity about homosexuality. She seemed unexpectedly naïve; her neighbour read her books and wondered how she could have written them. Marin got on with Jack, too, thinking he was 'a pretty cluey bloke'. All this made for a free and easy four-way friendship when they met over meals with Marin's more intellectual partner, Michael.

Thea and Jack were often at odds with each other over seemingly petty things, Marin could see, though Thea never really confided anything about the marriage. Thea could be very contrary. Marin asked Astley one day, 'How on earth did you two get married?' to which she answered simply that she didn't know, a characteristic seriously-not-serious quip.

Jack was starting to look physically much older than their ten-year age difference would suggest, his eyesight all but gone, yet he still appeared to their neighbour to be the carer. This impression was adjusted one day when Marin heard a racket coming from inside their house. 'I realised it was the two of them, chuckling away and shrieking with laughter.'[29] He was sure at that moment what many might have surmised: Thea could never have survived with a different person.

As someone entirely outside the literary world, Marin was better placed than most to see Astley's moods change. As they sat in the Nowra taxi rank, Thea's preferred 'smoko spot', he watched her scribbling constantly, taking down all the activities and conversations she was overhearing while at the same time conducting a perfectly intelligible conversation with him. Hers was a full mind, a busy mind, hardly surprising in a novelist, he thought.

But there was a worrying edge to it too. When Thea told him – and kept telling him for weeks – that she had driven hundreds of miles and then retraced her route because she was convinced she had run over a hitchhiker, it was difficult not to be concerned for her level of anxiety.

It did seem as though some things 'set her off', domestic and family matters certainly, but perhaps the chemistry was just set. It was difficult to separate genuine distress from 'Thea being Thea', as Jack said. In the house, Jack was his own man, though he did not stand firm when Thea worked herself up to tears. Ed's wife, Michelle, had no time for histrionics and could sense a 'Thea-being-Thea' moment coming on.

Michelle eventually came to understand that Thea was in fact being Thea out of compulsion, not especially from a desire for attention. Jack had always insisted that this was so. The blurting out, the one-liners – at any cost of offence – the complete inability to even carve a chicken or slice a cake were all of a piece. Of course, in the eyes of the public, Thea and Jack were now a celebrated Australian writer and her husband, but outside Astley's literary engagements, she preferred to be considered as one equal partner in a marriage. Jack never complained, was happy to go along with Thea's plans and was proud of her achievements. In return she was fiercely loyal to Jack, but also felt guilty about him.

It was a guilt that stretched back to all-but-forgotten days with Don Whitington and the years immediately following. How could Thea ever repay Jack for accepting the person who was 'just being Thea'? Nothing would ever be enough. She seemed to grab any opportunity to even things out, to make things at least seem more equal. A few years after Thea and Jack moved to Cambewarra, Jennifer and Bryan Bruty moved in next door after long careers at the ABC. They never saw a power struggle, rather a marriage that had always been one of equals. Thea talked of 'fitting the writing in' around family. The Jack of her youth was reprised in romantic reimaginings of their first meeting at a classical music concert in 'civilised' wartime Brisbane.[30]

To these neighbours Thea seemed fun, with little talk of unhappy memories. They did, however, see some of that spirit dwindle as her life changed. Before too long Jack was unable to read at all, and material from the Blind Society piled up on the bench. Thea now seemed to be doing all the (hated) driving. To neighbours she seemed absurdly modest about writing, about her various talents, to the point of secrecy. In the lounge room stood a piano whose main function as far as the Brutys knew when they looked after the place, was to hide Thea's cheque books in the bottom pedals. They never heard her play a single note.[31]

Cambewarra afforded Astley the ultimate in the twin modes of existence necessary to her writing. When Irene Stevens from the Literature Board visited, she was well aware that Thea 'wanted to be in things – but away from them'. Thea was at her happiest sitting outside having a cup of tea in a blue cloud of cigarette smoke. Irene knew Thea from Macquarie days in the 1970s when Astley had been her tutor; the two shared a Catholic background. Irene, who had dealt with writers for many years, was uniquely placed to understand Astley's peculiar mixture of bombast and diffidence. She did not take seriously the litany of petty complaints that generally greeted her. Thea, she said, was always complaining about something – either starting on a high and getting to a low or vice versa, and what lay at the heart of this was the lot of the writer. Thea looked forward to seeing Irene; like so many writers, she badly needed someone who listened with real and undemanding awareness.[32]

By 1986 Astley was working very hard on *It's Raining in Mango*, with her usual anxiety intensified by the feeling that she was indeed on a new writing journey, even if the setting for her work had not changed. Though tropical northern Australia had become Astley's favoured locus, she could still be hypersensitive about it. When the publisher Bob Sessions dealt with later editions of the novel he made the mistake of casually asking her, 'Isn't it about time you moved locale?' Astley bit back sharply, saying, 'I don't have any control over what I write ... you can either publish it or not.'[33] Sessions had seen Astley's letters to Penguin on file and probably wondered whether a grudge was in the making. Fortunately for him, it was not.

In her old love-hate habit, Astley was missing the north despite being immersed in it through her writing. She was always susceptible in this way; a trip up north was likely to be followed by her conviction that she could live there again, and she might even put an improvident deposit on a beach shack that appealed to her. Irene Stevens recalled an over-friendly greeting from a real estate agent when she and Astley were in Townsville, and felt she should have a quiet word to Jack to make sure that sense prevailed.[34] Ed and Michelle dined out on stories like these: Thea's new 'beach shack', usually absurdly ill-placed or a poor buy; Thea's insistence on travelling in the most uncomfortable way, arriving exhausted, dumping her old-style solid card suitcases and desperate for a cigarette.

Travel in trains and buses gave Astley ample opportunity to observe people and their idiosyncrasies, and to begin working them up as characters. Travel on public transport added to her long list of petty irritations: loud music in buses joined grainy breads that couldn't be properly chewed and snooty descriptions of food on restaurant menus. These fired up many of her award speeches. And when asked as a member of Paul Keating's Creative Nation panel in the mid-1990s what was the most important thing she would like to see change in the arts, she replied, 'Lowering the volume of rock music on buses.'[35] Rodney Hall, who was there at the time, remembers how it broke the whole solemnity of the moment.

Astley liked planning adventures on public transport. 'Don't forget writers on trains,' she wrote to Laurie Muller. 'I keep thinking more and more that I want to attend a train conference on Aust.Lit. heading out to Charleville or Cunnamulla. Doesn't the west deserve something. Maybe Kingaroy, even! How about that Joh ...'[36]

Trains gave her one of her most characteristic short story titles: 'Diesel Epiphany' was pure Astley, with its odd yoking of a classical word and sluggish locomotive. Titles were very important to Astley, though she was not always good at picking commercially successful ones: 'Come Home People' became the much better *A Kindness Cup*. In the early 1980s D'Arcy Randall, her editor at UQP, had worried about the title of *An Item from the Late News* but agreed to it when Astley suggested 'Myth-fits' – which Randall thought appropriate but too cute.[37] When Penguin tried to change the title of her early novel *The Slow Natives*, she would have none of it. *It's Raining in Mango* was unusual in being a working title that was retained. It was good, and nobody questioned it.

Astley needed that certainty, worried that Penguin might consider the novel's family saga too much like Peter Carey's novel *Illywhacker*. Given the brouhaha about the coming 1988 bicentennial year, Astley didn't want to appear merely modish – 'Hell, are all writers on the same wave length!'[38]

By now Astley's insecurities were a kind of pathology that couldn't be shifted by facts. She was, however, more in charge of the commercial decisions about her work than she had ever been. She might protest that legalese made her eyes cross and that contracts made her think of Chico and Groucho Marx in *A Night at the Opera*, but she now understood a great deal about writer–publisher commerce.[39]

While in the US she had engaged American literary agents Arnold and Elise Simon Goodman of Goodman Associates. Elise soon discovered that Stacy Creamer, editor at G.P. Putnam's Sons, loved Astley's writing, seeing it as entirely fresh and a welcome break from the recommended lists of the *New York Times Book Review*. Creamer would go on to publish many Astley titles in the US. Elise Goodman and Thea became firm friends; as contracts and documents flowed across the hemispheres, Elise would look out from her desk in her Manhattan apartment, 'wondering what Thea was doing all the way over there'.[40] She did not know that the leaves on the locust tree outside her apartment in New York were almost identical to the Australian jacaranda Astley had grown up with.

In the next few years Astley acquired an Australian agent and was published in the US and UK, with a steady stream of new paperback editions of her earlier works by Penguin and UQP, and even A&R who had retained some rights to her early novels.

Astley had encyclopaedic recall of the editions and sales of her works. She remembered how even the two editions of the 1967 US paperback of *The Slow Natives* had pretty much sank without a trace: she would not let that happen this time. She insisted on hardback publication and reprints for her titles in the US. In this she had the support of Elise Goodman, who wrote to Penguin: 'It does still – alas – make a difference to the reviewers.'[41] In late 1986 as Astley was working on the third draft of *It's Raining in Mango*, Penguin was asked to 'hold off' sending Astley paperbacks to interested US publishers to make way for the serious hardback career in the US that Astley longed for.[42]

By early 1987 the drafts of *Mango* had taken their toll and Astley found herself with ulcer problems and exhausted, 'like a returned serviceman from Beirut when I got to Xeroxing stage'.[43] After four or five drafts she certainly did not wish to re-read the novel or make any more major changes. Within a month of her finishing, she had signed a contract for paperback publication with Viking/Penguin in the US. Chasing up details of contracts and royalty statements was preoccupying and made writing feel like 'drain-digging fitted in between' but Astley kept a keen eye on how transnational rights operated.[44] She was also dealing from time to time with film treatments and rights, which troubled her even more – she'd had 'hell with *Descant*' – and *Item*'s treatment had been like 'a junior high school boy's masturbatory fantasy'. Astley also wondered why a scriptwriter's name should go ahead of the writer whose idea the book had been, and why putting together a screenplay might take five years to complete.[45]

Astley's direct manner and occasionally waspish tongue could cause offence – like telling the Penguin rights editor 'her telephone voice was brunette' – which she would try to smooth over with a joke.[46] Astley was still unsure of what banter she could take for granted between women. It was easier with writers: Helen Garner hadn't seemed to mind when Astley observed that she looked as if she had 'a new bloke'.[47]

When the cover for the Australian Penguin edition of *It's Raining in Mango* finally arrived, she already had Putnam's US hardback version as a comparison, which she preferred, complaining that the Australian cover was 'too busy in all its gloss'.[48]

She continued to be – without really needing to be – an agitator for her work. When Brian Johns left Penguin in 1987 Astley lost another key publisher–author relationship. She admired his successor Susan Ryan, former federal Minister for Education, and 'longed to have a good debate' with her 'on the Education bit' – but had not actually met her.[49]

In the meantime, Elise Goodman was angrily questioning some Penguin decisions about the sales of Astley's earlier titles. This was enough to rattle Astley and make Penguin invite their US publisher to explain the rights and sales of Astley's works as they stood. Australian authors were increasingly agitating for separate contracting of works by US publishers but were not necessarily going to find publishers willing to pay a separate advance. It was a lost opportunity with past titles, something Astley did not forget.

Response to the publication of *Mango* consumed Astley; so much depended on it because she wanted to honour the American interest in her work. She was to be a writer-in-residence at Memphis State University early in 1988, where Fay Zwicky would later report that she had been 'a smash hit'.[50] In another ten years the novel would be selected by a German publisher as part of a collection exploring Australian identity.[51]

When the novel was reviewed positively in *The New York Times* Astley immediately wrote to UQP begging them to let Putnam's UK produce a hardback 'Two by Astley', a joint volume of *The Acolyte* and *A Kindness Cup*. Penguin asked her for an old copy of *Natives* to work from for the paperback but she said – pointedly – that she really must hang on to the 'last American hardback published by M. Evans in 1967'.[52] Astley was well into her 'post-book low, why-do-I-bother-writing mood'.[53] At the same time she was endorsing books by other writers, such as Kate Grenville's bicentennial novel *Joan Makes History*.

Her mood was real. She and Jack were ageing. Ed was now working in television as a music producer, researcher and scriptwriter, putting in long hours at the Channel Nine network in Sydney. It wasn't a secure job in the way that she and Jack would have preferred. Despite their love of music and encouragement of Ed's musical talents, Thea and Jack shared a suspicion of the entertainment industry, a view common to many parents of their generation. To others, Ed's working life would have seemed a successful one – he was now being offered jobs at other studios. Ed and Michelle were doing what they had always done, travelling, working, and there were no grandchildren on the horizon. Astley never mentioned this to either of them.

Writing was her ballast, perhaps especially now. In the years to come it would give Astley little breaks from caring full-time for Jack, and there was continuity in seeing so many literary people she knew in Australia and the US. Late in 1989, serendipitously, a new fan emerged – 'a skin specialist who came into our lives from the blue,' Astley wrote. Geoff Cains collected Australian first editions and wanted Thea to sign his books. He and his wife, Sarah, invited Thea and Jack to spend a weekend at their bush home in Mittagong. Astley delighted in 'sneaking out to pee in early morning Mittagong on the salubrious lawns and dodging the affronted glances of joggers'.[54]

When the Cainses had first met Jack and Thea at Cambewarra, it seemed to them that Thea 'was lacking in stimulation', although entertaining, 'it was as if she didn't want to discuss the books at all, as if she'd said everything' and she could be quite 'repetitive in her conversation'.[55] Like Helen Garner, Geoff had picked up Astley's tendency to act out set scenes. Astley even revisited projects: in a letter to Garner, Astley suggested a joint writing exercise, much as she had with the novel she had mentioned more than twenty years before to Thelma Forshaw.[56]

Geoff thought Ed and Michelle's money-making activities in real estate were greeted without much joy; to others it seemed bizarre that these successful ventures were bitter disappointments to Thea. It was as if she viewed people almost with cruelty, even when she loved them. He also wondered whether Thea felt personally exposed by her writing – she had said to him 'it's almost as if I have no self left'. Thea and Jack as a couple now seemed 'totally dependent' by this stage of their lives. Thea was beginning to panic about Jack's health, including his frequent skin cancers; Geoff helped organise health cover.[57]

By the beginning of 1989 Astley had a draft of the next novel, 'Rubbertime' (it would become *Reaching Tin River*), and she had already begun to think of finding an Australian agent and offering her work on the open Australian market. Susan Ryan at Penguin was bitterly disappointed to lose Astley but it was well known in publishing circles that there could be further changes at the Penguin helm.[58] Astley chose to give the new manuscript to literary agent Jill Hickson of Hickson Associates in Sydney. The agency had begun more than five years before and had quickly established a reputation for energetic promotion of Australian authors. Hickson's written response was warm, intimate and emotional; to Astley it must have seemed irresistibly simpatico, with its deep understanding of 'the artful yet unselfconscious and completely satisfying way you have told Belle's story' and, 'the tension in the telling of the sexual epiphanies'.[59]

A new voice of support had come at just the right time: Astley now had someone who understood her work and who would promote sales of her books overseas. She knew the agency already handled many key Australian writers such as Tom Keneally, Janette Turner Hospital, and Robert Drewe, as well as more commercially popular writers such as Bryce Courtenay. Hickson astutely avoided the question of the manuscript's title, a further sign perhaps that here was someone with the kind of clever tact that Astley still valued so much, the kind Beatrice Davis had always had.

Davis was now in hospital enduring hip surgery, but she still handwrote a letter of thanks for Astley's 'generous praise' on an ABC arts show. She remembered that almost thirty years before she had experienced 'the shock of finding a real writer springing out of the general stodge: the individual imagination that marked *Girl with a Monkey*'. Now she wrote, 'I'm very proud of you Thea Deah', a sentiment that almost nobody but Davis could have expressed without Astley taking offence.[60]

16

Inventing her own weather

I must tell you: I have invented the weather. My personal weather.
Vanishing Points by Thea Astley, 1992[1]

The 1990s brought more success to Astley than she had known for thirty years. Her personal weather was changing; she was now surrounded by approbation that even she could hardly ignore. Astley had often joked that to write about Queensland she would have to leave the state first, but in 1988 *It's Raining in Mango* picked up Queensland's Steele Rudd Award for short story collections.[2] Penguin paperbacks of her earlier works were in production, including reprints of *Mango*, the earlier *Beachmasters*, and in the next year *A Kindness Cup*; the cover of *The Slow Natives* featured Queenslander houses, which pleased Astley.[3] She had accepted an honorary degree from the University of Queensland. The momentum of success was sweeping Astley forward.

In her new agent, Jill Hickson, Astley had chosen someone with excellent overseas publishing contacts (though this would lead to the end of the US Goodman connection) as well as local influence: Hickson was married to New South Wales Labor Premier Neville Wran, which suited Astley politically. Agency commissions were settled efficiently and an invitation to the exclusive Woollahra home of the Wrans was in the offing. Hickson worked quickly, placing Astley's new novel, *Reaching Tin River*, and tracing the position of all rights to her new author's books.

Overseas rights sold through Penguin in the US and in the UK led to editions of most of Astley's works being published and available in those countries. These included *Mango*, but also *Beachmasters*, *An Item from the Late News*, *A Kindness Cup*, *The Acolyte*, *A Boat Load of Home Folk*, *The Well Dressed Explorer* and *Girl with a Monkey*. No author, let alone one like Astley who had been writing for forty years, could fail to appreciate this moment: her entire oeuvre was in print and highly visible across the world.

Overseas exposure was much on Astley's mind, not least because she was now in regular contact with a number of writers and academics outside Australia. Letters and cards arrived regularly from University of California writer and academic Carolyn See, who wrote an occasional 'Literary Letter from Australia' for *The New York Times Book Review* and promised, 'You're in it and you're wonderful.'[4] See admired Astley's work and was thinking of teaching *A Kindness Cup* in her Australian literature course – all reminders for Astley that she had made her mark and would be welcome when she went to the US again.

Most significantly, Astley had won the Patrick White Award for 1989. This annual award had been established by White with his money from the 1973 Nobel Prize in Literature, and was given to a writer who has been creative over a long period but has not necessarily received adequate recognition. Astley was at lunch with Rodney Hall when the news came through. She said quietly to Hall, 'Ya know what it's for; it's for people who fail … question is do I take it or not? Think I'll take the money and run.' Her response did seem perverse but Hall knew some of the undercurrents here. Astley had talked dismissively of prizes before; she was happy to have them but according to Hall 'she felt her serious purpose had not been recognised'.[5] Of course, this had by now simply become an *idée fixe*.

What did Astley want? She had won all major literary national awards, her work was being published outside Australia, academic scholarship on her novels and short stories was increasing (it had never been as thin as she liked to imagine). By the end of the 1980s, it was true to say that Astley's novels were not widely set on school or university syllabuses, but some were. *Hunting the Wild Pineapple* was a particular success, set as a senior text for the New South Wales HSC in 1986, 1988–89 and 1994. The growth in postcolonial literature university studies saw *Beachmasters* appear on several courses. Astley had become a much-fêted interviewee, as well as featuring in two prominent collections of interviews with Australian writers (Candida Baker's *Yacker* collection and Jennifer Ellison's *Rooms of their Own*), published in 1986. Critical attention of her novels via academic journals now included articles in nearly all of the major ones: *Westerly*, *Australian Literary Studies*, *Southerly*, *Hecate* and *Ariel*. Robert Ross, the US academic, was now working on an edited book of essays, one of which would be about Astley, to be published in a year or so. All of this activity had emerged despite the fact that she had always professed scorn about literary scholarship; in 1972, when asked to speak at a conference on Patrick White, she replied, 'I'm not able to dig out those transcendental themes university critics are so good at; merely able to discuss form.'[6] Patrick White had personally endorsed the award in his name – something he knew Astley would know – and it was the final reparation for White's letter to Astley nearly thirty years before.[7] It was an acknowledgement that Astley had survived what he had called 'the rackety career of novel writing'.

There were many endings now in Astley's life. Hal Porter had died in 1984, and Douglas Stewart had gone the following year, a loss that affected Beatrice Davis badly. Other friends were becoming frail, including Beatrice, now eighty (she had been born in 1909), who had suffered a fall at home and was in hospital. There were tales of

Beatrice smuggling cigarettes and whisky into the hospital, but within a year she would be in a nursing home. Barrett Reid from Barjai days was dying, and of course Jack's health remained the dominant issue at home. He had recovered from his hip replacement surgery in 1989 but that seemed like the beginning of health issues, not the end. Astley often made light of the situation: 'He has X-rays of the prostheses that would make a cubist foam with envy,' Astley observed.[8]

Astley was still writing. As letters of congratulation for the Patrick White Award poured in from writers from all over the country, she concentrated on what was happening with her new work. *It's Raining in Mango* and now *Reaching Tin River* extended a whole visionary landscape that she had begun to explore decades before. Now, the practical question that played on Astley's mind was what to do about an Australian publisher.

Penguin had played an important role in her US visibility and her sales figures were seriously growing. But the change of publishing director in the company had made her a little less comfortable there. A new publisher, Louise Adler, had been appointed at Heinemann. She was already well known as an arts broadcaster, but now she was planning a strong Australian fiction list. Adler, who had considered Astley a loyal Penguin author, was surprised when Astley decided to break away, which she knew was a big decision. Jill Hickson was strongly in favour of the move, and they both liked what Heinemann was trying to do for Australian authors. Astley also liked the fact that Heinemann was prepared to offer a better deal than Penguin. Adler suggested that it wasn't just about the money, and Astley did feel loyal to Penguin, but she cared about being a professional writer and the money was tied to that.[9]

Astley was enjoying this new world of successful women; for the first time in her life her agent and publisher were both women. There was also genuine rapport between Astley and Adler. Astley had never seen herself as part of the sisterhood and though Louise was young enough to be her daughter and part of that generation who talked about feminism, their relationship was never political in that way. Together they went 'skipping arm in arm down Melbourne's Toorak Road dress shops' looking for a brown corduroy suit that Astley insisted she must have. Hours of pursuit failed to produce such a thing and Adler had to step in: 'Look Thea, it's not really the *year* of the corduroy suit!'[10]

Having arrived at Heinemann as such an experienced writer, Astley also appreciated Adler's light editorial touch.[11] Like Beatrice Davis before her, Adler had the knack of urging Astley towards the next book, and the next: *Vanishing Points* (1992) and *Coda* (1994) over the next four years. The settings were still Queensland, the natural site for Astley's creative vision.

For *Reaching Tin River*, she drew upon her years of living in the lush tropics, a landscape she knew intimately. Astley had once said that 'writing is bit like painting – putting a dab of colour down to get a whole effect' and she knew those little dabs needed to be made in intricate detail.[12] Some years after *Reaching Tin River* was published Astley explained the novel's origins: 'News clippings – yes, yes – especially old photos of early settlers. Old photos of bank clerks standing outside a building – there's a shed, a dog disappearing 'round the corner, somewhere near Charters Towers – three men in ties – marvellous – gave me the whole novel – *Reaching Tin River*.'[13] Ever since she had coined the metaphor 'the hinterland of childhood' Astley had wanted the landscape to be emotional as well as physical geography for her characters.

This novel was about obsessions, but Astley was attempting to do more than just parody people who were trying to 'find themselves'. She continued to be preoccupied with relationships. Sometimes this must have been wearing for her: in writing so much about relationships in her novels Astley was forced to live through more intense versions of her own thoughts and fears. She was risking – almost recklessly – proximity to her own guilt. 'Writing out the things that bothered her' put her at risk of harm all over again.

At the same time, Astley was having fun. Women could do things apart from marrying, and she was enjoying writing about them. In *Mango* Nadine and Chloe of the Dancing Bears whorehouse treat their business with weary disdain. In the *Multiple Effects of Rainshadow*, Mrs Curthoys regards marriage as 'legalised prostitution'.[14] If you chose to marry, as Boobs McAvoy had in *Tin River*, you were in for the 'the despair of lushness'.[15] In each of her later books Astley was building bridges between ideas about love, sex and responsibility that she had spent a lifetime in her writing trying to understand.

In *Reaching Tin River* Belle is caught between admiration of her mother's eccentricity and independence, and resentment for its effect on her own childhood. Astley was now into her mid-sixties, with her son in his thirties, and was facing such things. What had been the effect of her choices on Ed? Whenever she got the chance, especially with someone of roughly Ed's age, she would express these thoughts. At a café meal in Melbourne during a book tour, Astley overheard a young woman confess rather sheepishly that her mother had been a 'stay-at-home' mum. Astley cut in, rather too abruptly, 'Perhaps if she'd done anything else, you might have resented her?'[16] It was not really a question.

Tellingly, in *Tin River*, young Belle affirms her mother's unorthodox womanhood: 'Bonnie is right, I tell myself, in her committed obsessions, attached emotionally only to the abstract problems of life-style and drums, or even me in a tangential way.'[17] 'Tangential' is not a word Astley would ever have used to describe her attachment to her son but she obviously wondered about such things still. She remained convinced that parental love was the only love that lasted.

Being older meant that she was often reminded of this by other parents. Jill Hickson sent her a note saying that she hoped to have the 'wonderful relationship' with her children later in life that Astley clearly had with Ed.[18] Astley knew that her views on love and marriage spawned books that appealed to women on both sides of the age divide. She relished her opportunity to reverse the status quo, creating the character Julie Truscott in 'Inventing the Weather' (one of the novellas in *Vanishing Points*), who is so calm and formidably logical about the needs of her children that she leaves them in the full care of her unfaithful husband and his mistress.

Astley wanted to give voice to women's great unheard moments in marriage, silent from years of disengagement. This was a new arc of representation of women for her: from victims to passive resisters to those energised by self-interested protest. Increasingly the animus became not just anger but revenge, of 'disaffected and drifting protagonists' who fight back.[19]

Astley's tart comedic style attracted new readers. Her portrayal of women had bothered critics in the past: the language describing them could be harsh and judgemental. One critic described this aspect of her work as 'linguistically unstable'.[20] Was this part of Astley's 'feminist evasion tactics'?

A letter from the feminist author Dale Spender gave Astley vindication. In 1992 Spender wrote to say how much she liked *Vanishing Points*. Astley wrote back 'delighted to get a tribute from someone of your caliber … it was private, unsolicited and it made my day!' Even so, Astley couldn't help herself: 'It's funny, you know, but all the nice things critics have said about *V.P.* rather stun me. I guess after years of critical mauling of books that I feel are somewhat better, I'm confused. Maybe someone thinks I deserve a break after all these years!'[21]

It was thirty years since Astley had stated that 'women are sad things'; now she saw a 'vanishing point' for women when they aged that didn't seem to exist for men. She was still expressing old anger, really: anger for her years of teaching on half the male salary; for having to retire upon marriage; for the anti-female hierarchy of the Catholic Church she had grown up with; with the idea that sexual women are somehow selfish. There were no easy answers. Even the character Julie Truscott, who escapes to 'invent her own weather', does so to a low-paying job, all the while fighting off the unwelcome sexual attentions of a former boss.[22]

Sexuality and women's choices were still on Astley's mind when she talked with Martinelli next door, when she thought about her brother and the Church, but at other times, too, reflected in nervous phrases and throwaway lines.

Astley was tightening the circle of her personal history around herself, enabling her to shift female experience from the edge to the centre of her work. In *Vanishing Points* and *Coda* she telescoped past, present and ageing. In *Reaching Tin River*, her eccentric, self-willed female characters made the men seem tame and tiresome. Astley was now scattering details of her own past playfully: Villa Marina is the name of a boarding house like the one in Shorncliffe where she had boarded as a young student teacher; Julie Truscott speaks of her maternal forebears who 'lived in a world of women', as Astley's own mother had.[23]

The year 1990 was one of travel for Astley. She was to visit the US but there was another journey close to Astley's heart. After years of planning and as part of the International Year of Literacy, the Writers' Train she had continually discussed with Laurie Muller at UQP was about to depart from Central railway station in Brisbane for remote parts of Queensland, with Astley aboard. The Queensland government, as part of their decade of reviving arts funding, supported the innovative travelling writers' show.

Phil (now living in Rome and loving it) had been reminding her of their Queensland childhood, writing about their early years and the Latin Mass. Astley could not help but be reminded of teaching the 'kiddois', as she would pronounce it, as she had all those years ago.

The train would go to Toowoomba, Dalby, Chinchilla, Roma, and even more remote towns such as Charleville. These were places where she had given literary talks back in the early 1960s as a Commonwealth Literary Fellow. She was to travel with other writers, some of whom she knew and liked: Tom Keneally, Janette Turner Hospital, Rodney Hall, Tim Winton, Hugh Lunn, Victor Kelleher and poets Bruce Dawe and Komninos Zervos.[24] Not since the days of Barjai in the

1940s had Astley enjoyed this kind of writerly camaraderie. It was a perfect Astley expedition: locomotives, distance, travel, and country hotels in remote places.

The train pulled out after a convivial breakfast provided by UQP. Rodney Hall recalls that the whole trip was a 'rather strange full-on experience. All of us in the one carriage'. He sat next to Astley most of each day and the two found themselves very much the 'senior people'. It suited him, especially since he found that Astley could 'talk all day, never dry up, ranging over so many things'. She could start a conversation with a fixed view but end up unsure, and vice versa.

But it was the way Astley behaved towards children that told Hall a great deal about her. She never tried to be one of them or talk down to them. One scene stayed clearly in his memory. They were heading west out of Roma, and they passed a platform, not even a real station. On it stood about a dozen children holding up open books. Astley rushed up to the driver, desperately trying to get him to return: 'Quick, get on the radio, tell them there's kids here, you've gotta stop!'

The train returned, with those on board cheering and waving, but the children had left the platform and nobody was there. The driver blew the whistle and the writers saw the children almost a kilometre away, running towards them from a small schoolhouse and still clutching the books, with the teacher behind them. Astley insisted they all sign the children's books, whatever they were – even picture books.[25]

Astley couldn't wait to introduce Tim Winton to her friend Jeff McMullen, who was making a short film of the trip for television. 'You've got to meet this young bloke with the ponytail,' she told McMullen. Winton was by no means a household name at that time and Astley wanted to show off this new Australian writer who explored the themes of country, coast and character and who wasn't pushing himself forward. She herself did not want to be in the film, and McMullen couldn't help thinking of how strangely shy she could be. He knew the

Writers' Train had been her idea. It struck him that she might have been more comfortable about the whole project in a foreign setting, presenting an 'authentic take on who we are', but from afar.[26]

But his camera did manage to catch Astley once. She was in high spirits: 'I'm taking over. We're going to Warwick first. This is a hijack, everyone!' When asked about the trip, she was ready: 'I think people inland have been neglected. As if we've forgotten about them. I come out here with the utmost respect. I hope they get some fun out of us. I hope they get something.'[27] She had been moved by knowing what books meant to the people in the outback, particularly the children. Theirs was an isolation she understood.

Eventually Astley even agreed to a photograph, but only because it was taken in front of an outback dunny door lavishly covered by ivy. Typical Thea, thought McMullen. When Astley returned to the city, a letter in a child's handwriting said it all: 'I hope when I get older that I can buy a book of yours and read it. I really enjoyed meeting you and hope to see you again someday. Yours sincerely … (the girl in the pink jacket)'.[28]

Life was getting busier all the time, and Thea and Jack were often apart, though he had come on the earlier US trip. This was the year of further investigation of his eye problems by the specialist. The situation worried Phil – he wondered how Thea would cope – but he had his own problems. Back at Campion House in Melbourne he was nervous about having to say a less familiar but 'beautiful, reverent form of the Mass'.[29]

Astley, who had to look after Jack, was not what friends would call a natural nurse, and some actually felt sorry for her. As one commented, 'She had to do it and she did, but she had to learn it.' It was the same with the driving, 'she got into the car like a little old lady'.[30] Jack still wanted Thea to go on working. He was not just tolerant of her eccentricities, he was fiercely proud of her.

Astley continued to embrace literary activity other than writing. She had been asked to talk at the Australian Booksellers and Publishers

Association in March; she had agreed to launch a monograph on Beatrice Davis by Anthony Barker later in 1991, and she was still in demand at writers' festivals. At the ABPA dinner, she was in a good mood about the business of writing, saying, 'Writers must admit that without publishers and distributors they (the writers) would exist under what Maxwell Smart called the Dome [actually Cone] of Silence.'[31]

But she really wanted to talk about writers and how increasing age didn't matter. The speech brought together all the old irritations as well as new fears: that question of style and her status as a 'senior' writer. Quoting from an article advising writers not to write in a 'style of and for a readership 30 or 50 years ago', Astley launched into a list of all the 'Greats' that this advice would 'cut out', as well as herself. It begins as a list as close to Astley's literary preferences and influences as one might get: Flaubert, Balzac, McCullers, Flannery O'Connor, Virginia Woolf, Borges, Calvino, Lowry, Joyce, Sterne, Austen, Eliot, Rimbaud, Baudelaire, Kafka, Proust, Dostoyevsky, Dickens, Twain. By this stage of course, as she acknowledged to the audience, the list would have no end. Astley was still sensitive: maybe she herself would fall under that Cone of Silence.

But shortly afterwards in 1991 came the news that *Tin River* had won the Christina Stead Prize for Fiction, one of the major New South Wales literary awards. The book had also been received favourably by the US literary press. Astley was enjoying a very strong relationship with her editor at Putnam's, who had already contracted for US rights to several of her previous works. Within a couple of years these older titles, spanning thirty years of Astley's writing career, were also being reviewed in the US, and favourably. Here was the extended assessment she longed for. 'The prolific Australian novelist,' wrote one *New York Times* reviewer, 'could be an antipodean cousin to Muriel Spark or Iris Murdoch.'[32]

At home in Australia, her profile continued to grow. Astley was being rediscovered. Interviewers easily related the concerns of *Tin River* to her earlier works, especially to music. The 'Rustle of Spring' parody had amused music buffs. Helen Garner – who was writing to Thea quite often – even joked that she might learn the piece.[33]

Louise Adler was playful, wondering 'how fecund' Astley was feeling with all her 'gallivanting around'.[34] She knew her author well: Astley would want to capitalise on the success of *Tin River.* She had two novellas that could be published in one volume. Early in 1992 the 'twinned' novellas of *Vanishing Points* were settled for publication later in the year and Astley turned her thoughts to a last book with the significant title *Coda*.

Endings are a feature of late life. Vida Horn from Barjai days had written and invited her and Jack for a last visit to see an ailing Barrett Reid in Melbourne in January of 1992.[35] A letter arrived from Sister Mary Claver, now infirm and in Charitis Christi, where Phil gave the Friday Benediction of the Sacrament. Sister Mary was a reminder to Astley of the special relationship they had shared; the young nun had always taken a special interest in her. 'It wasn't difficult to learn,' wrote the sister in what would be her last letter, 'that you'd been blessed with special talents, especially in the literary line.'[36] She sounded almost like Beatrice Davis, who was also fading.

Astley knew Beatrice was not religious in her thinking about death. She had instructed those planning her memorial, 'Don't put too much God into it, darling.'[37] Astley and Beatrice had always enjoyed the same bleak humour: they joked how Beatrice's fall and emphysema from years of chain-smoking hadn't quite killed her off. Astley knew Davis simply wanted to die peacefully, ever the background figure, like the judicious and self-effacing editor Astley had known for over thirty years.[38] The announcement when it came was not unexpected. Davis had died in her sleep on 24 May 1992, aged eighty-two. It was an important loss.

Astley did not care for funerals and did not attend Beatrice's. All her life she had avoided these ritual occasions of grief, save for her close family. The mixture of formality and possible outward displays of emotion was clearly unsettling for Astley. She did not fear witnessing other people's vulnerabilities; she feared exposing her own.

But she had Phil's letters for consolation. In a couple of years his health would start failing, but he had a better way of dealing with death and loss. His letters about their earliest loves in music and poetry were a delight.[39] Astley herself was not ready to give up writing, and she resisted any honours that suggested she might be – such as *The Courier-Mail*'s mid-year 'Top 100' Queensland Day celebration of writers.[40] She was healthy, she was writing, that was all anyone needed to know.

These ruminations always put Astley in a bad mood, which influenced her behaviour in ways that troubled others. Louise Adler wanted to make her happy, and found herself trying. She arrived at Cambewarra. The house was clean-lined and functional yet somehow 'felt unloved, plain'. She unpacked her carefully selected Melbourne gourmet delicacies, looking at Astley's face: she accepted the goods but with little more than polite interest. Didn't she want a taste? Astley found indulgence impossible: she was like eighteenth-century writer Samuel Johnson who said that 'music is the only sensual pleasure without vice'.[41] This apparent determination not to take pleasure in such things was foreign to Adler.

Adler knew Astley to be a complex and intelligent woman who could be highly critical and prone to resentment. She felt that her reputation had been hard won and she could seem jealous of other writers getting prizes.[42] Her feelings could take a perverse form if modish ideas about her work irritated her or she just didn't want to be there. At the 1992 Melbourne Writers Festival, Astley sat grimly, and was terse in her interview with Rosemary Sorensen (who later confessed to tears afterwards), stonewalling her polite and engaging questions about the writing life and Astley's books in particular. It was impossible – on a public stage – for the interviewer to dig herself out of such a predicament with such a well-known writer, especially as Astley would turn to the audience with a facial expression that invited them to join her in frustration at the stage-managed life of the literary festival. But it was Astley's conduct that became the talk of the festival.[43]

However, she could demonstrate a genuine rapport with interviewers, for example with the ABC's Caroline Jones on the radio program *The Search for Meaning*. ('Caroline, the hotel they've chosen for me certainly isn't the answer to the search for meaning.')[44] And ABC radio's *Books and Writing* presenter Robert Dessaix had appreciated Astley's support for his autobiography *A Mother's Disgrace*. He wrote to her, grateful for her conviction that he could go on to write something else. Astley had also been personally kind to his mother when they met.[45]

Astley should have been sanguine: a new wave of scholarly interest in her was happening and the academics were moving in. Letters arrived regularly about books, her work, and books about books; there was talk of research grants. Then there was that blonde woman who was starting something biocritical. It was 'always strange to see whimsy in a blonde', Thea had said when they met. This woman had brought home-made lamb shank soup, soft white bread and real butter to Astley's hotel apartment, causing Thea to whisper to Jack: 'This girl's gotta really want something!'[46] These new younger readers meant well but Astley was still bored or affected boredom with theoretical debate about feminism, for instance. But she was still angry about women and about men's control over women's lives. For her feminism was about justice, not '-isms'. What gave her public remarks such a snarky aspect was of course her own sense of having been hard done by.

Astley was now approaching seventy. She had spent her sixties turning on its head her comment that 'women are sad things after forty'. It remained to be seen what the next years would bring.

17

Curving

Tracking a peculiar logical sorites he attached the infallibility of the Lord to himself.

The Multiple Effects of Rainshadow
by Thea Astley, 1996[1]

Though all readers and writers are obviously on a journey towards old age, it takes a brave novelist to tackle the subject of nursing homes. But Thea Astley almost ran towards the topic. Though she had already dealt with 'granny dumping', in *Coda* (1994), she was still collecting advertisements featuring aged-care facilities with 'Special Spring Offers' and resort-style activities. It was as though Astley saw the final descent into old age as her last writerly high point, an opportunity to visit the ultimate self-delusion.

Old age may be the saddest expression of unfounded self-belief: we forget in the moment – we have to – that we don't live forever. To Astley death was predictable, boring even, and pretending it did not exist was pathetic, if human. It wasn't death that bothered Astley; it was the extinction of consciousness. Death was much on her mind, as it had been for a long time. In one poignant scene from *Beachmasters*, published in 1985 when she was sixty, the vulnerable teenager Gavi Salway is in conversation with his grandfather:

> '... as we get older it's as if we draw a circle round ourselves, make the boundary smaller and smaller until maybe, one day we find ourselves at the very centre.'
>
> 'What's that?' the boy had asked. 'What's the centre?'
>
> 'It might be death,' grandfather had said, softening the word with a smile.[2]

The naming of death could be softened with a smile – but the fact of it could never be changed.

Astley had long since ceased attending Mass, but still prayed to a God – not necessarily the God of the Catholic Church.[3] Remembering, being remembered, was important. In Astley's new 1996 novel, *The Multiple Effects of Rainshadow*, the schoolteacher Vine muses how the memory of lost relationships is 'as fragile and unmemorable as most fiction is'.[4] Her words perfectly capture how Astley felt about relationships – beyond the very few she had maintained – during this period in her life.

What remained? Astley was asking. Was it family? Was it books? She had just received a strange parcel from Michael McGirr. He had found a copy of her first novel, *Girl with a Monkey*, in the Toowong Jesuit library, her hand-written inscription to her own parents still intact. She did not like to think about how it got there. But love was never simple: 'First rule of family. Love is loathing,' she scribbled on her manuscript. Astley was currently 'finding writing sheer effort'. 'These days I wonder why I bother. Something drives me, I guess.'[5]

In 1988 Thea and Jack bought a house at Sussex Inlet on the New South Wales south coast, and in 1999 they decided to move there. It was a godsend. The place was only half an hour away from Cambewarra, but it offered a complete change of scene. The house was like their first home in Dorset Street, being clad in a similar style of timber and of similar proportions. The exercise of tasteful remodelling was a journey back in time for Thea and Jack. It was another opportunity, too, to be a couple among couples, with pleasant neighbours. It was an escape: a quiet home by the water in old age was an ironic celebration of the predictable.

'Vanishing points', as Astley called them, had become a set of skilfully placed allusions throughout her books. The phrase dates back to her first novel. To Astley the phrase came to stand for the singular and disturbing moments of a terror of consciousness, which she confronted in her work, as she did here in her first novel: 'There was some vanishing point for all these things, a point where they actually met with dagger-like acuteness and drove the mind further than it dared.'[6]

In this Astley is being true to the credo of the Orphic artist, concerned to map, reach, or breach historical time and the poetic infinite. Astley's 'vanishing point' (and much of her other mystical symbolism) is thus an overriding Orphic metaphor that supports the other numerous Orphic 'moments' throughout her work. Perhaps this is best illustrated in the epigraph she chose from 'Le Voyage' by one of her favourite Orphic poets, Charles Baudelaire, which she used in *Vanishing Points*. It illustrates Astley's sense of the phrase, but also perhaps the poetic company she liked to keep:

> *Ah! que le monde est grande à la clarté des lampes!*
> *Aux yeux du souvenir que le monde est petit!*
>
> Ah! How large the world is by lamplight!
> In the eyes of memory, how small it is!

In *The Well Dressed Explorer* she had written of the 'merciful vanishing point of perspective that in its alchemy causes the fact to become insubstantial. Remaining. Vanishing. Both at once'.[7] That was the key: being present and absent. Everything had its equal and equivalent opposite. These phrases inverted beautifully to reflect the central paradox of consciousness Astley experienced. It would become a trademark of her later prose style: 'Peace is explicable. Is inexplicable.'[8] This was her mathematics of despair – she was miming Charles Baudelaire, who also wrote of 'certain delicious sensations which are no less intense for being vague; and there is no sharper point than that of Infinity'.[9]

Astley's metaphors for life more or less suspended between the two tendencies. The rather ethereal images of vanishing points have their energetic counterpoint, in 'a natural synchronism in the world. All things crash together'.[10] Indeed at this time, for Astley, they certainly seemed to.

Heinemann was in a state of corporate flux, with Louise Adler about to depart after five years, as she did in 1994, to become arts and entertainment editor for the Melbourne *Age*. Theirs had been an important personal relationship for Astley; professionally, it had changed the way her books were published and built her readership by drawing in new readers. Much as she liked the journalist Jennifer Byrne who was taking over, things would not be the same. Other pressures edged in too. Phil had cancer and was facing a protracted terminal illness; Jack had prostate cancer, not itself a killer but needing to be managed; she and Jack were now 'an aged pair', she wrote in a letter; and always there was the concern about moving closer to Ed.[11] The tone of complaint meant that this was a letter the seventy-year-old Astley could have written at any time during the previous five decades of her life. Doubtless she knew it.

In Donal O'Shea's book *The Poincare Conjecture: In Search of the Shape of the Universe*, he writes that 'nothing illustrates the tension between precision and dreaminess better than Euclid's *The Elements* …' Writing about the universe and the way we imagine space and time, he asks the question: 'If our universe doesn't go on forever, and if it has no walls, doesn't that mean that the universe must be bent or curved somehow? … Come to think of it, what do we mean by curving?'[12] Thea Astley, who once said the Catholic Church stimulated 'metaphor glands', was writing a geometry of living more in keeping with Euclid.

Astley would have loved the concept of curving. But the real attraction of lines, shapes, movements across space was the visual richness it offered Astley. Hers was a visual imagination that she possibly inherited from her grandfather, the artist Charles Astley. Increasingly Astley saw the shape of her writing in images: 'a series of overlapping photos, negatives … with bits of one view superimposed on the next or others'.[13] She moved gently around the territory that she had made hers in her writing, looking for a final resting place. Her return to her old publisher Penguin in 1996 might have had something to do with this. Astley and Bob Sessions, now publishing director there, went back twenty years to the days of Nelson and Beatrice Davis and the *Pineapple* story collection. She wanted to call her new novel *The Multiple Effects of Rainshadow* and she discovered a new ally in Meredith Rose, her young editor at Penguin. She and Astley clicked; Rose had her own 'crazy Methodist upbringing' to rival her author's Catholicism, and they shared a similar sense of humour. Astley always knew how to play many roles almost simultaneously: friend-teacher-parent. On first impression she seemed to Rose more like an impish schoolgirl than anything else.[14]

Author and editor met in a hotel room for a one-off editing session on *Rainshadow* and Rose brought a teapot so they could have real leaf tea. 'We spent as much time laughing as editing,' said Rose. 'She didn't need a lot of editing.' The manuscript had already been worked on in the process of being bought by Penguin. Rose soon understood that she was working with an author who was 'scrupulously sensible', not at all the tricky customer she had been warned about.[15]

Astley was in any case happy about being with Penguin again, 'loved the whole iconic thing of Penguin', would laugh at herself for loving also the bright orange bulb that overhung the entrance at the publisher's large outer-suburban Melbourne office. Rose and Astley enjoyed endless phone calls, catching up on episodes of *The Bold and the Beautiful*, the plots of which Astley would relate in hilarious detail. But Rose saw that Astley was also suffering. She seemed in fact to be consumed by guilt about Jack and whether she was doing enough for him.

Her sense of responsibility seemed all the more pressing because Phil was now gravely ill. Astley might not have known it, but her brother was struggling with more than illness. In August of 1996 he had asked to be released from the Jesuits, but his wishes were regarded as a temporary aberration induced by stress related to his cancer treatment.[16]

Ageing makes life seem less linear, more like a series of patterns that crisscross back and forth. Once, years before, Astley had given a speech about writing. The transcript is undated, but mentions 'Gabby', the main character from the 1982 novel *Item from the Late News*, assuming audience familiarity with that text. She mentioned Chekhov's short story 'Ariadne', where one of the characters refers to a novel by Weltmann in which one man says, 'What a story'; the other replies, 'No, it's only the beginning to my story.' 'Most of life,' said Astley, 'is a series of multiple beginnings. To grasp even a few of those beginnings and weave them into some sort of form is what the writer's craft is all about.'[17]

By the end of 1996, as the fortunes of *Rainshadow* rose, Phil was ill enough to be taking morphine. He scribbled a last note to his sister: he was sleeping a lot, and perhaps it was 'time for a phone call or two'.[18] Ed and Michelle had decided to visit him in Melbourne. Astley was tentative about seeing her brother that one last time; the arrangements, the flights seemed too difficult. She put the trip off for several months. Then a nurse rang her to say that Phil was close to death. Ed organised flights quickly and Astley was in Melbourne that night. Phil was looking dreadful in a way Astley had never previously seen. She was shocked, and escaped for a cigarette outside.[19]

Just over half an hour later Astley saw Ed walking towards her and immediately knew the worst. As well as dealing with the finality of that news, she was appalled at her selfishness. She went back to Phil's home in Campion House, Kew – she would be near him there – and three days later, on 19 June 1997, attended his Memorial Mass at the Church of the Immaculate Conception, Hawthorn.

At the service Astley was confronted by the past that she and Phil had shared. The liturgy, rightly or wrongly, was also a litany, an honest account of Phil's life and his many stages in the Church, at odds with himself, struggling with his God and his religious responsibilities. Why, Astley wondered, was there such sanctimonious insistence on the ways the Church had helped him in all the phases of his misfortune? Did they think his life was a failure? Astley sat silently fuming, unable to see quite how the Church had been a place of nurture for her brother.

Conversations after the ceremony didn't help, with one or two brothers offering accounts of Phil's naïve approach to cheeky primary schoolboys and how the boys had outsmarted him. Michael McGirr remembers Astley pronouncing defensively, 'Well, at least he tried.' Back in the car, she blurted out to McGirr, 'He suffered for fifty-five years, so much loneliness.' But McGirr knew this was not so: Phil had touched lives, made genuine friendships. Astley was projecting her own feelings about Phil's life: she knew she could never have stood it.

McGirr also knew that Astley was protective of Phil and he could see how much of a strain the day had been for her. In the car, every conversation seemed to turn on guilt. After coffee, Astley and McGirr went to a bookshop, where McGirr was a little astonished to see Astley taking her books off the shelves to sign them. He heard her lean over to the girl behind the counter: 'I'll give you a piece of advice. A signed book is a sold book. Once they are signed, they can't be returned to the warehouse.'

Business on the day of your brother's funeral: it was very odd behaviour, thought McGirr. After the funeral Astley wanted to visit Helen Daniel, the editor of *Australian Book Review*, whose partner had just died. They arrived at the office in Carlton unannounced and Thea immediately embraced Helen and said, 'You feel like *you* did it, don't you?' It seemed she did. It was a rapport, but it was built on guilt; McGirr could see this was Thea's way of 'drawing poison from the wound'.[20] By the time they travelled out to Penguin's offices, Astley's defences were falling away. Meredith Rose was called down to the foyer to find Thea distressed and in tears.

It was one thing to travel back in your own mind, another to be propelled there by the fates. Astley, who had lived largely outside her home state, found that despite *Rainshadow*'s main award being the Melbourne-based *Age* Book of the Year, many things continued to take her back to Queensland. There was to be a plaque with her name in the Albert Street library trail in Brisbane; Diane Cilento was hoping to perform an adaptation of *It's Raining in Mango* with her community theatre group Karnak in north Queensland. It only took one letter like that for real estate fantasies to bubble to the surface. A house had been bought in Cairns three years before, in 1994, and sat empty. When Astley heard Meredith Rose was going up north for a holiday, she asked her to bring back the real estate brochures for Mossman where Cilento lived.

Increasingly, signs of multiple endings – rather than the 'multiple beginnings' Astley had previously been concerned with – were now the norm. People Astley had known well for many years were now leaving publishing or other roles, reminding her that time was doing its work. The most significant was Irene Stevens's departure from the Literature Board. For more than twenty years she had seen Astley throughout the stages of writing, all her 'before and after' moods. Even closer to home was the question of Jack's various illnesses – involving his eyesight, prostate and heart, the long-term effects of two hip replacements he had had as far back as the 1980s – and how best to manage the end. Would she even have the chance to write just one last book? Astley's near contemporary, the short story writer and novelist Elizabeth Jolley, had said that the writing in *Rainshadow* was 'poetical and musical', 'vivid and haunting' and above all endorsed the title.[21] 'Haunting' was the word that stood out for Astley.

The house near Sussex Inlet was still a refuge, from Jack's health problems as much as for Astley's writing. Ed's wife, Michelle, and her sister had stayed there for long periods after Thea and Jack first bought it in 1988 but before they had moved in, and suggested that near neighbours Kevin and Pat McHugh were people she and Jack might befriend. By 1996 Thea and Jack planned to live there permanently. The house had been gradually altered, with the addition of a bedroom and a bathroom that had a bath – a necessity in Astley's view – so it was now suitable for friends to make it their own from time to time. Above all it was the best house for family.

Ed, Michelle and Michelle's wider family, including her siblings and their young children, made Christmas seem almost picture-perfect and easy, with everybody sitting in the sun on the new decking and Thea matching cigarettes one to one with Jack's scotch. At such gatherings Astley was at her most immediately present but still, as always, not completely. She still had the world of words in her head, the words in the world. What would her world have been like without them? What would the world be like without them? Here was the kernel of an idea for that last book, a book for the world's last reader.

Astley was not fond of last words of the kind spoken at funerals; a writer might scatter her own ashes better in a final book. Time might be running out. If Astley was headed for 'dry lands', why not have *Drylands* as a title?

From the end of 1996 until 1998 Astley was writing this novel, about a small Queensland town where little had changed in fifty years, where 'loneliness is almost a religion, and still everyone knows your business'.[22] It was the same subject as *Girl with a Monkey* but this time the writing was more savage. She was finely calibrating all the fifty years of her anger for one last expression – about men and women, small minds, the violence and hedonism of a philistine culture that liked to pretend it was 'knockabout' while in fact being driven by consumerism and corruption. It was an anger Astley found herself defending after the book came out in 1999: 'You haven't got to be angry – you can be amused – but it needs to be strong enough as an impulse.'[23] If hers was an ill-tempered view then that was how Astley was feeling. The book was bleak: 'I might have to agree – maybe I was feeling bleak.'[24] This last instalment was a strong indictment of the world, but in interviews Astley kept talking about 'magic', the magic of words.

The same low mood prevailed all year. Cairns City Library was using quotes from her work for their Literary Trail – but misspelling them. There was to be a series of plaques dedicated to writers, created by local artists, with quotations from the chosen works of the writer. Astley wrote a stinging letter:

> I might have felt differently, perhaps, had I been consulted on the actual choice of extracts; but what incensed me was the inability of the typist to transcribe accurately. The first quotation contains two spelling mistakes in four lines; the second has one mistake in three lines; the fourth extract has the page wrong. This does not inspire confidence.[25]

The library had meant to celebrate her. People were still getting her wrong and no amount of apology would persuade her not to point this out. Astley knew that such acerbic reactions seemed extreme to others but she was unable to respond any other way when the mood took hold of her. She wrote this flaw into some of her characters, unveiling alter egos spanning fifty years of writing – the '90% ME' she had declared her books were.

In the new novel – the one she intended to be her last – many of Astley's lifelong preoccupations and attitudes had their final expression. The character of Franzi Massig is a man with a 'flippancy' he can't control. The character Janet loves reading; she is the child who 'learned about the warfare of married couples' and found corners in which to hide. Paddy Locke is a collector and protector of the underdog, particularly the Aboriginal underdog, and nurturer of the screwball outsider. Evie is a creative writing tutor who deplores the wrongs inflicted on her own sex. Lannie Cunneen, after twenty years of marriage, hardly knows what sex she is. All were logical sorties in an argument whose premise was Thea. Astley was travelling backwards fast: author, mother, wife, woman, girl.

Penguin's team was bowled over by the novel from the outset.[26] By October of 1998 the usual tussle over the title had begun. Astley was toying with 'Almost There' or 'Almost Home' (the title of the last-but-one section of the novel) or 'Dry Lands'.[27] Her original title stuck, though as one word, and Meredith Rose, now in Broome working as editor for Magabala Books, agreed to take on the editing, sending pages of minor edits from there for Astley to consider. Astley was surprised that Rose had said little about the book itself – just the edits coming through. She was still unusually sensitive and easily undermined, and Rose knew this, sending a note praising the book's 'undeniable feeling of the emptiness of everything. And the fullness of it'.[28] Only an editor who knew Astley well and understood her work could have made such an observation, close to something Astley would have thought of herself. The matter of title settled, Astley prepared to enjoy this last beginning that was also an end.

Ambient sadness gentle as death's dust had settled on her despite the shimmer of activity caused by the move in 1999 to Sussex Inlet. The flatness of the land and its proximity to the sea were attractive to both her and Jack, especially as Jack now needed more care. Michelle had been right about the McHughs a couple of doors down; Thea had introduced herself as 'Mrs Gregson' and Pat McHugh soon learned how suspicious and touchy Thea was about being identified as Thea Astley the writer. Soon afterwards she had said hello only to find Thea forgetting they knew each other: 'How do you know me?' They had a shared Catholic upbringing and both enjoyed heated discussions. Marital spats raised no eyebrows in this company. 'Thea would come around the block smoking furiously muttering, "I'm gettin' away from 'im in there."'[29]

The McHughs had been married as long as Thea and Jack and the two couples enjoyed an easy camaraderie. This was not literary friendship but, importantly now, personal. Astley warmed to her new audience, one that understood her gibes about Catholicism. To the McHughs these seemed to hinge on very particular rules that Thea had grown up with and they led to absurd stand-up arguments, monologues and inquisitions. Astley was determined to subject the rituals of faith to pure logic. In her childhood it had been a sin to eat meat on Friday: you went to Hell. Once it was allowed, 'Thea got stuck into whether they were all going to Hell'. She laid the argument out as neatly as a tablecloth: How did it work, then? Maybe the others hadn't gone to Hell. Ergo, it was a lie. Ergo, lying was a sin. Conclusion: there was no Hell.

In this mood she refused to let go of the topic, her attitude ranging from mock-seriousness to genuine anger.[30]

Behind it all was worry: Jack. Thea joked that his eyesight wasn't as bad as he made out and they played games along that line. Astley would move the pepper or salt, just to see whether Jack knew where it was. On her own Thea would confess she felt she must have caused the macular degeneration from which Jack was suffering by forcing him to live in the Queensland sun during the 1980s. Astley had a way of convincing herself of these things: it was almost as if she needed guilt to justify her concern for his wellbeing.[31]

Pat McHugh was the kind of woman Astley had always liked: unfussed by status and preoccupied within her own private sphere and family. She might visit the mobile library and go for coffee wearing a man's blue-checked pyjama top. Somehow Pat understood that Thea could not be talked into or out of anything; anyone who tried was likely to strike a sore point. Driving was a good example. Thea had always hated driving and dealing with gears, but the suggestion that she should get an automatic car would provoke a tirade about the way men tried to restrict women from driving. The typewriter could never be replaced with a computer. If she went shopping – 'Let's have a bit of a perve,' she would say – she always looked for caftans. Loose-fitting garments were not in fashion, and the search would be another version of the hunt for the brown corduroy suit with Louise Adler in Melbourne.

Sport was another touchy topic. The McHughs happened to be friends with Tom Keneally, who had been at school with Pat's husband, Kevin. They met him skiing and mentioned it to Thea: 'What's he doing skiing!' she answered, as if writers were letting the side down by taking part in such pursuits. For someone whose main outing was to Nowra to buy cigarettes in large cartons, perhaps that reaction was to be expected. It was a relief to Thea not to have to talk about her writing, but she was probably enjoying the chance to express her views one more time.

Astley's life now centred on caring for Jack. In May 1999, she herself had been ill with stomach pain; she had had to cancel the launch of *Drylands* at the Melbourne Writers Festival. Astley had not given much attention to her own health until now – only Jack's – and she knew she was facing a couple of years of doctors and hospitals, disruptions to the life they were used to leading. At the back of her mind was always how these things would affect Ed.

It was time to walk away from certain things. Her agent Jill Hickson had decided to sell her business to agents Curtis Brown. In May of 2000 Astley wrote to them: 'I feel it is rather pointless continuing to have an agent at this stage of my life. I don't intend writing any more novels.'[32] 'This stage of my life' was not an Astley phrase; the shadow of cliché had just crept across her life.

The only thing that broke the literary silence of this time was news that *Drylands* was a joint winner of the 2000 Miles Franklin Award for fiction – Astley's fourth. The other winner was Kim Scott, an Indigenous writer, for *Benang*, a novel about Aboriginal disinheritance, an epic subject Astley would have endorsed. To be sharing the award was another one of those synchronous happenings: she had shared her first Miles Franklin nearly forty years before.

In 2002, at the New South Wales Premier's Literary Awards, she was given a special award for her lifetime achievement. This did cheer her up and the McHughs had sparkling wine ready for a celebration. However, Thea was now so concerned for Jack he wasn't allowed any of it – she had to get him up the few stairs to their house afterwards. Jack, who used to be able to leap up stairs, was now extremely ill. Astley decided not to attend the award ceremony in Sydney and to use the award money to fly Ed up to see Jack.

By the end of 2002 Jack was clearly failing. He was admitted to hospital, drifting in and out of consciousness. Astley sat with him on New Year's Day 2003 and was told to go home: the hospital rang soon after with the news she had been dreading.

No foreknowledge of death protects from its impact. Ed suddenly realised how little either of his parents had ever talked of it. Jack had not wanted a formal funeral and Thea was of like mind. The decision was made to scatter his ashes near the house at Sussex Inlet. On the appointed day, Thea, Ed and Michelle braved a fierce wind in the wrong direction – with some welcome laughs – before heading for a calm spot near the park at the edge of Swan Lake. Thea read a poem from Bruce Dawe's 1971 *Condolences of the Season*, 'Any Shorter and I'd Have Missed It Altogether', a final tribute to irony and the lives lived, and shared, in its presence.

Astley had been independent in her early twenties but this was the first time she had been alone. Of course, she had travelled to writers' festivals and carried out residencies, but not alone, not like this. In the last ten years she'd been writing passionately about women striking out on their own, which she admired, yet she had not lived like that herself. Even when Astley had a short residency in Denmark, Jack and Ed had tried to convince her to extend her trip, to travel freely on her own, but she had come straight home. Ed had long understood this anxiety; things needed to be, and stay, in place. Plans were not for altering. 'You could never say to Thea, "Look, there's been a change and we might have to do it differently." It would cause real angst.'[33]

Like most people suddenly bereaved after a long relationship, Astley was left to wonder what there had been before Jack. What could she go back to? In her mind there was only that lonely young schoolteacher in a small Queensland town. With Jack gone, everything was gone: argument, music, jokes. They had fought each other fiercely and often but never over the future, because they knew each of them was the other's future. Being so bound together had actually liberated them.

They were people of their time. Technology, in most of its guises, had never much appealed to Astley, and both she and Jack took pride in being technically intolerant. Ed would recall, 'If you tried to explain email Thea would just close down.'[34] She remained attracted to the spiritual calm of their special kind of merging of consciousness, because it foretold of death; in *Drylands* she had written of Chardin's Omega Point and 'the ultimate integration of all individual consciousness', anticipating her own such moment.[35]

In the days after Jack's death there was much to face and at such times all the writing in the world is useless. Astley, in great distress, took to calling friends repeating endlessly what she saw as her failure to support Jack in his time of need. 'I've been a terrible wife, I've been shocking,' she told Michael McGirr. Her reaction did not fit the facts but somehow she needed to say such things. People became seriously worried about her. Mark Macleod, still a close friend, knew that her feeling this way was also partly the consequence of all those years when Thea and Jack removed themselves to such remote places, making life more difficult for them.[36]

Within weeks of Jack's death, Ed and Michelle organised for Thea to move to a rented holiday apartment near the town of Brunswick Heads in northern New South Wales, close to them and not too far from Byron Bay. She was to be there temporarily while the house that had been purchased at Suffolk Park, with its little strip of shops and bush nearby, was settled formally. Thea said little about the arrangements.

Staying at the same holiday apartments were former Epping neighbours Margaret and Allan Smith. During dinner they spotted their old friend looking rather lost. When they visited her in her room the next morning, there she was, sitting on the bed in the familiar cross-legged pose, smoking furiously under the 'Smoking Prohibited' sign. This was reassuring, a sign that the old Thea was still there. But she was desperately unhappy, a little spiteful with it, and not inclined to pretend to please. There was a litany of complaints: There was no square bread in Byron Bay; the new house was 'a good investment for when I'm gone'.

The velocity of the changes seemed too much for her. The Smiths wondered whether Thea should have stayed in the Sussex Inlet house temporarily, to grieve quietly. But when Astley rang them a year later, at Christmas, they could hardly believe the difference in her. This time they got a typical 'Thea account of the new house, its absurd design'; the steps she had to negotiate just to 'get to the loo' and the lush bush surrounding the lovely decking that she might just set on fire with her early morning fag.[37] If anyone had happened to move to Suffolk Park for the tranquillity of fresh air and bush, Astley was clearly not the ideal neighbour.

Astley knew she was, as she said to the writer Marele Day, in 'the end zone'.[38] However, she discovered that she really enjoyed Byron Bay. The place might have been pretentious in its trendiness in ways she had satirised all her life in novels, but it was also home to a strong community writing culture, with its own literary festival and a writers' centre. Its director, Jill Eddington, remembers the day a woman whose face she was sure she recognised walked in, and said, 'G'day. I'm Thea Astley. You probably don't know me. Listen, I don't drink, but I do smoke.'[39] They went up to the balcony to talk books.

Astley had already started to enjoy the frisson of surprise in meetings like this. It had been fun to see the look on the librarian's face at Brunswick Heads when Astley presented her library card. She made an instant friend in Lisa Morrison, who was happy to show off the neighbouring libraries, such as the newer one down the road at Ballina.

This tip-off led to a vintage Astley cameo. Her visit coincided with the 'Loud in the Library' week, an initiative encouraging young people back into the spaces of reading. The noise did not go down well with the novelist-visitor, who could be seen in a corner writing a rather long passage in the library's suggestion book: 'Once the library was a place of silent reading. Is there *nowhere* youth can be taught that some things deserve respect. And rock music? A moronic noise. I'm shocked a librarian would permit it. P.S. Pity to mar a beautiful library. Thea Astley'.[40]

Astley sought comfort in taking out works of Australian literature she knew well, often novels by writers she knew personally or remembered from her Literature Board days. She re-read some Rodney Hall. Books about Brisbane were on her top shelf, including *The Motorcycle Café* by the young writer Matthew Condon.

They had met. Her *Pineapple* stories in the 1980s had spoken to him, making him realise that this was the kind of voice he could have in writing about a place many would have considered unsuitable for literary purposes. Twenty years later Condon reviewed *Drylands* and thanked Astley for her work, telling her how important she had been to him as a writer, that she was a 'writer's writer'. A return letter didn't arrive but Condon heard via a publisher that Astley was desperate for him to phone. They spent time together at the last two Byron Bay Writers Festivals Astley would attend, smoking and talking and drinking coffee under a tree.

Condon could see Astley was ailing, which made her running commentary on the passers-by, complete with comic idle speculation, all the more astounding. They smoked 'like trains' and 'laughed and laughed'. Condon learned that every year she re-read *The Motorcycle Café* about a bygone Brisbane. They shared the link of being Queenslanders, could chat about the strangeness of the place, the details of Brisbane such as the brothels in Albert Street; they were 'like two children in the same clubhouse'.[41]

In Byron Bay Astley settled into a sort of routine. She visited the writers' centre and held court at the regular Friday café lunches. Writers and interested readers passing by would join in. Astley expressed her long-held views, but sometimes she risked alienating the very crowd that held her in such high esteem. Arguments broke out around the table about creative writing. 'You can't teach it,' Thea would declare, although she had done so, as most people there knew.

She was aware of being among a new generation of writers. The years had given Astley's contrariness new licence but many in the group were pleased that she wanted to mix with younger people, to talk seriously to practising writers who were working, engaged in life.[42] She argued over definitions, labels, that cliché male–female divide of the literary critical world. 'Why should there be such a thing as chick-lit?' Astley asked. 'What about men writing utter crap, would you call it cock-schlock?'

Astley greatly enjoyed living near Byron Bay. The weather was balmy, the conversation casual and unafraid, and she was finding intelligent kindness. Byron Bay saw a woman in her late seventies getting about in men's checked flannel shirts, trying to avoid the young footpath-hoggers who rudely refused to give way. Astley would arrive at the local Woolworths very early in the morning, using Jack's disabled parking sticker to park nearby. She was still acting out and, even if she didn't admit it, she had arrived in the right town to do that.

Still, she was facing the extreme challenges of isolation, and her health was deteriorating. She had suffered several minor strokes. And her eyesight was failing: she needed the large print books in the library. She was forced to give up driving altogether. Dislike it as she did, the independence that driving offered was an important thread connecting her to her previous life and to Jack. Like most people of her age, Astley worried about being a burden. 'A person who dies young shows great foresight' is the kind of rueful whimsy Astley would have enjoyed in expressing this anxiety.

Donna McLaughlin, a broadcaster from the ABC who had grown up in Mackay, north Queensland, and whom Astley knew, was in touch about an interview. It was a choice moment for Astley to open up. She was finding life very difficult, not being able to do all the things she once could. Two of the strokes she had suffered had been 'sharp pointed pains in the side of her head. A headache really,' she joked.[43] In fact, she had had a number of x-rays that she tried to keep quiet. The scans had been inconclusive, a word whose vague import Astley would have understood as a death sentence. She knew that smokers – and she had been one for forty years – could expect aneurysms, or bulges in the walls of weakened blood vessels: something was wrong.

Irritability sometimes broke through her sociability. Astley oscillated between wanting to be left alone – 'I've had enough' – and secretly enjoying being recognised and valued. Privately, post-Jack, Astley was emotionally raw, but still able to form closer friendships than at other times in her life. A near neighbour, Ingrid Loewy had a mixed European heritage and a life in broadcasting that intrigued Astley. They listened to lieder together. To have music in common was to Astley the only cure worth having. If she listened to Richard Strauss's song cycle 'Vier letzte Lieder', then for the moment she, too, could be weightless, floating.

By this time, according to Loewy, 'Thea was well on the way to idolising Jack' but her new friend saw, beyond the wisecracks, a distraught wife who had lost her life partner and who was also physically frail – a frustrated and angry person.[44]

Some of this volatility was also on public display. On a writers' festival panel in 2003 with Richard Flanagan, Astley misfired badly when she described his latest novel *Gould's Book of Fish* as 'a nice book but a bit of a wank'. Her comment inspired the kind of for-or-against press argument that many authors dread, reducing discussion to a school debate. At the time Flanagan did his chivalrous best to laugh off Astley's comment, but he looked a bit nonplussed, as did many in the audience.

Did Astley really mean what she had said? Her comment was bafflingly rude unless people realised how flippancy had dogged her all her life. Now there was no Jack to call up offended parties on her behalf to explain she hadn't meant her words. Astley had been embarrassed at the time, had tried to insist she hadn't known what the word 'wank' meant, but people were looking less than convinced. That didn't prevent her from feeling misunderstood.

Astley was not 'losing her nouns', to quote the ageing Kathleen in *Coda*, but she had lost her bearings in life. Her anchors were the same as they had always been: books and writing. She felt most comfortable, unsurprisingly, in the home of words.

In Byron Bay Astley would prop herself on the rotting council bench outside the library. She had everything she needed: books and cigarettes and people. From here she could invent narratives. She grumbled out loud about the pathetic neglect of public property; she complained to the council, demanding a better, newly painted seat to restore dignity to the library. It hadn't occurred to her that they would remove the entire seat. When they did she was enraged.

Life went on. Astley had agreed to a public reading of her work at the 2004 Byron Bay Writers Festival. She was feeling surprisingly well despite planned surgery to remove the aneurysm. It was better to have that, everyone agreed – no point letting your body play Russian roulette with you.

She stuck with her professional decision about the reading. Always it seemed the shorter pieces worked – she could read several. It was almost twenty-five years to the day since she had read 'Diesel Epiphany' to an Adelaide Writers' Festival crowd. It had been onc of the first of such readings for her, before the writer-as-entertainer became commonplace. She knew the story extremely well; she could still read it with comic timing. It was a crowd-pleaser. Reading it now, after such an interval, had its own pleasing symmetry.

Astley was accepting with greater alacrity than she could ever have imagined being the 'older revered writer'. She might have wished for recognition sooner in life but now she was greeting it with equanimity. Early in her writing life she had almost hated writers' festivals, the fanfare aspect of them, but now she was enjoying the social aspect of such events. She was looking forward to seeing Mark Macleod, too, and to him seeing her in her new life; their previous phone conversation had been all tears and recriminations over Jack.

The day arrived. The crowd at the reading recognised the elderly woman who slowly made her way towards the stage. Some were fellow writers who had come to know Astley now that she was a Byron local; some were old neighbours, including Betty Judd from Epping days. There were new neighbours and new friends, but Astley was most recognisable because of a lifetime of writing. She faced the audience with a direct gaze and the room slipped quickly into a deep hush. It was an atmosphere electric with the promise of something unique.

Astley began reading in much the same crackling, acrid style of her time in Barjai in the 1940s, but the years had added a composure made altogether exotic when expressed in her broad Queensland drawl. The reading was a story about a journey. Halting now and then at the side-cuttings of narrative, Astley waited just long enough for the audience to catch up with her. When they did, the room exploded with recognition and laughter. Without looking up, except to spot where Mark Macleod was sitting, Astley read on, pacing herself until the end. The crowd erupted: there was applause, cheering, stamping feet. It was hard at first for her to take it all in and Astley looked startled. On her way out, passing Mark, she couldn't resist one last deflection. 'It was you leading that cheering, wasn't it?' she said. He hadn't been, but he could see she was touched.[45] It was a new feeling – no resistance required.

It was 'primary magic'.

Epilogue

The phone rang, and Ed picked up. A nurse from the Gold Coast hospital asked whether he could come straightaway, as 'things hadn't quite gone to plan'. His heart started to beat fast. Car keys were grabbed, doors bolted at speed, decisions revisited. What had gone wrong? Should he have encouraged Thea to risk the operation? Had they understood the odds? He and Michelle had spent many days and nights discussing at length how they would care for an elderly invalid mother; now they were leaving for the Gold Coast hospital dazed by the urgency of the call.

When Ed arrived in Thea's room it was obvious that she was heavily sedated. He stepped into the corridor to speak to the doctor and find out what had happened. The explanation was as abrupt as it was simple: an aneurysm in the aorta behind her heart, not previously detected by the angiogram, had ruptured. The end was now a matter of time.

Ed walked back to Thea and sat motionless. After what seemed a long time she began to move, then faced him. One look at his face must have told her that all was not well. Her mind, with customary acuity, turned quickly on the issue.

A moment.

'They stuffed it up, didn't they?' she said in her smoker's rasp.

Typical Thea, thought Ed, but he knew she would want plain truths told plainly. He had to think of something quickly, some way of intimating what might be next.

'You'll be joining Jack soon,' he blurted, immediately terrified he had said the wrong thing.

Thea's eyes widened with all that she knew. It was the last look from a mother to a son. 'That moment', as she called it in her novels, was now coming to her. Within a few minutes, she found the strength to turn over, carefully, to face the blank wall. She never turned back.

Ed and Michelle left the hospital exhausted. They decided to head for nearby Kirra Beach, the scene of so many happy childhood memories for Thea, moments frozen in albums under the caption: 'Family Holiday'. Here they saw the rocks Thea had perched on, where Eileen, overdressed in her 1920s clothes, complete with parasol, sat proud and upright next to her. Here were the rock pools, where Thea had been innocently happy while she and Phil quietly poked at shells and small sea creatures; over there was a dilapidated timber beach shack high up on stilts, its paint flaking in the tropical heat that Astley described with such nostalgia. Here Thea's father, Cecil, finally relaxed enough away from the newsroom, had sung sea shanties.

Where was Thea now?

The formal announcement would come soon enough: Thea Astley had died at the John Flynn Hospital on the Gold Coast on 17 August 2004. Later, much later, Ed would scatter some of Thea's ashes at Nudgee in Brisbane, near her parents Cec and Eileen, and some near Phil's grave in Melbourne Catholic Cemetery, North Carlton.

Now, there was silence.

Illness has momentum: there's something to worry about, things to do, places that must be visited. Death brings stillness, a presence not an absence. After he left the hospital Ed got into the car to drive back to Byron Bay. The sound of the sea roared in his ears.

He entered the roundabout near Byron's public library. There in fresh, glorious green paint was Thea's smoking bench, as Ed called it, the one she'd 'roughed up' the council about, the object of her last concerted agitation against slack officialdom. She wasn't holding her breath, she said loudly to anyone who asked about progress with the council. Comic in her moroseness, she liked to think the worst, rather enjoyed being able to say that she never expected it to materialise – as in fact it hadn't when she had last been well enough to visit the library.

But now it was there. Newly painted, it shone brilliantly in the noonday sunshine, perfectly placed in front of the library itself. This house of books had been the ideal backdrop for Thea, sitting, smoking and enjoying the passing parade, ever the 'people freak'. And now this empty seat seemed a tribute to Thea Astley: to her life in literature, to the courage of all writers.

Acknowledgements

This biography has been many years in the making but it has brought unique pleasures to me. The first has been the opportunity to live for so many years alongside the challenging ideas and writings of a novelist as talented as Thea Astley. Over years of research and writing, I have been very grateful for the candour with which people spoke about Thea Astley. By any standards, this has been a rich and privileged writing experience.

I did meet Thea Astley on several occasions, at writers' festivals and public readings and also at her home in Cambewarra, New South Wales, with her husband, Jack. I have my own memories, but impressions of others who knew Astley have also helped shape this portrait of her. Their recollections of Thea Astley are as varied as the many roles she played in her life: part of the couple 'Jack and Thea', a mother, a neighbour, a friend, a teacher, a colleague, above all a writer.

This book has involved the support of many. My daughter has

spent years of her life living with this project without questioning its importance: thank you, Laura. I also wish to thank Jill Hickson, Astley's literary agent in the 1990s. When I first envisaged a biography she was very encouraging. To my agent, Fiona Inglis, at Curtis Brown, and my publisher, Alexandra Payne, thank you. Thanks also to UQP staff, especially Cathy Vallance, who managed the book with such meticulous care. I am also particularly grateful to publisher Bob Sessions, a longtime admirer of Astley's work as well as her publisher over many years. In 2006 it was he who put me in touch with Astley's son, Ed.

In a Sydney suburban café Ed and I met and drank coffee for three hours in appalling heat and humidity. I could never have imagined his magnanimity in the face of so many personal intrusions, nor the patience of his partner, Michelle. Ed and Michelle: I cannot thank you enough. My time spent with you both has been a total pleasure.

In the long years of research, libraries provide vital support for researchers and writers. I particularly thank the staff at the Fryer Library, University of Queensland, where Astley's papers are held. Astley had been depositing her manuscripts, some early poetry and other aspects of her writing life in the library for many years. This material was the basis for my research on Astley in the mid-1990s, which was supported by funding from Monash University, which I acknowledge with thanks. In 2005, a year after Astley's death, her son was able to pass over her remaining papers, completing the full collection as it is today. It was this second archive that I have most drawn from for the writing of this biography.

It has also been rewarding to work on papers in the Mitchell Library, State Library of New South Wales, and at the University of Melbourne Archives; also on the Bohemia Society papers at the State Library of Victoria. I thank all those librarians who assisted me. I'd also like to thank the staff at Ballina Library, and school archivists at All Hallows' and Gregory Terrace in Brisbane. Help from the staff at the Australian Broadcasting Commission Radio and Television Archives in

Sydney was also expert and invaluable. A small research grant towards the latter stages of this work from the Australian Catholic University also assisted me.

To the people who made time to talk to me, in face-to-face interviews and telephone conversations, or in emails and letters, I owe you a great deal. If I have overlooked anyone, I do apologise.

Barbara Abouchar, Louise Adler, the late Father Phil Astley, the late Thea Astley, June Barbour, Michelle Barbour, John Bernard, Carmel Bird, Barbara Blackman, Wendy Blaxland, Veronica Brady, the late Sir Theodore Bray, Jennifer and Bryan Bruty, Tony Buckley, Jennifer Byrne, Geoff and Sarah Cains, Matthew Condon, Glenn Cook, Peter Corris, Michael Costigan, Helen Dash, Marele Day, John Docker, Robert Drewe, Jill Eddington, Gerald Fitzgerald, the late Thelma Forshaw, Helen Garner, Arnold and Elise Simon Goodman, Ed Gregson, Jacquie Griffiths, Rodney Hall, Michael Head, Jill Hickson, Janet Hutchinson, Caroline Jones, Betty Judd, Alla Kammaralli, Tom Keneally, Joan Kirkby, Moira and Sheila Knudson, Sue LeGanza, Elaine Lindsay, Ingrid Loewy, the late Sister Lourda, Hugh Lunn, Margaret McEniery, Michael McGirr, Kevin and Pat McHugh, Mark McKenna, Mark Macleod, Jeff McMullen, David Malouf, David Marr, Susan Marshall, the late Sister Mary Martin, Marin Martinelli, Ruth Mawson, Lisa Morrison, Laurie Muller, Marcia Price, D'Arcy Randall, the late Barrett Reid, Jill Roe, Meredith Rose, the late Hazel Rowley, John Ryan, Mary Sainty, Robert Sessions, Patricia Sheehan, Jim Shute, Margaret and Allen Smith, Irene Stevens, Sister Patricia Sullivan, Chris Wallace-Crabbe, Richard Walsh, Margery Watsford, Elizabeth Webby, Richard Whitington, Yvonne Wyndham, Fay Zwicky.

Notes

Prologue

1 Thea Astley in Lenore Nicklin, 'Thea Astley: Writing in the Rainforest', The Good Weekend, *The Sydney Morning Herald*, 13 October 1979, p. 14.

2 Thea Astley, 'Writing in North Queensland', *LINQ*, 9(1), 1981, p. 3; Thea Astley in Jennifer Ellison (ed.), *Rooms of Their Own*, Penguin, Ringwood, Victoria, 1986, p. 51; Astley in Robert L. Ross, 'An Interview with Thea Astley', *World Literature Written in English*, 26(2), 1986, p. 268.

3 F. Scott Fitzgerald and Henry James in Dennis W. Petrie, *Ultimately Fiction: Design in Modern American Biography*, Purdue University Press, Indiana, 1981, p. 2.

4 Christina Stead in Hazel Rowley, *Christina Stead: A Biography*, William Heinemann, Melbourne, 1993, p. xi.

1 The hinterland of childhood

1 Thea Astley, *Drylands: A Book for the World's Last Reader*, Penguin, Melbourne, 1999, p. 106.

2 Thea Astley, *A Kindness Cup*, Penguin, Melbourne, 1989, p. 112.

3 Thea Astley, Wordfest sound recording, Canberra, 9 March 1985, ABC Radio Archives.
4 Thea Astley, 'Diesel Epiphany', *Antipodes*, 1(1), 1987, pp. 10–11.
5 Thea Astley, 'Why I Wrote a Short Story Called "Diesel Epiphany"', *Meanjin*, 45(2), 1986, p. 193.
6 David Malouf, 'A First Place: The Mapping of a World', in James Tulip (ed.), *Johnno, Short Stories, Poems, Essays and Interview*, UQP, St Lucia, 1990, p. 262.
7 Sister Mary Martin to author, Melbourne, 17 July 1995.
8 ibid.
9 Thea Astley, reading in Jimmy Watson's Wine Bar, Melbourne, February 1993.
10 Father Phil Astley to author, Melbourne, 1 July 1995.
11 Immortalised as the character Cornelius in Thea Astley, *It's Raining in Mango*, Penguin, Melbourne, 1987.
12 Lance Loughrey, 'Last of the Bush Balladists', *Southerly*, 42(1), 1982, p. 91.
13 Obituary of Charles Astley, *The Queenslander*, 27 June 1929, p. 62; Glenn Cook, *Charles Astley: The History of an Art Instructor on the Darling Downs*, PhD draft (typescript of work-in-progress).
14 Artnet website, details of auctions, accessed 11 July 2013.
15 Thea Astley to author, Cambewarra, 28 May 1995.
16 C. (Cecil) B. Astley, 'Comin' into Work', *The Bulletin*, 36(1856), 9 September 1915, p. 44.
17 Sir Theodore Bray to author, Brisbane, 21 September 1995.
18 Hugh Lunn to author, Brisbane, 20 September 1995.
19 Thea Astley in Candida Baker (ed.), *Yacker: Australian Writers Talk about Their Work*, Picador, Woollahra, New South Wales, 1986, p. 39.
20 Thea Astley in Graeme Kinross-Smith, 'Thea Astley', *Kunapipi*, 4(1), 1982, p. 23.
21 Astley in Baker (ed.), *Yacker*, p. 33.
22 Thea Astley in Peter Craven, 'Written in Her Genes', *Sunday Herald*, 8 April 1990, p. 3.
23 Thea Astley in Amanda Smith, 'Thea Astley', *Publishers Weekly*, 30 March 1990, p. 42.
24 Michael McGirr, *Things You Get for Free*, Grove Press, 2003, p. 10; Michael McGirr, letter to author, 23 March 2008.
25 Phil Astley, *Gregory Terrace Newsletter*, 1938, St Joseph's Gregory Terrace Archives.

[26] David Malouf, 'Confessions of an Only Child', *Neighbours in a Thicket*, UQP, St Lucia, 1974, p. 5.
[27] Thea Astley, *A Boat Load of Home Folk*, Penguin, Melbourne, 1983, p. 124.
[28] Michelle Barbour to author, New Brighton, 2007; Michelle Barbour, email to author, 10 February 2014.
[29] Astley, *Drylands*, p. 106.
[30] David Marr, *Patrick White: A Life*, Random House, Melbourne, 1991, p. 357.
[31] Thea Astley, *Words with James Griffin*, ABC TV, 17 August 2003, ABC Television Archives.
[32] Brian Matthews, 'Life in the Eye of the Hurricane: The Novels of Thea Astley', *The Southern Review*, vi, 1973, p. 171.
[33] Sister Mary Martin to author, Melbourne, 17 July 1995.
[34] ibid.
[35] Thea Astley in Susan Duncan, 'The Thrill of It All', *Australian Women's Weekly*, February 1990, p. 49.
[36] Sister Mary Martin to author, Melbourne, 17 July 1995.
[37] Father Phil Astley to author, Melbourne, 1 July 1995.
[38] Thea Astley to author, Cambewarra, 28 May 1995.
[39] Thea Astley, *The Well Dressed Explorer*, Thomas Nelson, Melbourne, 1977, p. 21.
[40] Thea Astley in Robert L. Ross, 'An Interview with Thea Astley', *World Literature Written in English*, 1986, p. 264.
[41] Clifford Tolchard, 'Novelist and Teacher', *Walkabout*, June 1969, p. 14.
[42] Thea Astley in Ray Willbanks (ed.), *Australian Voices: Australian Writers and Their Work*, University of Texas Press, Texas, 1991, p. 37.
[43] Astley in Ross, *World Literature Written in English*, p. 264.
[44] Astley in Willbanks (ed.), *Australian Voices*, p. 37.

2 Suspected of reading

[1] Thea Astley, *Beachmasters*, Viking/Penguin, Melbourne, 1985, p. 60.
[2] Pat Ryan, letter to Sister P. Sullivan, 1991.
[3] Thea Astley, 'Going Home', *Brisbane Herald*, 16 January 1986.
[4] Thea Astley in Graeme Kinross-Smith, 'Thea Astley', *Kunapipi*, 4(1), 1982, p. 24.
[5] Betty Burrows, letter to author, 20 November 1996.
[6] Thea Astley, Thea Astley papers, UQFL97, Fryer Library, University of Queensland.
[7] Sister Lourda to author, Brisbane, 14 September 1995.

8 Thea Astley, 'Unrest', *Jottings* (All Hallows' magazine), 1940, p. 38, All Hallows' Archives.

9 Thea Astley in Amanda Smith, 'Thea Astley', *Publishers Weekly*, 30 March 1990, p. 43.

10 Thea Astley in Ray Willbanks (ed.), *Australian Voices: Australian Writers and Their Work*, University of Texas Press, Texas, 1991, p. 35.

11 Michael McGirr to author, Melbourne, 14 March 2008.

12 Thea Astley in Jennifer Ellison (ed.), *Rooms of Their Own*, Penguin, Ringwood, Victoria, 1986, p. 64.

13 Thea Astley, 'To You – The Poet', *Jottings* (All Hallows' magazine), Brisbane, 1942, p. 58, All Hallows' Archives.

14 T. P. Boland, *James Duhig*, UQP, St Lucia, 1986, p. 297.

15 Thea Astley, 'The Monstrous Accent on Youth', *Meanjin Quarterly*, xxvii, March 1968, p. 109.

16 There is just one school photograph of Astley from this period.

17 *Jottings* (All Hallows' magazine), 1942, All Hallows' Archives.

18 Thea Astley, *The Slow Natives*, Penguin, Melbourne, 1990, p. 77.

19 Thea Astley, *Girl with a Monkey*, Angus & Robertson, Sydney, 1958, p. 12.

20 Moira Knudson to author, Cairns, 19 February 2008.

21 Astley, *Girl with a Monkey*, p. 129.

22 Thea Astley in Rosemary Sorensen, 'Perfectly Calm until She Writes', *Australian Book Review*, 144, 1992, p. 10.

23 ibid.

24 Robert L. Ross, 'Thea Astley's Long Struggle with the Language of Fiction', *World Literature Today*, (67)3, p. 507 – an extensive discussion of the Mass and its meaning to Astley.

25 ibid., p. 506.

26 Thea Astley, *The Search for Meaning* with Caroline Jones, ABC radio, 17 April 1994 (repeated 8 January 1995), 64732, ABC Radio Archives.

27 Thea Astley, 'The Curate Breaker', *Hunting the Wild Pineapple and Other Related Stories*, Thomas Nelson, Melbourne, 1979, pp. 37–38.

28 Helen Garner to author, Melbourne, 6 June 2011.

29 Patricia Sheehan to author, Melbourne, 3 December 1996.

30 Astley, *Brisbane Herald*, 1986.

31 Moira and her sister Sheila re-met Astley almost fifty years later when Astley moved to north Queensland.

32 Examination results, 'Leaving and Matriculation', All Hallows' magazine, 1942, All Hallows' Archives.

33 Astley, *The Slow Natives*, p. 141.

34 Thea Astley, *Books and Writing* with Robert Dessaix, ABC radio, 8 March 1990, 48609, ABC Radio Archives.
35 Thea Astley in Robert L. Ross, 'The Shape of Language in Astley's Work', *World Literature Written in English*, (28)2, p. 265.
36 Thea Astley, *A Boat Load of Home Folk*, Penguin, Melbourne, 1983, p. 98; Thea Astley, *It's Raining in Mango: Pictures from the Family Album*, Penguin, Melbourne, 1987, p. 130.
37 Astley, *The Search for Meaning* with Caroline Jones, ABC Radio Archives.
38 Teilhard de Chardin (1881–1955) published *The Future of Man* in 1950.
39 Thea Astley, *The Coming Out Show* with Jill Lennon, ABC radio, 3 July 1976, ABC Radio Archives.
40 Astley, *The Slow Natives*, p. 76.
41 Thea Astley, *The Well Dressed Explorer*, Thomas Nelson, Melbourne, 1977, p. 11.
42 Astley, *A Boat Load of Home Folk*, p. 218.
43 Astley, *The Well Dressed Explorer*, p. 74.
44 Thea Astley in Robert Drewe, 'Profile of a Prize Novelist', *The Age*, 28 May 1966, p. 22.
45 Astley, *It's Raining in Mango*, p. 15.
46 Thea Astley in Doug Aiton, 'The Getting of Wisdom', *Sunday Age*, 4 October 1992.
47 Astley in Drewe, *The Age*, p. 22.
48 Thea Astley, *Reaching Tin River*, William Heinemann, Melbourne, 1990, p. 87.
49 Astley, *It's Raining in Mango*, pp. 75–76.

3 Barjai: A meeting place

1 Barbara Blackman, *Glass after Glass: Autobiographical Reflections*, Penguin, Melbourne, 1997, p. 112.
2 Thea Astley, 'Going Home', *Brisbane Herald*, 16 January 1986.
3 Thea Astley, *Spoken Word* with Peter Couchman, ABC radio, 24 February 1994, 57078, ABC Radio Archives.
4 *Semper Floreat*, xi(1), 23 March 1942, p. 1.
5 David Malouf, 'Johnno' in James Tulip (ed.), *Johnno, Short Stories, Poems, Essays and Interview*, UQP, St Lucia, 1990, p. 27.
6 I am grateful for these details of the teacher training college given in letters from Mr Jim Shute, who was a junior in Brisbane at the same time Astley was a senior (matriculated).
7 Astley, *Brisbane Herald*, 1986.

8 Thea Astley to author, Cambewarra, 28 May 1995.
9 Thea Astley, *A Boat Load of Home Folk*, Penguin, Melbourne, 1983, pp. 91–92.
10 David Malouf, 'The Year of the Foxes', *Bicycle and Other Poems*, UQP, St Lucia, 1970, p. 1.
11 Judith Wright, 'Brisbane in War-time', *Overland*, 100, 1985, p. 65.
12 Joan Colebrook, *A House of Trees*, Corgi, United Kingdom, 1989, p. 181.
13 Thea Astley, *Books and Writing* with Robert Dessaix, ABC radio, 8 March 1990, 48609, ABC Radio Archives.
14 Astley, *Brisbane Herald*, 1986.
15 *Semper Floreat*, xi(1), 23 March 1942, p. 1.
16 *Semper Floreat*, xii(2), 18 March 1943, p. 1.
17 Amy Witting in Jane Sullivan, 'The Hard Slog and the Little Knack', Books Extra, *The Age*, 9 March 1996, p. 7.
18 ibid.
19 *Semper Floreat*, xi(1), p. 3.
20 *Semper Floreat*, xii(19), 28 July 1943, p. 1.
21 Thea Astley, letter to Paul Grano, 15 July 1944, Martin Haley papers, UQFL48, Fryer Library, University of Queensland.
22 'Review of *Meanjin Papers*', *Semper Floreat*, xii(16), 8 July 1943.
23 Blackman, *Glass After Glass*, p. 108.
24 ibid., pp. 108–109.
25 Thea Astley to author, Cambewarra, 28 May 1995.

4 We've Freud and Nietzsche at our finger-tips

1 Thea Astley, 'Culture, 1945', *Galmahra*, 1945, p. 25.
2 Barrie Reid, editorial, *Barjai*, 8, p. 1.
3 Paul Grano & M. Fogarty & C. Rinstead, 'A Letter to Members from the Committee', Martin Haley papers, UQFL48, Fryer Library, University of Queensland.
4 Barrie Reid, 'These Leaden Weights', *Barjai*, 13, 1944, p. 3.
5 Sister Lourda to author, Brisbane, 14 September 1995.
6 Judith Wright, 'Brisbane in War-time', *Overland*, 100, 1985, p. 66.
7 Barrie Reid, editorial, *Barjai*, 10, p. 1.
8 Barrie Reid, editorial, *Barjai*, 19, 1945, p. 3.
9 Barrie Reid, editorial, *Barjai*, 13, 1944, p. 1.
10 C. H. Sisson, *Edgar Allan Poe: Poems and Essays on Poetry*, Fyfield Books, Manchester, 1995, p. 93.

11 Edgar Allan Poe, *Selected Writings*, Penguin, Middlesex, England, 1967, pp. 481–482.
12 Barrie Reid, editorial, *Barjai*, 16, 1944, p. 1.
13 Thea Astley in Amanda Smith, 'Thea Astley', *Publishers Weekly*, 30 March 1990, p. 43.
14 Thea Astley, 'From Troy', *Barjai*, 13, 1944, p. 12.
15 Thea Astley, 'Saturday Night', *Barjai*, 14, 1944, p. 3.
16 Thea Astley in Jennifer Ellison (ed.), *Rooms of Their Own*, Penguin, Ringwood, Victoria, 1986, p. 58.
17 Thea Astley, 'Poetic Fire', *Barjai*, 13, 1944, p. 6.
18 ibid.
19 Thea Astley, 'Culture, 1945', *Galmahra*, 1945.
20 Vivian Smith, 'Australian Modernism: The Case of Kenneth Slessor', in Margaret Harris & Elizabeth Webby (eds.), *Reconnoitres: Essays in Australian Literature in Honour of G. A. Wilkes*, Oxford University Press, Melbourne, 1992, pp. 131, 141.
21 Thea Astley, 'Two Poems' (I), *Barjai*, 18, 1945, p. 13.
22 Thea Astley in Robert Drewe, 'Profile of a Prize Novelist', *The Age*, 28 May 1966, p. 22.
23 Thea Astley in Graeme Kinross-Smith, 'Thea Astley', *Kunapipi*, 4(1), 1982, p. 35.
24 Barrie Reid, editorial, *Barjai*, 18, 1945, p. 3.
25 Julian Croft, 'Australian Responses to Modernism', in Laurie Hergehan & Bruce Bennett (eds.), *The Penguin New Literary History of Australia*, Penguin, Ringwood, Victoria, 1988, pp. 411, 427.
26 Barrie Reid in Michele Elizabeth Anderson, Honours thesis (Art History), 'Barjai, Miya Studio and Young Brisbane Artists of the 1940s: Towards a Radical Practice', University of Queensland, 1987, p. 34.
27 Thea Astley, *The Search for Meaning* with Caroline Jones, ABC radio, 17 April 1994 (repeated 8 January 1995), 64732, ABC Radio Archives.
28 Reid in Anderson, Honours thesis, University of Queensland, 1987, p. 32.
29 Thomas Hardy, 'Christmas: 1924', *Barjai*, 21, 1946, p. 43.
30 Vida Horn & Thea Astley, 'Barjai Days', *Overland*, 142, 1996, p. 36.
31 Thea Astley, 'Juvenilia', *Barjai*, 20, 1946, p. 17.
32 Clem Christesen, letter to Dr Frederick Robinson, 28 September 1944, Frederick Robinson papers, UQFL5, Fryer Library, University of Queensland.
33 Barrie Reid, *Barjai*, 22, 1946, p. 40.

5 Dream Country

1 Thea Astley in Graeme Kinross-Smith, 'Thea Astley', *Kunapipi*, 4(1), 1982, p. 22.

2 Thea Astley, *Spoken Word* with Peter Couchman, ABC radio, 24 February 1994, 57078, ABC Radio Archives.

3 Thea Astley, *Arts Talk* with Ramona Koval, ABC radio, 9 June 2000, 84762, ABC Radio Archives.

4 Thea Astley, *Books and Writing* with Robert Dessaix, ABC radio, 8 March 1990, 48609, ABC Radio Archives.

5 Thea Astley, *Reaching Tin River*, William Heinemann, Melbourne, 1990, p. 32.

6 Thea Astley in Robert Drewe, 'Profile of a Prize Novelist', *The Age*, 28 May 1966, p. 22.

7 Thea Astley in Ray Willbanks (ed.), *Australian Voices: Australian Writers and Their Work*, University of Texas Press, Texas, 1991, p. 30.

8 Thea Astley, *The Search for Meaning* with Caroline Jones, ABC radio, 17 April 1994 (repeated 8 January 1995), 64732, ABC Radio Archives.

9 Astley, *Books and Writing* with Robert Dessaix, ABC Radio Archives.

10 Thea Astley, *A Kindness Cup*, Penguin, Melbourne, 1989, pp. 5–6.

11 Thea Astley, letter to Martin Haley, 11 March 1947, Martin Haley papers, UQFL48, Fryer Library, University of Queensland.

12 Thea Astley, 'Poetic Fire', *Barjai*, 13, 1944, p. 6.

13 Thea Astley, letter to Martin Haley, August 1948, Martin Haley papers.

14 ibid.

15 Thea Astley, 'To My Brother', Thea Astley papers, UQFL97, Fryer Library, University of Queensland.

16 Notes from eulogy for Father Phil Astley, Requiem Mass, Immaculate Conception Church, Hawthorn, 19 June 1997.

17 Thea Astley, untitled poem, c. 1940s, Thea Astley papers.

18 Thea Astley, letter to Martin Haley, August 1948, Martin Haley papers.

19 Thea Astley, *A Descant for Gossips*, UQP, St Lucia, 1983, p. 25.

20 Astley in Willbanks, *Australian Voices*, p. 30.

21 Thea Astley, 'Love in Our Time', c. 1940s, Thea Astley papers.

22 Thea Astley, *The Multiple Effects of Rainshadow*, Viking/Penguin, Melbourne, 1996, p. 164.

23 Thea Astley, 'Revelation', 1944, Thea Astley papers.

24 Thea Astley, notebooks, Thea Astley papers.

25 Thea Astley, 'Writing in North Queensland', *LINQ*, 9(1), 1981, pp. 7–8.

26 Astley, *A Descant for Gossips*, p. 123.

27 Astley in Willbanks, *Australian Voices*, p. 32.
28 Thea Astley, letter to Martin Haley, n.d., Martin Haley papers.
29 Astley refers to this novel in her correspondence but no manuscript with this title survives in her papers, suggesting that it has been destroyed.
30 Thea Astley, letter to Martin Haley, 7 July 1947, Martin Haley papers.

6 Jack

1 John Milton, 'Arcades', *Poems of Mr John Milton, Both English and Latin*, 1645.
2 Thea Astley, letter to Hal Porter, 1958, Ann and Roger Jennings papers, MLMS7171, Mitchell Library, State Library of New South Wales.
3 Thea Astley, *Books and Writing* with Robert Dessaix, ABC radio, 8 March 1990, 48609, ABC Radio Archives.
4 Margaret Smith to author, Somersby, 25 February 2008.
5 Tom Keneally to author, Sydney, 12 June 2008.
6 Thea Astley in Robert Drewe, 'Profile of a Prize Novelist', *The Age*, 28 May 1966, p. 22.
7 John Bernard to author, Sydney, 5 February 2008.
8 Thea Astley, farewell speech for Sydney Conservatorium's Big Band, typescript, 1974, Thea Astley papers, UQFL97, Fryer Library, University of Queensland.
9 Thea Astley, untitled poem, May 1949, Thea Astley papers.
10 Ed Gregson to author, New Brighton, 30 November 2006.
11 Marcia Price to author, phone interview, 2008.
12 ibid.
13 Mary Sainty to author, Sydney, 8 February 2007.
14 ibid.
15 ibid.
16 Barbara Abouchar to author, Sydney, 7 February 2008.
17 Ed Gregson to author, New Brighton, 30 November 2006.
18 Thea Astley, 'Sulpicia III', *The Sydney Morning Herald*, 19 October 1957, p. 12.
19 Mary Sainty to author, Sydney, 8 February 2007.
20 Thea Astley, *Girl with a Monkey*, Angus & Robertson, Sydney, 1958, pp. 26, 49.
21 Thea Astley, *Spectrum*, ABC radio, 25 June 1966, ABC Radio Archives.
22 Thea Astley in Graeme Kinross-Smith, 'Thea Astley', *Kunapipi*, 4(1), 1982, p. 22.

7 The Gorgon of Epping North

1 Thea Astley, letter to Beatrice Davis, n.d., Angus & Robertson Archives, MLMSS3269, State Library of New South Wales.
2 Sidney Baker, letter to 'Phillip Cressy' (Thea Astley), 30 July 1956, Thea Astley papers, UQFL97, Fryer Library, University of Queensland.
3 Susan Sheridan, *Who Was That Woman? The Australian Women's Weekly in the Postwar Years*, UNSW Press, Sydney, 2002, p. 43.
4 Thea Astley in Candida Baker, 'Cooler, Calmer and More Collected', *The Age*, 31 March 1990, p. 6.
5 Thea Astley, *The Coming Out Show* with Jill Lennon, ABC radio, 3 July 1976, ABC Radio Archives.
6 Betty Judd to author, Coffs Harbour, 25 November 2006.
7 ibid.
8 ibid.
9 Yvonne Wyndham to author, Sydney, 8 January 2006.
10 Betty Judd to author, Coffs Harbour, 25 November 2006.
11 Thea Astley, letter to Beatrice Davis, n.d., A&R Archives.
12 Thea Astley in Ray Willbanks (ed.), *Australian Voices: Australian Writers and Their Work*, University of Texas Press, Texas, 1991, p. 37.
13 ibid.
14 Thea Astley, letter addressed 'To the Editor', Angus & Robertson Publishers, 30 January 1957, A&R Archives.
15 Beatrice Davis in Anthony Barker, *One of the First and One of the Finest: Beatrice Davis, Book Editor*, Society of Editors (Vic.), Carlton, 1991, p. 45.
16 Beatrice Davis, letter to Thea Astley, 4 May 1957, A&R Archives.
17 Beatrice Davis in Jacqueline Kent, *A Certain Style: Beatrice Davis, A Literary Life*, Viking/Penguin, Melbourne, 2001, p. 10.
18 Bob Sessions to author, Melbourne, 13 March 2008.
19 Thea Astley, Beatrice Davis tribute volume, 1974, Beatrice Davis papers, State Library of New South Wales.
20 Kent, *A Certain Style*, p. 10.
21 ibid.
22 Patrick White in David Marr (ed.), *Patrick White: Letters*, Random House, Sydney, 1994, p. 171.
23 Beatrice Davis, letter to Thea Astley, 4 May 1957, A&R Archives.
24 Beatrice Davis, publishing memo, A&R Archives.
25 Thea Astley, letter to Beatrice Davis, 9 July 1957, A&R Archives.
26 Thea Astley in Robert Drewe, 'Profile of a Prize Novelist', *The Age*, 28 May 1966, p. 22.

27 Betty Judd to author, Coffs Harbour, 25 November 2006.
28 ibid.
29 Thea Astley, letter to Beatrice Davis, 8 June 1958, A&R Archives.
30 Thea Astley to author, Cambewarra, 28 May 1995.
31 ibid.
32 Thea Astley, letter to Beatrice Davis, 17 March 1957, A&R Archives.
33 Beatrice Davis, letter to Thea Astley, 21 March 1957, A&R Archives.
34 Caroline Jones, *The Search for Meaning* with Caroline Jones, ABC radio, 17 April 1994 (repeated 8 January 1995), 64732, ABC Radio Archives.
35 Thea Astley, *Spoken Word* with Peter Couchman, ABC radio, 24 February 1994, 57078, ABC Radio Archives.
36 Thea Astley, notebook, Thea Astley papers.
37 Michael McGirr to author, Melbourne, 14 March 2008.
38 Beatrice Davis, letter to Thea Astley, 26 May 1958, A&R Archives.
39 Thea Astley, letter to Beatrice Davis, 21 June 1958, A&R Archives.
40 Beatrice Davis, letter to Thea Astley, 25 June 1958, A&R Archives.
41 Richard Walsh to author, Sydney, 29 May 1995.
42 Beatrice Davis, letter to Thea Astley, 10 September 1958, A&R Archives.
43 Douglas Stewart, letter to Thea Astley, 28 August 1958, Thea Astley papers.
44 Thea Astley, letter to Martin Haley, 1958, Martin Haley papers, UQFL48, Fryer Library, University of Queensland.
45 ibid.
46 Thea Astley, letter to Martin Haley, 9 August 1958, Martin Haley papers.
47 Thea Astley, letter to Martin Haley, 1958, Martin Haley papers.
48 Barbara Abouchar to author, Sydney, 7 February 2008.
49 ibid.
50 ibid.
51 Bob Sessions to author, Melbourne, 13 March 2008.
52 Hal Porter, letter to Thea Astley, 19 November 1958, Thea Astley papers.
53 Barbara Abouchar to author, Sydney, 7 February 2008.
54 ibid.
55 Michael McGirr to author, Melbourne, 14 March 2008.
56 Cecil and Eileen Astley, letter to Thea Astley, c. 1960, Thea Astley papers.
57 ibid.
58 ibid.

8 An armed neutrality

1 Thea Astley, *The Slow Natives*, Penguin, Melbourne, 1990, p. 40.
2 Advertisement, *The Sydney Morning Herald*, 16 July 1957.
3 Bryan and Jennifer Bruty to author, Mittagong, January 2007.
4 Yvonne Wyndham to author, Sydney, 8 January 2007.
5 Thea Astley in Ray Willbanks (ed.), *Australian Voices: Australian Writers and Their Work*, University of Texas Press, Texas, 1991, p. 35.
6 Yvonne Wyndham to author, Sydney, 8 January 2007.
7 Thea Astley, letter to Beatrice Davis, c. 1958–59, Angus & Robertson Archives, MLMSS3269, State Library of New South Wales.
8 Thea Astley in Rosemary Sorensen, 'Perfectly Calm Until She Writes', *Australian Book Review*, 144, 1992, p. 10.
9 Tom Keneally to author, Avalon, 12 June 2008.
10 ibid.
11 Patrick White, letter to Thea Astley, 24 March 1960, Thea Astley papers, UQFL97, Fryer Library, University of Queensland.
12 Patrick White, inscription in book *Selected Writings of Gérard de Nerval*, Grove Press, New York, 1957, Thea Astley papers.
13 Hal Porter, letter to Thea Astley, 27 November 1960, Thea Astley papers.
14 ibid.
15 Judy Ogilvie, *The Push: An Impressionistic Memoir*, Primavera Press, Sydney, 1995.
16 Thea Astley in Jennifer Ellison (ed.), *Rooms of Their Own*, Penguin, Ringwood, Victoria, 1986, p. 60.
17 'A Correct Compassion', (author not known), *Times Literary Supplement*, 1 April 1960, p. 205.
18 Sidney J. Baker, 'Social Satire', *The Sydney Morning Herald*, 7 May 1960, p. 14.
19 Kathryn Purnell, *Luna*, 18, 1984, pp. 40–43.
20 Patrick White, letter to Thea Astley, 20 March 1961, Thea Astley papers.
21 Robert Gray, 'White Mischief', *The Australian*, September 13–14 2008, pp. 4–5.
22 Jesuit Society, letter to Phil Astley, 1 June 1961, Jesuit Archives, Melbourne.
23 Eileen Astley, letter to Phil Astley, 29 June 1961, Jesuit Archives.
24 Jesuit Society, letter to Phil Astley, 24 November 1961, Jesuit Archives.
25 Obituary, *The Journalist*, Australian Journalists' Association, August 1961, p. 3.
26 Patrick White, letter to Thea Astley, 20 March 1961, Thea Astley papers.

27 Thea Astley, *Books and Writing* with Robert Dessaix, ABC Radio, 8 March 1990, 48609, ABC Radio Archives.
28 Thea Astley, *The Well Dressed Explorer*, Penguin, Melbourne, 1988, p. 26.
29 Astley in Willbanks, *Australian Voices*, p. 37.
30 Ed Gregson to author, New Brighton, 30 November 2006.
31 Fay Zwicky, *Lingua Franca* (obituary compilation with Fay Zwicky and Mark Macleod), ABC radio, 28 August 2004, ABC Radio Archives.
32 Yvonne Wyndham to author, Sydney, 8 January 2007.
33 Ed Gregson to author, New Brighton, 30 November 2006.
34 ibid.
35 ibid.
36 Hal Porter in Mary Lord, *Hal Porter: A Man of Many Parts*, Random House, Melbourne, 1994, p. 293.
37 Thea Astley in Graeme Kinross-Smith, 'Thea Astley', *Kunapipi*, 4(1), 1982, p. 21.
38 Barbara Abouchar to author, Sydney, 7 February 2008.
39 Thea Astley in Candida Baker (ed.), *Yacker: Australian Writers Talk about Their Work*, Picador, Woollahra, New South Wales, 1986, p. 50; Thea Astley in Clifford Tolchard, 'Thea Astley: Novelist and Teacher', *Walkabout*, June 1969, p. 14.
40 Astley in Ellison (ed.), *Rooms of Their Own*, p. 60.
41 Carole Ferrier (ed.), *As Good as a Yarn with You*, Cambridge University Press, 1992.
42 Astley in Baker (ed.), *Yacker*, pp. 42–43.

9 I merely crave an intelligent buddy

1 Thea Astley, letter to Thelma Forshaw, 14 January 1963, MLMSS3431, State Library of New South Wales.
2 Thea Astley, letter to George Ferguson, 12 April 1962, Beatrice Davis papers, State Library of New South Wales.
3 Thea Astley in Clifford Tolchard, 'Thea Astley: Novelist and Teacher', *Walkabout*, June 1969, p. 14.
4 Thea Astley, 'Authors and Publishers Panel', *This Day Tonight*, 13 November 1967, 218894, ABC Television Archives.
5 Thea Astley, letter to Beatrice Davis, 27 May 1962, Angus & Robertson Archives, MLMSS3269, State Library of New South Wales.
6 Thea Astley in Rosemary Sorensen, 'Perfectly Calm Until She Writes', *Australian Book Review*, 144, 1992, p. 10.
7 Beatrice Davis, letter to Thea Astley, 9 December 1964, A&R Archives.

8 Thea Astley, letter to Beatrice Davis, c. 1957, A&R Archives.
9 Thea Astley, letter to Beatrice Davis, 25 February 1965, A&R Archives.
10 Reader's report, *The Well Dressed Explorer*, A&R Archives.
11 Kylie Tennant, review of *The Well Dressed Explorer*, *Meanjin Quarterly*, 21, 1962, p. 509.
12 Bob Burns, review of *The Well Dressed Explorer*, *Prospect*, 1, 1964, p. 29.
13 Miles Franklin, letter to Criena Rohan, Jill Roe (ed.), *My Congenials: Miles Franklin & Friends in Letters*, vol. 2, 1939–1954, Angus & Robertson/HarperCollins, Sydney, 1993, p. 351.
14 Thea Astley, quoted from a scene re-created in David Marr, *Patrick White: A Life*, Random House, Melbourne, 1991, p. 357.
15 Barbara Abouchar to author, Sydney, 7 February 2008.
16 ibid.
17 Thea Astley, *A Boat Load of Home Folk*, Penguin, Melbourne, 1983, p. 198.
18 Christina Stead in Hazel Rowley, *Christina Stead: A Biography*, William Heinemann, Melbourne, 1993, p. 319.
19 Thea Astley, letter to Beatrice Davis, n.d., A&R Archives.
20 David Marr to author, Melbourne, September 1996.
21 Thelma Forshaw to author, phone interview, 30 May 1995.
22 Thea Astley, letter to George Turner, 29 April 1963, Thea Astley papers, UQFL97, Fryer Library, University of Queensland.
23 Thea Astley, letter to Thelma Forshaw, 14 January 1963, MLMSS3431, SLNSW.
24 ibid.
25 ibid.
26 Astley in Marr, *Patrick White: A Life*, p. 356.
27 Patrick White, letter to Thea Astley, 16 May 1963, Thea Astley papers.
28 Patrick White, letter to Thea Astley, 18 June 1963, Thea Astley papers.
29 ibid.
30 ibid.
31 Eileen Astley, letter to Thea Astley, 18 April 1963, Thea Astley papers.
32 Thea Astley, letter to Thelma Forshaw, 14 January 1963, MLMSS3431, SLNSW.
33 Thelma Forshaw to author, phone interview, 30 May 1995.
34 Yvonne Wyndham to author, Sydney, 11 January 2008.
35 Astley, *A Boat Load of Home Folk*, p. 194. 'The silence of old marriage' is a typical 'Astley-on-marriage' phrase.
36 Beatrice Davis, letter to Thea Astley, 1 June 1962, A&R Archives.
37 Thea Astley, letter to Beatrice Davis, n.d., A&R Archives.

38 Patrick White, letter to Laurie Collinson, 27 November 1964, in David Marr (ed.), *Patrick White: Letters*, Random House, Sydney, 1994, p. 273.

39 White to Collinson, in Marr (ed.), *Patrick White: Letters*, p. 274.

40 Thea Astley, letter to Thelma Forshaw, 14 January 1963, MLMSS3431, SLNSW.

10 Writing as a neuter

1 Thea Astley in Candida Baker (ed.), *Yacker: Australian Writers Talk about Their Work*, Picador, Woollahra, New South Wales, 1986, pp. 42–43.

2 Ed Gregson to author, New Brighton, 30 November 2006.

3 ibid.

4 Thea Astley in *The Bulletin*, 85(4328), 26 January 1963.

5 Thea Astley, postcard, n.d., Thea Astley papers, UQFL97, Fryer Library, University of Queensland.

6 Thea Astley in Ray Willbanks (ed.), *Australian Voices: Australian Writers and Their Work*, University of Texas Press, Texas, 1991, p. 40.

7 Thea Astley, *Arts Today* with Louise Adler, ABC radio, 1 January 1996, 69976, ABC Radio Archives.

8 Thea Astley, *The Slow Natives*, Penguin, Melbourne, 1990, p. 28.

9 ibid., p. 157.

10 Thea Astley, *The Coming Out Show* with Jill Lennon, ABC radio, 3 July 1976, ABC Radio Archives.

11 Astley, *The Slow Natives*, p. 16.

12 Fay Zwicky to author, phone interview, 20 January 2009.

13 Ed Gregson to author, New Brighton, 30 November 2006.

14 ibid.

15 Thea Astley, review of *The Brigadier and the Golf Widow* by John Cheever, *The Sydney Morning Herald*, c. 1964.

16 ibid.

17 Thea Astley, *A Descant for Gossips*, UQP, St Lucia, 1983, p. 172.

18 Jessica Anderson, *Taking Shelter*, Penguin/Viking, Ringwood, Victoria, 1989, p. 22.

19 Julia Kristeva saw this as both 'self-assurance and nihilistic self-observation'. Julia Kristeva, *Powers of Horror: An Essay on Abjection* (trans. Leon S. Roudiez), Columbia University Press, New York, 1982, p. 194.

20 Astley, *The Slow Natives*, p. 67.

21 ibid., p. 161.

22 Margaret Smith to author, Somersby, 25 February 2008.

23 ibid.

24 Ed Gregson to author, New Brighton, 30 November 2006.
25 Lisa Morrison to author, Byron Bay, 27 November, 2007.
26 Beatrice Davis, letter to Thea Astley, 9 December 1964, Angus & Robertson Archives, MLMSS3269, State Library of New South Wales.
27 Thea Astley, dedication, *The Acolyte*, UQP, St Lucia, 1980.
28 Neil Jillet, 'Australian Suburban Agony', review of *The Slow Natives*, *The Age*, 6 November 1965, p. 21.
29 ibid.
30 Thea Astley in 'Soul for Sale: Just for Jazz', 18 July 1966.
31 ibid.
32 Tom Keneally to author, Avalon, 12 June 2008.
33 ibid.
34 Tom Keneally, 'A Novelist Looks at Prose Writing', *Opinion*, August 1967, p. 36.
35 J. M. Couper, 'The Novels of Thea Astley', *Meanjin Quarterly*, xxvi, September 1967, pp. 332–337.
36 Ezra Pound, *ABC of Reading* quoted in 'Music', *Collins Thesaurus* (new 1st ed.), HarperCollins, Glasgow, 1995, p. 642.
37 Thea Astley in Amanda Smith, 'Thea Astley', *Publishers Weekly*, 30 March 1990, p. 43.
38 Arthur Phillips, letter to Thea Astley, 23 February 1965, Thea Astley papers.
39 Astley in 'Soul for Sale: Just for Jazz', 1966.
40 Robert Drewe to author, Melbourne, 2009.
41 Thea Astley in Robert Drewe, 'Profile of a Prize Novelist', *The Age*, 28 May 1966, p. 22.
42 Tom Keneally to author, Avalon, 12 June 2008.
43 ibid.
44 Richard Whitington to author, Sydney, 6 February 2009.
45 Tom Keneally to author, Avalon, 12 June 2008.
46 Yvonne Wyndham to author, Sydney, January 2007.
47 Richard Whitington to author, Sydney, 6 February 2009.
48 Betty Judd to author, Coffs Harbour, 25 November 2006.
49 Richard Whitington to author, Sydney, 6 February 2009.
50 Margaret Smith to author, Somersby, 25 February 2008.
51 Ed Gregson to author, New Brighton, 30 November 2006.
52 Principal Celebrant at the Requiem Mass for Father Philip Astley S.J., 19 June 1997, notes provided by Michael McGirr.
53 Margaret Smith to author, Somersby, 25 February 2008.

54 Astley, *The Coming Out Show* with Jill Lennon, ABC Radio Archives.

55 Beatrice Davis, letter to Mr A. J. T. Ford (registrar at Macquarie University), c. 1966, A&R Archives.

11 The oldest senior tutor in the Commonwealth

1 Thea Astley, letter to Professor A. Gibbs (School of English and Linguistics, Macquarie University), 30 November 1976, Thea Astley papers, UQFL97, Fryer Library, University of Queensland.

2 Bruce Mansfield & Mark Hutchinson, *Liberality of Opportunity: A History of Macquarie University 1964–1989*, Macquarie University/Hale & Iremonger, Sydney, 1992, pp. 58, 60.

3 Sue La Ganza to author, phone interview, 2 October 2014.

4 Leigh Dale, *The Enchantment of English: Professing English Literatures at Australian Universities*, Sydney University Press, Sydney, 2012, p. 298.

5 Joan Kirkby to author, Sydney, January 2008.

6 John Ryan to author, Sydney, 13 February 2008.

7 J. M. Couper, 'The Novels of Thea Astley', *Meanjin Quarterly*, xxvi, September 1967, pp. 332–337.

8 Thea Astley, letter to Clem Christesen, 9 October 1967, U84, box 4, Melbourne University Archives.

9 Joan Kirkby to author, Sydney, January 2008.

10 Tom Keneally to author, Avalon, 12 June 2008.

11 ibid.

12 ibid.

13 Reader's report, *A Boat Load of Home Folk*, Angus & Robertson Archives, MLMSS3269, State Library of New South Wales.

14 Mark McKenna, *An Eye for Eternity: The Life of Manning Clark*, The Miegunyah Press, Melbourne University Publishing, Melbourne, 2011.

15 Thea Astley in Ray Willbanks (ed.), *Australian Voices: Australian Writers and Their Work*, University of Texas Press, Texas, 1991, p. 36.

16 Thea Astley, *The Multiple Effects of Rainshadow*, Viking/Penguin, Melbourne, 1996, p. 65.

17 Thea Astley, *A Kindness Cup*, Penguin, Melbourne, 1989, p. 1.

18 Thea Astley, *The Slow Natives*, Penguin, Melbourne, 1990, p. 128.

19 Thea Astley, *A Boat Load of Home Folk*, Penguin, Melbourne, 1983, pp. 2, 142, 92, 3, 194, 23.

20 Thea Astley, *The Coming Out Show* with Jill Lennon, ABC radio, 3 July 1976, ABC Radio Archives.

21 Reader's report, *A Boat Load of Home Folk*, A&R Archives.

22 Hal Porter, letter to Thea Astley, 13 February 1968, Thea Astley papers.
23 Anne Baxter, letter to Thea Astley, n.d., Thea Astley papers.
24 *Time* magazine comment on *The Slow Natives* quoted in Beatrice Davis, letter to Alec Bolton, 26 July 1968, A&R Archives.
25 Christina Stead, letter to Alec Bolton, 21 September 1968, A&R Archives.
26 Alec Bolton, memo to Beatrice Davis, n.d., A&R Archives.
27 Alec Bolton, letter to John Abernethy, 18 October 1968, A&R Archives.
28 Thea Astley, 'Writing in North Queensland', *LINQ*, 9(1), 1981, p. 4.
29 Joan Kirkby to author, Sydney, January 2008.
30 John Ryan to author, Sydney, 13 February 2008.
31 Eileen Astley, letter to Thea Astley, 5 November 1968, Thea Astley papers.
32 ibid.
33 Thea Astley in Amanda Smith, 'Thea Astley', *Publishers Weekly*, 30 March 1990, p. 42.
34 Astley in Willbanks, *Australian Voices*, p. 37.
35 Thea Astley to Andrew Olle, ABC radio, 7 March 1990, ABC Radio Archives.
36 Thea Astley, 'The Author as a Critic of Society', typescript, 1970, Thea Astley papers.
37 Thea Astley, *Books and Writing* with Robert Dessaix, ABC radio, 8 March 1990, 48609, ABC Radio Archives.
38 Hal Porter (ed.), *It Could be You*, Rigby, Adelaide, 1972.
39 Thea Astley, *Beachmasters*, Viking/Penguin, New York, 1986, p. 48.
40 Thea Astley, *The Acolyte*, UQP, St Lucia, 1980, p. 88.
41 Thea Astley, 'Après Baudelaire', unpublished sonnet, Thea Astley papers.
42 *Sorites* (defn.): a form of pure logical argument with several premises, one conclusion, resolvable into a number of syllogisms, the conclusion of each of which is the premise of the next.
43 John Docker to author, Sydney, 31 May 1995.
44 Eileen Astley, letter to Thea Astley, 15 March 1969, Thea Astley papers.
45 Michael McGirr to author, Melbourne, 14 March 2008.
46 Eileen Astley, letter to Thea Astley, 15 March 1969, Thea Astley papers.

12 North of nostalgia

1 Thea Astley, *Hunting the Wild Pineapple and Other Related Stories*, Thomas Nelson, Melbourne, 1979, p. 1.
2 Thea Astley, *The Coming Out Show* with Jill Lennon, ABC radio, 3 July 1976, ABC Radio Archives.

3 Thea Astley, *Books and Writing* with Robert Dessaix, ABC radio, 8 March 1990, 48609, ABC Radio Archives.
4 ibid.
5 ibid.
6 Such as Mark Macleod, Jeff McMullen, Wendy Blaxland, Jenny Brockie.
7 Jenny Brockie in Jane Wheatley, 'Invisible Ink', *HQ*, Mar/Apr, 1994, p. 66.
8 Mark Macleod in Jane Wheatley, 'Invisible Ink', *HQ*, Mar/Apr, 1994, p. 66.
9 Thea Astley in Clifford Tolchard, 'Thea Astley: Novelist and Teacher', *Walkabout*, June 1969, p. 14.
10 Leigh Dale, *The Enchantment of English: Professing English Literatures at Australian Universities*, Sydney University Press, Sydney, 2012, p. 216.
11 Professor Ruth Mawson to author, phone interview, 25 September 2014.
12 Mark Macleod to author, Blue Mountains, 7 December 2007.
13 ibid.
14 Jeff McMullen to author, Sydney, 2 February 2008.
15 ibid.
16 Wendy Blaxland to author, Sydney, 20 February 2008.
17 ibid.
18 John Bernard to author, Sydney, 5 February 2008.
19 ibid.
20 ibid.
21 John Ryan to author, Sydney, 13 February 2008.
22 Thea Astley, *The Australian*, 31 August 1970.
23 Brian Matthews, 'Before Feminism … After Feminism', *Romantics and Mavericks: The Australian Short Story*, Foundation for Australian Literary Studies, 1987, p. 18.
24 Cherry H. Grimm, 'Always the Twelfth Man', *The Australian*, 14 October 1972, p. 35.
25 Thea Astley in Candida Baker, 'Cooler, Calmer and More Collected', *The Age*, 31 March 1990, p. 6.
26 Thea Astley in Candida Baker (ed.), *Yacker: Australian Writers Talk about Their Work*, Picador, Woollahra, New South Wales, 1986, pp. 42–43.
27 Henrietta Drake-Brockman quoted in J. A. Hay, 'Betrayed Romantics and Compromised Stoics: K. S. Prichard's Women', *Who is She? Images of Women in Australian Fiction*, UQP, St Lucia, 1983, p. 115.
28 ibid.
29 Thea Astley in Robert Drewe, 'Profile of a Prize Novelist', *The Age*, 28 May 1966, p. 22.

30 Mark Macleod to author, Blue Mountains, 7 December 2007.
31 Thea Astley, 'The Author as a Critic of Society', typescript, 1970, Thea Astley papers, UQFL97, Fryer Library, University of Queensland.
32 Patrick White, letter to Geoffrey Dutton, 1 February 1971, in David Marr (ed.), *Patrick White: Letters*, Random House, Sydney, 1994, p. 376.
33 Hal Porter, letter to Thea Astley, December 1971, Thea Astley papers.
34 Beatrice Davis, reader's report, 6 October 1971, Angus & Robertson Archives, MLMSS3269, State Library of New South Wales.
35 Readers' reports, *The Acolyte*, A&R Archives.
36 Thea Astley, letter to Beatrice Davis, 23 November 1971, A&R Archives.
37 Thea Astley, 'Thurlow's Answer' manuscript, Thea Astley papers.
38 Thea Astley, *The Acolyte*, UQP, St Lucia, 1980, p. 76.
39 Thea Astley in Graeme Kinross-Smith, 'Thea Astley', *Kunapipi*, 4(1), 1982, p. 35.
40 Thea Astley in Peter Fuller, 'To the Islands with Thea Astley', *The Canberra Times*, 8 March 1985, p. 17.
41 Richard Walsh to author, Sydney, 29 May 1995.
42 Jacqueline Kent, *A Certain Style: Beatrice Davis, A Literary Life*, Viking/Penguin, Melbourne, 2001, p. 157. In recording the history of Davis with A&R, Kent uses 'retirement' (p. 157), then later, quoting Richard Walsh, who offered a kind of consultancy that was refused, his phrase 'we had to let her go' (p. 273).
43 Beatrice Davis, letter to Thea Astley, 6 June 1972, A&R Archives.
44 Thea Astley, letter to Richard Walsh and Michael Johnston, Easter Monday 1973, A&R Archives.
45 Richard Walsh to author, Sydney, 29 May 1995.
46 Thea Astley, letter to Richard Walsh, 8 October 1975, A&R Archives.
47 Bob Sessions, letter to Richard Walsh, 17 February 1976, A&R Archives.
48 Richard Walsh, letter to Beatrice Davis, 8 December 1980, Beatrice Davis papers, State Library of New South Wales.
49 Richard Walsh, letter to Bob Sessions, 28 April 1980, A&R Archives.

13 Living is serial

1 Thea Astley, 'A Man Who is Tired of Swiper's Creek is Tired of Life', *Hunting the Wild Pineapple and Other Related Stories*, Thomas Nelson, Melbourne, 1979, p. 175.
2 John Bernard to author, Sydney, 5 February 2008.
3 Yvonne Wyndham to author, Sydney, 11 January 2008.
4 ibid.

5 Thea Astley, *A Descant for Gossips*, UQP, St Lucia, 1983, p. 18.
6 Alan and Margaret Smith to author, Somersby, 25 February 2008.
7 Sister Claver, letter to Thea Astley, 4 July 1973, Thea Astley papers, UQFL97, Fryer Library, University of Queensland.
8 Hal Porter, letter to Thea Astley, 20 April 1971, Thea Astley papers.
9 Lenore Nicklin, 'Thea Astley: Writing in the Rainforest', *The Sydney Morning Herald*, 13 October 1979.
10 Thea Astley, 'Being a Queenslander: A Form of Literary and Geographical Conceit', 6th Herbert Blaiklock Memorial Lecture, University of Sydney, 23 June 1976, The Wentworth Press, 1978, p. 13.
11 Eileen Astley, letter to Thea Astley, 5 February 197[?], Thea Astley papers.
12 Moira and Sheila Knudson to author, Cairns, 19 February 2008.
13 Rodney Hall to author, Melbourne, July 2011.
14 Michael Costigan to author, Sydney, 2011.
15 Thea Astley, 'Review', *The Sunday Telegraph*, 2 September 1973, p. 25.
16 Thea Astley, *A Kindness Cup*, Penguin, Melbourne, 1989, p. 6.
17 Thea Astley, 'The Author as a Critic of Society', typescript, 1970, Thea Astley papers.
18 Thea Astley, *Interim Spoken Word*, ABC radio, 1 January 1974, ABC Radio Archives.
19 Jeff McMullen to author, Sydney, 2 February 2008.
20 Thea Astley in Graeme Kinross-Smith, 'Thea Astley', *Kunapipi*, 4(1), 1982, p. 22.
21 Thea Astley, 'Writing in North Queensland', *LINQ*, 9(1), 1981, p. 5.
22 Kerryn Goldsworthy, 'Thea Astley's Writing: Magnetic North', *Meanjin*, 42(4), 1983, p. 482.
23 R. F. Brissenden, 'Going Back to Taws', *The Australian*, 15 February 1975, p. 19.
24 Richard Walsh to author, Sydney, 29 May 1995.
25 Thea Astley in Peter Craven, 'Written in Her Genes', *Sunday Herald*, 8 April 1990, p. 35.
26 Sue Ebury, letter to Beatrice Davis, 9 June 1978, Beatrice Davis papers, State Library of New South Wales.
27 Brethwyn Weyland, 'In Their Own Write', *New Idea*, 3 November 1973, p. 92.
28 Mark Macleod to author, Blue Mountains, 7 December 2007.
29 Eileen Astley, letter to Phil Astley, 22 February 1975, Jesuit Archives, Melbourne.
30 Thea Astley, card to Jack Gregson, 1975, Thea Astley papers.

31 Thea Astley, *Survey of Australian Universities* with John Pringle, ABC radio, 17 July 1977, ABC Radio Archives.
32 Thea Astley, 'The Higher Illiteracy', *The Australian*, n.d. 1975[?].
33 A. D. Hope, letter to Thea Astley, 10 January 1975, Thea Astley papers.
34 Eileen Astley, letter to Thea Astley, 19 March 1976, Thea Astley papers.
35 ibid.
36 Thea Astley in Amanda Smith, 'Thea Astley', *Publishers Weekly*, 30 March 1990, p. 42.
37 Beatrice Davis, memo draft of a cover blurb for *Hunting the Wild Pineapple*, n.d., Beatrice Davis papers.
38 Beatrice Davis, memo to Bob Sessions, n.d., Beatrice Davis papers.
39 ibid.
40 Thea Astley, letter to Professor A. Gibbs, 30 November 1976, Thea Astley papers.
41 Phil Astley, letter to Eileen Astley, 24 February 1978, Thea Astley papers.
42 Eileen Astley, letter to Thea Astley, 21 November 1977, Thea Astley papers.
43 Phil Astley, letter to Eileen Astley, 24 February 1978, Thea Astley papers.

14 Jane Austen of the rainforest

1 Thea Astley, 'Writing in North Queensland', *LINQ*, 9(1), 1981, p. 5.
2 Thea Astley, 'Revelation', 1944, Thea Astley papers, UQFL97, Fryer Library, University of Queensland.
3 Thea Astley in Lenore Nicklin, 'Thea Astley: Writing in the Rainforest', *The Sydney Morning Herald*, 13 October 1979.
4 Thea Astley, letter to Jack Gregson, n.d., Thea Astley papers.
5 ibid.
6 Jack Gregson, letter to Thea Astley, n.d., Thea Astley papers.
7 Phil Astley, letter to Thea Astley, 2 October 1980, Jesuit Archives, Melbourne.
8 Thea Astley, speech, n.d., Thea Astley papers.
9 Leonie Kramer, letter to Thea Astley, 16 July 1980, Thea Astley papers.
10 Richard Walsh, letter to Thea Astley, 24 December 1980, Thea Astley papers.
11 Thea Astley, letter to Beatrice Davis, 26 July c. 1982, Beatrice Davis papers, State Library of New South Wales.
12 Astley, *LINQ*, pp. 2–10.
13 Patsy Adam-Smith, card to Thea Astley, 8 August 1980, Thea Astley papers.

14 Tom Keneally, 'A Novelist Looks at Prose Writing', *Opinion*, August 1967, p. 40.

15 Neil Jillett, 'Atmosphere of Moods and Tension', *Age Saturday Extra*, 24 November 1981, p. 27; Hilma Wolitzer, 'Tales Told by a Monopod', *New York Times Book Review*, 23 December 1990.

16 Thea Astley, reading in Jimmy Watson's Wine Bar, Melbourne, February 1993. Astley introduced Mrs Waterman as 'one of her personal favourites'.

17 Thea Astley, *The Search for Meaning* with Caroline Jones, ABC radio, 17 April 1994 (repeated 8 January 1995), 64732, ABC Radio Archives.

18 Thea Astley, *Coda*, William Heinemann, Melbourne, 1994, p. 114.

19 Fay Zwicky, *Lingua Franca*, ABC radio, 28 August 2004, ABC Radio Archives.

20 Thea Astley, letter to Jackie Yowell, 14 September 1980, Penguin publishing files, Penguin Pty Ltd, Victoria.

21 Thea Astley, letter to Jackie Yowell, 15 December 1980, Penguin publishing files.

22 John Bernard to author, Sydney, 5 February 2008.

23 Thea Astley, *An Item from the Late News*, UQP, St Lucia, 1982, p. 19.

24 ibid., p. 5.

25 Cherry Grimm, review of *The Acolyte*, *The Australian*, 14 October 1972, p. 35.

26 Thea Astley, letter to D'Arcy Randall, 25 January 1982, in D'Arcy Randall, 'Contrary Motion: The Publication of Thea Astley's *An Item from the Late News*', typescript kindly provided by D'Arcy Randall.

27 ibid.

28 Thea Astley, letter to Brian Johns, 9 August 1982, Penguin publishing files.

29 Thea Astley, letter to Brian Johns, 26 August 1982, Penguin publishing files.

30 Beatrice Davis, memo to Bob Sessions, c. 1980, Beatrice Davis papers.

31 Jacqueline Kent, *A Certain Style: Beatrice Davis, A Literary Life*, Viking/Penguin, Melbourne, 2001, p. 157.

32 Bob Sessions, letter to Jackie Yowell, 28 October 1982, Penguin publishing files.

33 Thea Astley, letter to Jackie Yowell, 25 November 1982, Penguin publishing files.

34 Beatrice Davis, letter to Thea Astley, 11 November 1982, Thea Astley papers.

35 Geoff and Sarah Cains to author, Mittagong, 7 February 2008.

36 Ed Gregson and Michelle Barbour to author, New Brighton, 30 November 2006.

37 June Barbour to author, Sydney, December 2011.

38 Thea Astley, letter to Julie Watts, 14 September 1983, Penguin publishing files.

39 Rodney Hall to author, Melbourne, July 2011.

40 Thea Astley, letter to Beatrice Davis, 14 September 1979, Beatrice Davis papers. Suggests Brian Matthews could review *Hunting the Wild Pineapple*.

41 Thea Astley in Norma Jean Richey, 'An Interview with Thea Astley', *South Central Review*, 3(2), 1986, p. 90.

42 Thea Astley, letter to Brian Johns, 4 October 1983, Penguin publishing files.

43 For a full discussion of this period of American–Australian publishing relations, see Robert Dixon and Nicholas Birns (eds), 'Rejected by America? Some Tensions in Australian–American Literary Relations', *Reading Across the Pacific: Australia–United States Intellectual Histories*, Sydney University Press, Sydney, pp. 309–322.

44 Thea Astley, letter to Ed Gregson, 9 April 1983, Thea Astley papers.

45 Thea Astley, speech, Canberra Wordfest, c. 1988–89, Thea Astley papers.

46 Thea Astley, letter to Jackie Yowell, 13 May 1984, Penguin publishing files.

47 Thea Astley, letter to Jackie Yowell, 2 April 1984, Penguin publishing files.

48 Thea Astley, letter to Carla Taines, 31 July 1984, Penguin publishing files.

49 Astley in Richey, *South Central Review*, p. 93.

50 Phil Astley, Christmas card to Thea Astley, c. 1983, Thea Astley papers.

51 Peter Dent, letter to Thea Astley, 16 May 1985, Thea Astley papers.

52 May-Liz Shaw, 'Stone's Best at Author's Fest', *The Strand*, Toronto, 31 October 1984.

53 Thea Astley, letter to Jackie Yowell, 12 December 1984, Penguin publishing files.

15 Pictures from a family album

1 Thea Astley, *It's Raining in Mango: Pictures from the Family Album*, Penguin, Melbourne, 1987, p. 15.

2 Marin Martinelli to author, phone interview, 27 January 2011.

3 Thea Astley, letter to Peg McColl, 11 March 1986, Penguin publishing files, Penguin Pty Ltd, Victoria.

4 Don Anderson, 'Writers Contrast in Age and Style', review of *Beachmasters*, *The National Times*, 5–11 April 1985, p. 31.

5 Thea Astley, letter to Don Anderson, 7 April 1985, Don Anderson papers, State Library of New South Wales.
6 Letter, 7 April 1982, UQP papers, UQFL198, Fryer Library, University of Queensland.
7 Thea Astley, letter to Craig Munro, 20 January 1985, UQP papers.
8 Craig Munro, letter to Laurie Muller, 23 January 1985, UQP papers.
9 Laurie Muller, letter to Thea Astley, 4 March 1985, UQP papers.
10 Thea Astley, letter to Brian Johns, 19 March 1985, Penguin publishing files.
11 Thea Astley, letter to Corrie de Klijn, 16 April 1985, Penguin publishing files.
12 Thea Astley, letter to Brian Johns, 19 March 1985, Penguin publishing files.
13 Fay Zwicky, letter to Thea Astley, 12 January 1981, Thea Astley papers, UQFL97, Fryer Library, University of Queensland.
14 Tom Shapcott, *The Literature Board: A Brief History*, UQP, St Lucia, 1988, p. 209.
15 ibid., p. 299.
16 ibid., p. 304.
17 Thea Astley, *Reaching Tin River*, William Heinemann, Melbourne, 1990, p. 35.
18 Thea Astley in Candida Baker, 'Cooler, Calmer and More Collected', *The Age*, 31 March 1990, p. 6.
19 Thea Astley, *An Item from the Late News*, UQP, St Lucia, 1982, pp. 51–52.
20 Thea Astley, *The Acolyte*, UQP, St Lucia, 1980, pp. 73–74.
21 Carmel Bird to author, Melbourne, 31 May 2006.
22 ibid.
23 Helen Garner to author, Melbourne, July 2011.
24 ibid.
25 Ed Gregson to author, New Brighton, 30 November 2006.
26 David Malouf to author, Strathfield, May 2010.
27 Thea Astley, letter to Laurie Muller, 29 August 1988, UQP papers.
28 Michael McGirr to author, Melbourne, 14 March 2008.
29 Marin Martinelli to author, phone interview, 27 January 2011.
30 Jennifer and Bryan Bruty to author, Mittagong, February 2007.
31 ibid.
32 Irene Stevens and Elaine Lindsay to author, Sydney, 24 February 2008.
33 Bob Sessions to author, Melbourne, 13 March 2008.
34 Irene Stevens to author, Sydney, 24 February 2008.

35 Rodney Hall to author, Melbourne, July 2011.
36 Thea Astley, letter to Laurie Muller, 21 January 1987 and 25 March 1987, UQP papers.
37 D'Arcy Randall, reader's report, 4 June 1982, UQP papers.
38 Thea Astley, letter to Peg McColl, 11 March 1986, Penguin publishing files.
39 Thea Astley, letter to Peg McColl, 6 February 1987, Penguin publishing files.
40 Email correspondence with Elise Goodman, June–October 2014.
41 Elise Goodman, letter to Brian Johns, 13 November 1986, Penguin publishing files.
42 ibid.
43 Thea Astley, letter to Susan Hawthorne, 18 February 1987, Penguin publishing files.
44 Thea Astley, letter to Peg McColl, 7 May 1987, Penguin publishing files.
45 Thea Astley, letter to Linda Ristow, 29 September 1987, Penguin publishing files.
46 Thea Astley, letter to Peg McColl, 29 October 1987, Penguin publishing files.
47 Helen Garner, letter to Thea Astley, 23 September 1986, Thea Astley papers.
48 Thea Astley, letter to Susan Hawthorne, 10 February 1988, Penguin publishing files.
49 Thea Astley, letter to Susan Ryan, 5 September 1988, Penguin publishing files.
50 Fay Zwicky, letter to Thea Astley, 18 May 1988, Thea Astley papers.
51 Schöningh publishers, letter to Goodman Associates re: *Exploring Australian Identities*, 10 January 2011.
52 Thea Astley, letter to Bruce Sims, 8 August 1989, Penguin publishing files.
53 Thea Astley, letter to Bruce Sims, 8 October 1989, Penguin publishing files.
54 ibid.
55 Geoff and Sarah Cains to author, Mittagong, 7 February 2007.
56 Thea Astley, letter to Helen Garner, 7 October 1986, Thea Astley papers.
57 Geoff and Sarah Cains to author, Mittagong, 7 February 2007.
58 Susan Ryan, letter to Thea Astley, 17 October 1988, Thea Astley papers.
59 Jill Hickson, letter to Thea Astley, 24 April 1989, Thea Astley papers.
60 Beatrice Davis, letter to Thea Astley, 29 May 1987, Thea Astley papers.

16 Inventing her own weather

1 Thea Astley, 'Inventing the Weather', *Vanishing Points*, William Heinemann, Melbourne, 1992, p. 157.

2 Helen Rosenman, letter to Thea Astley, 21 November 1989, Thea Astley papers, UQFL97, Fryer Library, University of Queensland.

3 Thea Astley, letter to Bruce Sims, 17 May 1989, Penguin publishing files, Penguin Pty Ltd, Victoria.

4 Carolyn See, letter to Thea Astley, 20 January 1989, Thea Astley papers.

5 Rodney Hall to author, Melbourne, July 2011.

6 Thea Astley, letter to John Beston, 19 February 1972, John Beston papers, UQFL429, Fryer Library, University of Queensland. Beston, who was at that time working on a script dealing with the early years of Patrick White's writing life, had invited Astley to give a conference paper on White.

7 Patrick White, letter to Thea Astley, 20 March 1961, Thea Astley papers.

8 Thea Astley, letter to Bruce Sims, 8 October 1989, Penguin publishing files.

9 Louise Adler to author, Melbourne, 5 July 2011.

10 ibid.

11 ibid.

12 Thea Astley, *Spoken Word*, ABC radio, 9 October 1985, ABC Radio Archives.

13 Thea Astley, *Spoken Word* with Peter Couchman, ABC radio, 24 February 1994, 57078, ABC Radio Archives.

14 Thea Astley, *The Multiple Effects of Rainshadow*, Viking/Penguin, Melbourne, 1996, p. 37.

15 Thea Astley, *Reaching Tin River*, William Heinemann, Melbourne, 1990, p. 134

16 Thea Astley in the presence of the author, Melbourne, 1993.

17 Astley, *Reaching Tin River*, p. 82.

18 Jill Hickson, letter to Thea Astley, 15 August 1989, Thea Astley papers.

19 Jim Shepard, review of *Vanishing Points*, *The New York Times Book Review*, 27 September 1992.

20 Elizabeth Perkins, 'A Life of its Own: A Deconstructive Reading of *A Kindness Cup*', *Hecate*, xi(i), 1985, pp. 11–18.

21 Thea Astley, letter to Dale Spender, 3 October 1992, Dale Spender papers 1972–1995, State Library of New South Wales.

22 Astley, *Vanishing Points*, p. 189.

23 ibid., p. 206.

24 Writers' Train, agenda notes, n.d., UQP papers, UQFL198, Fryer Library, University of Queensland.
25 Rodney Hall to author, Melbourne, July 2011.
26 Jeff McMullen to author, Palm Beach, 2 February 2008.
27 Thea Astley, *7.30 Report* with Heidi Rexa, ABC TV, 26 July 1990, ABC Television Archives.
28 Letter to Thea Astley from a primary school-aged child who met her on the Writers' Train trip, 24 July 1990, Thea Astley papers.
29 Phil Astley, letter to Thea Astley, 9 June 1991, Thea Astley papers.
30 Margery Watsford to author, Cairns, February 2008.
31 Thea Astley, speech for the Australian Booksellers and Publishers Association annual dinner, 14 March 1991, Thea Astley papers.
32 Ron Hanson, review of *Reaching Tin River*, *The New York Times Book Review*, 20 October 1993.
33 Helen Garner, postcard to Thea Astley, 25 August 1991, Thea Astley papers.
34 Louise Adler, letter to Thea Astley, 20 March 1991, Thea Astley papers.
35 Vida Horn, letter to Thea Astley, 16 January 1992, Thea Astley papers.
36 Sister Mary Claver, letter to Thea Astley, c. 1992, Thea Astley papers.
37 Jacqueline Kent, *A Certain Style: Beatrice Davis, A Literary Life*, Viking/ Penguin, Melbourne, 2001, p. 300.
38 ibid.
39 Phil Astley, letter to Thea Astley, 1 September 1994, Thea Astley papers.
40 *The Courier-Mail*, 'Our Top 100: A salute to the brilliant, the dreamers, the go-getters, the builders, the do-gooders and achievers who have helped shape Queensland', 6 June 1992, newspaper clipping, Thea Astley papers.
41 Dr Johnson quoted in 'Music', *Collins Thesaurus* (new 1st ed.), HarperCollins, 1995, p. 641.
42 Louise Adler to author, Melbourne, 5 July 2011.
43 Rosemary Sorensen in *Good Weekend* magazine, *The Age*, 6 February 1993, p. 26.
44 Thea Astley, pre-interview, *The Search for Meaning* with Caroline Jones, ABC radio, 17 April 1994, 64732, ABC Radio Archives.
45 Robert Dessaix, letter to Thea Astley, 12 April 1994, Thea Astley papers.
46 Thea Astley to author, Melbourne, May 1993.

17 Curving

1 Thea Astley, *The Multiple Effects of Rainshadow*, Viking/Penguin, Melbourne, 1996, p. 174.
2 Thea Astley, *Beachmasters*, Viking/Penguin, New York, 1986, p. 130.

3 Thea Astley, *The Search for Meaning* with Caroline Jones, ABC radio, 17 April 1994 (repeated 8 January 1995), 64732, ABC Radio Archives.

4 Astley, *The Multiple Effects of Rainshadow*, p. 285.

5 Thea Astley, letter to Michael McGirr, 29 September 1995, photocopy supplied by Michael McGirr.

6 Thea Astley, *Girl with a Monkey*, Angus & Robertson, Sydney, 1958, p. 42.

7 Thea Astley, *The Well Dressed Explorer*, Thomas Nelson, Melbourne, 1977, p. 169.

8 Thea Astley, 'Inventing the Weather', *Vanishing Points*, William Heinemann, Melbourne, 1992, p. 182.

9 Charles Baudelaire, 'Artist's Confiteor', *Paris Spleen* (trans. Louise Varèse), New Directions, New York, 1947, p. 3.

10 Thea Astley, *An Item from the Late News*, UQP, St Lucia, 1982, p. 69.

11 Thea Astley, letter to Michael McGirr, 29 September 1995, photocopy supplied by Michael McGirr.

12 Donal O'Shea, *The Poincare Conjecture: In Search of the Shape of the Universe*, Walker & Company, New York, 2007, p. 46.

13 Thea Astley, letter to Meredith Rose, 5 May 1996, Penguin publishing files, Penguin Pty Ltd, Victoria.

14 Meredith Rose to author, Melbourne, 14 March 2008.

15 ibid.

16 Bill Uren, letter to Phil Astley, 8 August 1996, Jesuit Archives, Melbourne.

17 Thea Astley, 'Problems of Writing', speech, c. 1982, Thea Astley papers, UQFL97, Fryer Library, University of Queensland.

18 Phil Astley, letter to Thea Astley, 13 November 1996, Thea Astley papers.

19 Ed Gregson to author, email correspondence, 25 January 2014.

20 Michael McGirr to author, Melbourne, 14 March 2008.

21 Elizabeth Jolley, letter to Thea Astley, 20 January 1997, Thea Astley papers.

22 Thea Astley, *Drylands: A Book for the World's Last Reader*, Penguin, Melbourne, 1999, back cover blurb.

23 Thea Astley, *Spoken Word* with Ramona Koval, ABC radio, 9 June 2000, ABC Radio Archives.

24 ibid.

25 Thea Astley, letter to Cairns City Library Service, 30 May 1999, Thea Astley papers.

26 Bob Sessions, facsimile to Hickson Associates, 18 September 1998, Penguin publishing files.

27 Thea Astley, letter to Bob Sessions, 21 October 1998, Penguin publishing files.

[28] Meredith Rose, letter to Thea Astley, c. 1998, Thea Astley papers.
[29] Pat and Kevin McHugh to author, Sussex Inlet, 4 January 2011.
[30] ibid.
[31] ibid.
[32] Thea Astley, letter to Fiona Inglis (Curtis Brown Literary Agents), 8 May 2000, Penguin publishing files.
[33] Ed Gregson to author, New Brighton, 30 November 2006.
[34] ibid.
[35] Astley, *Drylands*, p. 178.
[36] Mark Macleod to author, Blue Mountains, 8 December 2006.
[37] Margaret Smith to author, Somersby, 25 February 2008.
[38] Marele Day to author, Brunswick Heads, 29 November 2006.
[39] Jill Eddington to author, Byron Bay, 1 December 2006.
[40] Thea Astley, Ballina Library comments book entry, 20 August 2003.
[41] Matthew Condon to author, Brisbane, 2006.
[42] Jill Eddington to author, Byron Bay, 1 December 2006.
[43] Thea Astley quoted by Donna McLaughlin, *Books and Writing*, ABC radio, 22 August 2004, ABC Radio Archives.
[44] Ingrid Loewy to author, Byron Bay, December 2006.
[45] Mark Macleod to author, Blue Mountains, 8 December 2006.

Further reading

Books by Thea Astley

Girl with a Monkey, Angus & Robertson, Sydney, 1958.

A Descant for Gossips, Angus & Robertson, Sydney, 1960.

The Well Dressed Explorer, Angus & Robertson, Sydney, 1962.

The Slow Natives, Angus & Robertson, Sydney, 1965.

A Boat Load of Home Folk, Angus & Robertson, Sydney, 1968.

The Acolyte, Angus & Robertson, Sydney, 1972.

A Kindness Cup, Thomas Nelson, Melbourne, 1974.

Hunting the Wild Pineapple and Other Related Stories, Thomas Nelson, Melbourne, 1979.

An Item from the Late News, UQP, St Lucia, 1982.

Beachmasters, Viking/Penguin, Melbourne, 1985.

It's Raining in Mango: Pictures from the Family Album, G.P. Putnam's Sons, New York, 1987.

Reaching Tin River, William Heinemann, Melbourne, 1990.

Vanishing Points, William Heinemann, Melbourne, 1992.

Coda, William Heinemann, Melbourne, 1994.

The Multiple Effects of Rainshadow, Viking/Penguin, Melbourne, 1996.
Drylands: A Book for the World's Last Reader, Penguin, Melbourne, 1999.

Selected writings by Thea Astley

'Poetic Fire', *Barjai*, 13, 1944, pp. 6–7.

'Picaninny Thoughts', *The Bulletin*, 75(3878), 9 June 1954, p. 13.

'Cubby', in Cecil Hadgraft (ed.), *Coast to Coast*, Angus & Robertson, Sydney, 1961, pp. 6–11.

'After Tasman', *The Bulletin*, 83(4288), 21 April 1962, p. 60.

'Journey to Olympus', in Leonie Kramer (ed.), *Coast to Coast*, Angus & Robertson, Sydney, 1965, pp. 7–14.

'The Monstrous Accent on Youth', *Meanjin*, xxvii, March 1968, p. 109.

'The Idiot Question', *Southerly*, 30(1), 1970, pp. 3–8.

'Being a Queenslander: A Form of Literary and Geographical Conceit', The Wentworth Press, Sydney, 1978.

'On Writing Short Fiction', *Australian Literary Studies*, 10(2), 1981, pp. 186–187.

'Writing in North Queensland', *LINQ*, 9(1), 1981, pp. 2–10.

'Travelling Even Farther North: David Williamson, You Must Have Stopped at the Border', *Meanjin*, 41(4), 1982, pp. 439–441.

'Going Home', *Brisbane Herald*, 16 January 1986.

'Why I Wrote a Short Story Called "Diesel Epiphany"', *Meanjin*, 45(2), 1986, pp. 193–196.

'The Teeth Father Naked at Last: The Short Stories of Barbara Baynton' (extracts), in Gillian Whitlock (ed.), *Eight Voices of the Eighties: Stories, Journalism and Criticism by Australian Women Writers*, UQP, St Lucia, 1989, pp. 146–195.

Manuscript collections

Fryer Library, University of Queensland, St Lucia, Brisbane:

Thea Astley papers, UQFL97. (See also 'Thea Astley's Poems: Chronological Order of Writing', compiled by Cheryl Taylor, 2011)

Martin Haley papers, UQFL48
Catholic Writers Society papers
Catholic Poetry Society papers
University of Queensland Press papers, UQFL198

State Library of New South Wales (Mitchell Library), Sydney:
Angus & Robertson Archives, MLMSS3269
Beatrice Davis papers

State Library of Victoria, Melbourne:
Bohemia Society papers

Audio material

National Library of Australia
Australian Broadcasting Commission Radio and Television Archives

Selected readings about Thea Astley

Baker, Candida (ed.), *Yacker: Australian Writers Talk about Their Work*, Picador, Woollahra, New South Wales, 1986, pp. 28–54.

Baker, Candida, 'Hard Yacker on the Frontline', *The Sydney Morning Herald*, 24 June 1989, p. 82.

Ellison, Jennifer (ed.), *Rooms of Their Own*, Penguin, Ringwood, Victoria, 1986, pp. 50–69.

Genoni, Paul, and Sheridan, Susan (eds.), *Thea Astley's Fictional Worlds*, Cambridge Scholars Press, Newcastle, UK, 2006.

Kinross-Smith, Graeme, 'Thea Astley', *Kunapipi*, 4(1), 1982, pp. 20–37.

Ross, Robert L., 'An Interview with Thea Astley', *World Literature Written in English*, 26(2), 1986, pp. 264–269.

Sheridan, Susan, *Nine Lives: Postwar Women Writers Making Their Mark*, UQP, St Lucia, 2011.

Willbanks, Ray, *Australian Voices: Australian Writers and Their Work*, University of Texas Press, Texas, 1991, pp. 26–42.

Index